FLAMES AFTER MIDNIGHT

MONTE
AKERS

FLAMES
after
MIDNIGHT

MURDER, VENGEANCE, AND THE
DESOLATION OF A TEXAS COMMUNITY

REVISED EDITION

University of Texas Press AUSTIN

Requests for permission to reproduce material from this work
should be sent to
Permissions
University of Texas Press
P.O. Box 7819
Austin, TX 78713-7819

⊗ The paper used in this publication meets the minimum
requirements of American National Standard for Information
Sciences—Permanence of Paper for Printed Library Materials,
ANSI Z39.48-1984.

LIBRARY OF CONGRESS CATALOGING-IN-PUBLICATION DATA
(FROM THE FIRST EDITION)

Akers, Monte, 1950–
Flames after midnight: murder, vengeance, and the desolation of a
Texas community / Monte Akers
    p.   cm.
Includes bibliographical references and index.
ISBN 978-0-292-72633-8 (pbk.: alk. paper)
    1. Kirvin (Tex.)—Race Relations.   2. Afro-Americans—
Texas—Kirvin—History—20th century.   3. Lynching—Texas—
Kirvin—History—20th century.   4. Murder—Texas—Kirvin—
History—20th century.   I. Title.
F394.K57A4   1999
976.4′232—dc21   98-29775

ISBN: 978-0-292-72992-6 (E-book)

DEDICATION

To Mom, for planting the dream.
To Bill, for fueling the dream.
To Larry, for focusing the dream.
To David, for encouraging the dream.
To Patty, for supporting the dream.
To Nathan and Megan, for being dreams.

Contents

Acknowledgments

I would like to express my sincere appreciation for the help of the following people in researching, writing, and bringing this story to publication:

First and foremost, the witnesses to the events described in this book who willingly, generously, gave interviews, answered questions, and provided documentation about events that were sometimes painful to recall; next, my agent, Kathleen Niendorff, of Austin, who believed in this story and told the right people; Theresa May and the staff at the University of Texas Press, who are those right people; Mandy Woods, my editor, whose English upbringing and training polished this Texas tale; David McCartney, who helped me sort out the story and served as a moral compass, grating critic, and blaring supporter in its preparation; Harry Hughes, who provided more leads and clues than he realized; David E. Des Jardines, who provided more professional encouragement than he realized; Dr. Michael Ditto, the grandson of Horace Mayo, who provided help, advice, and a photo of his grandparents; B. J. Ausley who permitted publication of photos for this book; the scholarly readers for the university press, who found merit in the story; Joyce Burns, of Teague, who provided review and encouragement; Jeffrey M. Flannery, manuscript reference librarian for the Library of Congress, whose extra moment on the phone made all the difference; all the people who heard this tale and provided advice and inspiration, especially Frank Sturzl, Sheryl Cole, Carol Harris, Jack Battle, Lynda Lankford, Susan Horton, Shanna Igo, and Professor Charles Sullivan; Alan Bojorequez, for his assistance obtaining the photographs published in this book; Randy Overman, plus the wizards at Computer Stuff of Austin, who bailed me out when a computer virus struck; Dottie, Rose, Lance, Suzanne, Brad, Rachael, and all of my other co-workers and friends; and of course, most importantly, the members of my family, especially my wife, Patty, and children, Nathan and Megan, my parents, Edward and Leona Akers, my author brother, Larry, and his author wife, Susan, and my sisters, Sharon and Pam, as well as nephews, nieces, in-laws, and the rest of the tribe, all of whom encouraged and inspired me.

FLAMES AFTER MIDNIGHT

PART ONE

*It is not enough to say let bygones be bygones.
Indeed, just saying that ensures it will not be so.
Reconciliation does not come easy. Believing it does
will ensure that it will never be. We have to work
and look the beast firmly in the eyes. . . . Without
memory, there is no healing. Without forgiveness,
there is no future.*

—ARCHBISHOP DESMOND TUTU, 1998

Prologue to Part One

This is not a pretty story. It "skims the joy off the pan of conversation." It asks thistle questions and offers scorpion answers, but it needs to be told.

I lived in Freestone County, Texas, from 1981 to 1990, and heard a seven-word summary of this story the first week I was there. The words were whispered to me by an accountant, a fellow employee of Dow Chemical Company.

Like me, he was an outsider, a move-in, and he did not know any facts, but the story was the kind that needed whispering more than it needed facts. The story was the kind we each thought we understood in about seven words.

The seven words the accountant whispered to me were: *"Kirven is where they burned the niggers."*

I forgave the accountant his poor choice of words at the time, rather like I might forgive a new acquaintance for having bad breath or dismal table manners. Pointing out the fact that the N-word was offensive might not have been conducive to a future working relationship. Nonetheless, his use of the word told me eloquently that although he and I might be co-workers, we would not be close friends. We were too different.

I grew up in a place where race was rarely an issue. People in our little corner of the Panhandle of Texas seldom used words like "nigger" or "spick" or "kike" in the 1950s and 1960s. There were no separate facilities for "coloreds," because there were none to use them. There were no blacks, and few or no Hispanics, Oriental people, or American Indians.

Folks determined to be prejudiced against an entire category of people had to content themselves with resenting the numerous Germans who inhabited the area, but they were distinguishable from the rest of us only by their surnames and accents. Beyond that, the human penchant for discrimination had to be satisfied with more fragmentary antipathies, such as that of Methodists for Baptists, of ranchers for farmers, of haves for have-nots. As a result, I grew up with no preconceived notions about the inferiority of one race in comparison with another.

Instead, perhaps ironically, I grew up possessing a keen interest in the American Civil War, particularly in the heroes of the Confederacy. From an early age, I filled my imagination with tales of Stonewall Jackson, J. E. B. Stuart, and Robert E. Lee the way my peers were filling theirs with the deeds of Mickey Mantle, Wilt Chamberlain, and Joe Namath. The fighting prowess of the Southern soldiers, their string of against-all-odds victories, their underdog status, and the near-miss sweetness of their defeat fueled fires in me. I was particularly enchanted by their sense of obligation, duty, and honor. Lee, Jackson, and Stuart were willing to sacrifice all for what they believed. They did not drink, swear, or smoke. They were marble men who valued "unblemished reputations" and "the crowning excellence of exemplary Christian piety" above all other qualities.[1]

My complete and utter fascination with everything involving the Confederacy meant, of course, that I must come to terms with the pesky problem of slavery. I could ignore the subject when I was a child, but as I approached high school, still without abandoning the fascination, I gave the topic more and more thought. The national situation ensured I would, and nothing that was happening in the country at the time made me sympathetic toward the South's spotty record on racial matters.

The civil rights movement was at its pinnacle in my junior high and high school years. Martin Luther King was making his mark, and I was eighteen when he was killed. From my vantage point in the Panhandle, far from any hotbeds of racism, I could neither accept nor condone the racial attitudes and backlash against the civil rights movement that was being exhibited in Mississippi, Alabama, and other Southern states. The hatred and violence being practiced by some white Southerners made me believe they were a different breed of people from those I idolized.

College exposed me to many more types of people and notions, as college is meant to do. I majored in history, and my classes included courses on the Old South, the New South, intellectual history, and the Civil War and Reconstruction, all taught by insightful professors who eliminated much of my Panhandle naiveté. College was followed by law school, and law school by four years of state agency legal practice in Austin before being hired in 1981 to work for Dow Chemical in Freestone County.

Freestone County had a lot of outsiders in 1981. The energy crisis of the 1970s and the search for alternative fuel sources had attracted several large companies that were buying and leasing rights to mine lignite, a brown coal abundant in the region. The commerce and economic opportunity were welcome, but distinctions between natives and outsiders were carefully preserved. Anyone whose family arrived by internal combustion engine tended to be an outsider forever, in fact. There were also subjects the natives preferred outsiders not to probe. This story was at the top of the list.

In 1986, I was elected chairman of the Freestone County Historical Commission, an unexpected elevation for an outsider. The position resulted in my learning some of the county's darker secrets. That is when this story seized me and would not let go.

At first, I wanted only to preserve the recollections of those who had witnessed the events described in this book. Later, I was driven to learn more facts, to try to uncover what catalysts set the events in motion and drove them to their odd conclusions. I wanted also to discover the "why" of this tale from a human perspective. What occurred in the minds of white Southerners that caused them to commit such an outrage? What reasons would fuel the hatred necessary for men to burn other men alive? How could men who idolized Lee and Jackson and Stuart justify what was done in Kirven? What drove people to commit an act so unspeakable that it would still be whispered about after three-quarters of a century?

What I ultimately discovered was that nobody knew all the facts, that much of the truth had been lost or hidden, and that the story was more tragic, more ironic, and possessed more far-reaching impact than anyone had guessed. The truth was more than I could dream to understand in seven words.

My research occurred in two very distinct stages. In 1986, I talked to my first eyewitnesses and obtained a copy of the *Kirven Commercial Record* for May 7, 1922. The newspaper contained what appeared to be a full and detailed account of the crime and immediate aftermath which are at the heart of this tale. Shortly thereafter I interviewed other eyewitnesses, particularly J. C. Whatley and Bertha Williams. They told complete stories, most of which corresponded with the newspaper account—particularly Whatley, whose version was almost too detailed to be credible. By September 1987, I believed I knew the entire story.

In October, I turned my attention from the story to politics. A group of citizens convinced me to run against a ten-year incumbent district judge who had stepped on a few local toes. Our six-month campaign took on a flavor of native versus newcomer, old versus new, tradition versus change. The two counties in the district were evenly divided, and rife with disagreement. On election night, 9,011 votes were cast, and the incumbent was declared the winner by one vote. I asked for a recount and was declared the victor by three votes.

The incumbent challenged that outcome, and an election contest in district court followed. After a three-day political and evidentiary slug-fest, with the two counties' differences no closer to settlement, he and I reached a compromise—we would agree to a new election, would then both withdraw from the race, and would support a mutually agreeable third party.

During the course of the campaign, I met and made friends with hundreds of Freestone County residents, but I detected an undercurrent of distrust and wariness in some corners of the county, even hostility, that I had never known in other regions of the state. I wondered how much of it was simply dislike of outsiders, and how much, if any, was a lingering result of what happened in 1922.

After the election contest, I put the research project aside for a while. I thought I had found all there was to find, and had concluded, in fact, that the incident was not particularly unusual for the time in which it occurred. I doubted I could find more illuminating details. I was mistaken.

After I moved to Austin in 1990, my thoughts continued to return to the events of 1922. Even though racial violence and lynchings might have been common in 1922, there were aspects of this tale that continued to tantalize me, and caused me to keep digging. Then, while transcribing the tapes of my interview of Bertha Williams, I was presented with new information, and a new mystery. Lost among the elderly black lady's mumbled statements was a jewel of information I had not heard during the interview. It prompted me to begin the second stage of my research.

That jewel is described in more detail in the prologue to Part Two. At first, I did not believe that any more could be uncovered about what Bertha Williams said, but I ended up discovering more than I imagined possible.

I do not claim to be uniquely qualified to write about the history of Freestone County, and I am certainly not qualified to pass judgment upon it. Indeed, there are natives living there today who would pronounce me, an outsider who lived there only nine years and who was not reared around black people, particularly unfit to do so. Yet this may be a story only an outsider can write, for a native who knows all the intricate relationships and who must live with the descendants of those who were involved in the tragic events might never feel able to tell the tale fully. The fact that some of the names of living people have been changed, or omitted entirely, speaks of the lingering hesitancy some people in the county still feel about being identified with this tale.

Nor do I present this work as a scholarly analysis of the practice of lynching in America. While that subject may be the shiny white bone poking from beneath America's closet door, our nation's holocaust, the door has been pulled open and the skeleton examined hundreds of times. Numerous scholarly works exist on the subject, and the basic details of the killings in Freestone County are not radically different from those of hundreds of other lynchings.

Still, this particular story, details of which have never been published, deserves particular attention. Although neither the participants in the events nor those who live in Freestone County today were aware of it, the lynchings in Kirven received widespread, even international, publicity. They occurred at a time that was ripe for them to receive a degree of attention they would not have received at any other time, and that attention helped contribute, albeit indirectly and gradually, to the end of the practice of racial lynching in America.

To those who would say the telling of this tale serves only to open up old wounds, stoke the fires of racial debate, or promote feelings of resentment and victimization, I respond that I have thought long and hard about those possibilities. My hope, however, is that the telling of this tale may actually contribute in some small way to the healing of American racial relations. Indeed, the nature of some of the details of this story and the way in which some of the information was delivered into my lap make me wonder if there is not a larger purpose in the story's telling.

Such a claim may seem preposterous, but the idea has given me hope since it was first suggested by a bright young black attorney who heard this story and described how she believes it fits into our nation's racial history and the four stages of human grieving.

Born after the civil rights movement, she grew up in an area where racism was not overt, and in a household where adults did not talk about the old days or the old ways. "Those were hard times," her parents told her, "and there is nothing to be gained by talking about them."

She did not agree with her family's reticence, however, and tried to learn more about the past and present of racial relations. Today she views the subject with an analytical, objective point of view. Comparing America's aching racial past to the death of a loved one, she regards those people, black and white, who prefer that the past remain buried as being in the first stage of the grieving process, that of denial. Others in the country are in the second stage, that of anger, while others occupy the third stage—sorrow. Still others, many in the South, are in the final stage, which is healing. She believes, and I agree with her, that healing requires knowledge, as well as acceptance, neither of which can come until stories such as this one are finally told. When blacks and whites can rationally discuss events such as those which occurred in Kirven, the nation will be closer to acceptance, healing, and recovery.[2]

Finally, the tale is worth telling for its irony and poignancy. Indeed, some of the details, unintended consequences, and coincidences of the story are richer, fuller, and more incongruous than I can capture. I had to try to capture them, however. I have known about the events for seventeen years, and have been researching and writing about them for twelve. Yet I cannot speak of some of the details without emotion catching in my throat.

What follows, what now begins, is the story of Freestone County, Texas, in 1922. Events that year in this rural, previously unexceptional part of Texas—"this cold world of care"—affected, and changed, the nation. The tale is not complete, and never can be, but even if every illuminating truth and solution is not revealed, the story supplies the best that history can offer—a chance to study something that should never be repeated.

 *Eula*

Among the many unknowables in this story, one of the least mysterious is what Eula Ausley thought on her last ride.

The date was May 4, 1922, a Thursday, and the final full day of school in Kirven, Texas. Seventeen-year-old Eula was to graduate the next morning. Her Aunt Rena was sewing a new white dress for her to wear at the commencement ceremony in the school auditorium, and she had been given strict instructions to ride straight home to Shanks for a final fitting.[1] She had been riding three miles to school each morning and returning three miles home each evening for two years, but this was the final return trip, the last routine of her schoolgirl years.

The sky was a brilliant blue. Big, slow cumulus clouds were drifting north like migrating mountaintops. Cotton fields had been planted for a month, and green leaves covered the furrows. A gentle spring breeze rustled the new grass and Eula could smell a fragrant bouquet of flowers and weeds, crushed beneath her black gelding's hooves. The countryside had received several inches of rain during the previous week, but May 4 was clear and pleasant.[2]

Her mind was almost certainly filled with happy, excited thoughts and plans. Graduation was a singularly significant event in the area, "one of the most important days in the lives" of the participants, who would be presented to family and neighbors in an auditorium "filled to overflowing."[3] Completion of school was a major accomplishment for anyone, anywhere, in 1922. For Eula, graduation was the realization of a dream.

She had received the first eight years of her education in Shanks, where she lived with her grandparents, John and Permelia King, but the little village school went no further than eighth grade, and she had wanted more. The school at Kirven offered two more years, a typical maximum for towns in the county, and Eula begged to be allowed to attend. Convincing her grandfather she could ride the six miles every day, in any kind of weather, was a challenge. He feared for her safety, but, as always, she convinced him.

She had other reasons to celebrate that day in May, other cause to feel fulfilled. Just two months earlier, she had attended a week-long Baptist revival in a large, tan, circus-style tent pitched in a vacant lot in downtown Kirven.[4] When, on Thursday night, the evangelist V. B. Starnes asked who among the participants would accept Christ into their lives, she and a friend went forward. A few days later, both girls were immersed in the baptistery of the Kirven Baptist church located at the edge of town.[5]

Finally, there was her family, orbiting around her, doting on her, nearly smothering her with adoration. She knew, could not help but know, how special she was in their eyes, and the knowledge made her determined to live up to their expectations.

She was going out into a bright, pleasant world, feeling mature, buoyed up by the love of God and of a large, happy family. Life in Freestone County must have appeared particularly promising to Eula Ausley on May 4, 1922.

Like the rest of her family, Eula was tall and good-looking, with wavy brown hair and a stout, athletic build. Although the style for young ladies her age was short, bobbed hair, and local newspapers kept those in the county abreast of fashion, Eula wore her hair long, often topped with a hat. She looked much older than her seventeen years.[6] On that day she was probably wearing a long black riding skirt and lace-up boots, a white middy blouse, and a round-brimmed straw hat.[7] Her mature good looks and extra height would have made her noticeable anywhere.

On top of everything else lifting her spirits that day, she was also hoping her best friend, Mary, could spend the night.

Mary lived at the corner of the vacant lot where the tent revival had been held, less than three blocks from the school. She was only twelve, five years younger than Eula, but she had started the first grade at age five and Eula had started when she was seven. The Kirven School had only four rooms for its ten grades, so even though Mary was in the eighth grade and Eula was in the tenth, they shared the same classroom after Eula moved over from Shanks.

In addition, Eula's grandparents often invited Mary to their home in Shanks to play the piano and sing. Despite their age differences, friendship blossomed between the two girls.

Eula knew Mary enjoyed coming to the King home. The younger girl loved to ride horses there, and was particularly impressed with their large two-story house, the long, elegant dining table in the main room, and the huge claw-foot bathtub in the upstairs bathroom. Mary came from a small family and the Kings were anything but small. There was always plenty of bustle, good food, and laughter.[8]

As the only girl in a family of six boys, and the youngest child, Eula was the center of attention, everyone's favorite. Anything she did or wanted to do seemed like the entire family's purpose in being, and Eula may have wondered, secretly, if her grandparents encouraged her to have younger friends. Perhaps they wanted to keep Eula as childlike and dependent as possible, in the hope that doing so would keep her living at home longer.

When she arrived at Mary's house, however, her friend's mother declined Eula's invitation. Like Eula's aunt, Mary's mother was sewing a new dress for her girl to wear to the graduation ceremony, and Mary needed to stay home and be fitted. Besides, both girls had a lot to do to get ready, and would need to be in bed early. Any disappointment Eula felt was assuaged, however, when she heard that Mary could stay overnight the next day, Friday, instead.[9] Eula could not know that these would be the last friendly words she would hear.

Eula rode on. She knew her grandmother and Aunt Rena would be watching the clock. They always did, and knew exactly how long it took the girl to make the trip. They were very protective of her, and Eula understood why: Nobody wanted to make the mistakes they had made with Eula's mother.

Her thoughts may have returned to her favorite uncle, John T. King. For two years she had stabled her horse in the barn behind his elegant home in Kirven during school days. Today had been the last time she would do so, and he had been in the barn to help her get the big gelding saddled.[10] Then he had extended a hand to give her a boost up and into the sidesaddle.

She had ridden a few yards down the street and turned back to look at him. He looked forlorn, and she nearly rode back to hug him and promise nothing was ending except a routine. She would still ride over to visit. Nothing else would change. Today might be the last day of her girlhood, but she would still be there, still the same Eula.

Instead of going back, though, she gave him a happy wave and her best smile. He waved back and she continued on her way.

Perhaps she pondered over asking her grandfather to allow her to drive her new car into Kirven for the graduation ceremony the next morning—but she already knew the answer would be no. Grandfather King was strict, and very traditional. That he had given her the car was amazing in itself. She was the only girl her age in Shanks or Kirven who owned one, but Grandfather King was very particular about when she was allowed to drive.

He was old-fashioned, and tight with his money. He and Eula's grandmother also owned a car, but they would take Eula to town in their horse-drawn carriage. Mr. King would not waste gasoline, nor would he allow Eula to do so, on a three-mile trip from Shanks to Kirven, not even for Eula's graduation.[11]

She may have wished briefly that her mother or father could be at the ceremony, that they could see how well their little girl had done, but both were dead. There would be plenty of family there—grandparents, uncles, aunts, brother, nephews, nieces—but not parents.

For years after Eula's last ride, there would be whispers in some corners of the county that the girl's thoughts were entirely different that day, and that she hurried from the school in shame and anguish, toward a secret, hateful rendezvous. Those whispers and speculations described a boyfriend waiting between Kirven and Shanks,[12] and painted a tortured Eula hiding a terrible secret, a secret not unlike that of her mother.

In those corners of the county, such a secret and such a rendezvous were a way to explain what happened to Eula, and what took place thereafter. Such a story, such speculation, were a way for the people who repeated them to erase what they believed were untruths being told by others. Yet there is no evidence to support the story.

Between those speculations and what would be accepted later as fact, however, there is another explanation for what happened that is almost certainly correct. This explanation, which would become lost for more than seventy-five years, could not have changed Eula's thoughts from being happy, innocent, and excited on her last ride. Still, the correct explanation may finally accomplish what the story about a boyfriend was designed to do, and may finally erase the untruths.

The road from Kirven to Shanks was an unpaved wagon lane that ran parallel to the tracks of the Trinity and Brazos Valley railroad. Halfway between the two communities a small bridge, made of dark native stones overlaid with railroad ties, crossed Grindstone Creek. Barbedwire fences lined pastures and cotton fields on each side of the lane, but close to the creek the fields yielded to brush, post oaks, and shinnery. Grindstone was a small creek with little water.[13] Like most watercourses in that part of Texas, the banks were bordered with dense, nearly impenetrable brakes and underbrush.

Eula's gelding approached the bridge at a single-foot, a gentle gait between a walk and a trot. The horse had made the same trip every weekday for two years, and was a large, calm, dependable animal. A few yards short of the bridge, however, in a clear, sandy patch of ground, he pulled up short, snorted, and looked nervously into the brush.

Eula started to urge him forward, but then saw what had startled the horse. A man was standing beside the road, half-hidden in a clump of bushes.

Before she could say or do anything, the man stepped out and she recognized him. For an instant she was relieved, but just as quickly she became alarmed, for he grabbed the gelding's bridle just above the bit.[14]

The man may have spoken reassuringly to her, may have pointed to her saddle blanket and told her he could see a cocklebur underneath. According to one version of the story, he convinced her to dismount so he could remove the sticker.[15] Eula was not gullible, however. She would have known to look for burs herself, and would have known her horse was not acting as though there was such a problem.

More likely, the first man only stopped her, and once he had done so, his job was finished. The others could act.

Another man stepped out of the brush on her right, reached up, and grabbed her by the waist.

Eula screamed. That much is certain.[16]

The big gelding may have panicked and wheeled away to the left, unseating the girl as the second man pulled her backward from the sidesaddle. The first man probably maintained his grip on the frightened horse's bridle as a third came out of the brake to help the second, grabbing for the girl's legs as she came out of the saddle.

Eula surely struck and kicked at the two men, still screaming. Neither were particularly large, while she was strong and terrified. She may have struggled enough to cause the second or third man to lose his footing in the sandy soil.

One of the men, possibly the one who grabbed the horse's bridle, may have fallen and hit the barbed wire or a post of the nearest fence with his chest or back, snapping off a post at the base. Something, probably a struggling man or a plunging horse, broke the fence.[17]

The first man may have tied the horse's reins to a nearby bush then,[18] and at some point, Eula's straw hat was dislodged from her head and caught by the wind. The hat floated several yards north, the direction from which she had come.[19]

The efforts of two men, perhaps all three, were required to hold her thrashing feet and arms and carry her awkwardly into the brush along the creek. She continued to scream as they did so. The common practice in Freestone County was to locate one house on every fifty acres — the amount of land one man could farm[20]— and Eula's shrieks were heard by people in at least two of the nearest houses. Neighbors would come forward later who said they heard her. They would have dashed to her rescue if they had suspected the truth. Instead, they assumed a child was being disciplined at another house.[21] Nobody came.

The men carried Eula east, down the creek, stepped across it, and stopped in a small clearing on the bank. They threw her to the ground and began tearing the clothes from her body. As the first man looked on, one of the other two took a knife from his pocket and opened the blade. The third found a knotted cedar stick.

For the next half hour, the final thirty minutes of Eula Ausley's last ride, she experienced greater horror than she had believed could exist.

2 Kirven, the County, the Country, and the Kings

May 4, 1922 began as bright and promising for the other inhabitants of Kirven, Texas, as it had for Eula. Spring was the county's best season. The recent rains were what the cotton crops needed, and neither of summer's killjoys—sucking humidity and baking sun—were yet in attendance. The kiln that would be July was two months away, and the drudgery of chopping cotton was two weeks in the future. The first part of May was a time to play baseball, go to Caney Creek or Hinds Lake and barter worms for fish, or have a picnic in the butter-colored sunlight.

More important, more exciting, were the untold riches looming on the horizon for Kirven's inhabitants. Just as Eula had been ready to graduate and go out into the world, so Kirven was tottering on the brink of great wealth and modernization. Oil derricks from the Mexia field, twenty miles west, appeared to be marching steadily closer each week as more and more new wells were drilled.

On November 19, 1920, the Rogers Discovery Well had "blown in" for the Humphreys Company in neighboring Limestone County. Its gusher had started the largest oil boom in Texas' history since that following Spindletop in 1901. For a year and a half, production from the field had increased exponentially, and by May 4, 1922, the wells around Mexia were producing 200,000 barrels a day, half the entire production of Texas. The United States was leading the world in oil production, Texas was leading the nation, and the Mexia field was leading the state.[1]

Freestone County newspapers were filled with the bright news. Front-page banners trumpeted joyful predictions: "Freestone County to be Punched Full of Holes," "Oil Men Flocking to Freestone County by the Hundreds," and "Drills Going Down in Large Numbers of Freestone County Wells" were among the headlines from previous months.[2] "Let Us Make You Some Money," shouted a full-page ad for the Freestone County Oil and Drilling Company, published every week in the *Fairfield Recorder* for two months from December 1921 to February 1922.[3]

In October 1921, a county newspaper reported that "the little town of Kirven is putting on boom appearances and her people are wide-awake," and that "Kirven is seething with oil and civic progress nowadays." Six new wells were reported to have been "made" within the square mile that included Kirven.[4] In November, three wells were being drilled near town, and the newspaper reported that "perhaps six or eight other locations have been made. . . . Kirven will be thoroughly tested, and here's hoping we hit it!"[5] More wells were reported in February and April 1922.[6]

Their derricks could be seen from front porches, beacons of promise, lighthouses of hope.[7] In a matter of months, maybe weeks, maybe days, serious oil production and phenomenal wealth might come to anyone who owned land or ran a business in the area.

Adults were not the only ones who felt good that fourth of May. The last day of school was second only to Christmas on the list of children's most anticipated events. Summer in Freestone County might mean chores and hard work for many of them, but freedom and playtime were what they anticipated. Best of all, summer meant escape from the classroom.

But as bright and beautiful as the day began, it ended in total disaster. For Kirven, Texas, the world would stop turning in its ordinary course at the end of Eula Ausley's last ride.

Fourteen years earlier there had been no Kirven, no oil production, no bright hopes. An old, tiny community called Woodland was located three-quarters of a mile west of the townsite, while Shanks, previously called "Nip n Tuck," was located three miles to the south. The latter community boasted a post office, a blacksmith shop, a general store, a hard-shell Baptist church, and an eight-grade school.[8] Then, in 1906, the county's first railroad, the Trinity and Brazos Valley, came to the region.[9]

Tracks were laid within twenty-five yards of the Shanks cemetery, but no depot was constructed. Instead, the T. & B. V.—folks called it the Turnip and Bean Vine—placed a railroad station farther north, at the intersection of roads leading to the county's largest towns, Wortham, Teague, Fairfield, and Streetman.[10]

A village sprang from the earth at the crossroads. The site was in the heart of the county's cotton-growing region, an ideal location for ginning and shipping. Farther north than all but one other depot in the county, closer to Corsicana and Dallas, the depot was within a few miles of the borders of two other counties—Limestone to the west and Navarro to the north.

The new community was in the northwest part of the county, but was centrally located in relation to other towns. Teague was fourteen miles south, Wortham eight miles west, Streetman nine miles north, and Fairfield twelve miles southeast. Cotton Gin, a village where little boys waved good-bye to their mothers with both hands in 1864, marching off to fight Yankees on the Red River in Louisiana, was nine miles southwest.

The new village was named for a former county judge, Oliver Kirven, who donated land for the railroad right-of-way. The few existing businesses, as well as residents, of Woodland moved over to inhabit the new town. The Shanks post office was taken away from that unlucky community and reassigned to the growing new one.[11] The town's name was spelled variously Kirven and Kirvin, the latter becoming more popular in later years.

Modern businesses were established, some of them cutting-edge modern for the time—a telephone exchange, an electric plant, a movie theater, gas stations, a tailor shop, a ladies' dress shop, a confectionery, a roller-skating rink, a music store, and a pool hall. There were also two drug stores, two doctors' offices, a dentist's office, and three banks, as well as grocery stores, barber shops, blacksmiths, a newspaper, and anything else that might make a go.

One- and two-story brick buildings—some say there was one that was three stories—went up downtown. A new brick school, built in 1914, had two stories with a large auditorium on the second floor. Two cotton gins, three cottonseed houses, a 1,000-bale-capacity cotton warehouse, and two grist mills were erected near the depot to serve the county's major agricultural activity.[12]

People from Shanks, Fairfield, Cotton Gin, Streetman, Wortham, and every other Freestone County town except Teague flocked in. Teague, which was larger than Kirven, was the other boom town of the county. Many newcomers, particularly employees of the T. & B. V., built new homes there, but Kirven looked like the town with the brightest future to county natives. Freestone folks placed great stock in a person's background, family, and status. Teague was attracting the most newcomers, but many of the best and brightest of the county's old families chose to locate in Kirven.

Lura Bess Mayo, a resident of Kirven who taught school there in

1922, reminisced in 1994 about the people who came to Kirven, saying, "They just thought that it was the boom town of Freestone County. Everyone wants to go where it's new and invigorating and everything is new and everyone is exciting, and that's the feeling we had."[13]

Willie Mae Beaver, a young lady living in nearby Mexia in 1921 and 1922, recalled how young people of other Freestone and Limestone communities vied for invitations to social events in Kirven; in her words, "When you were invited to a party there, you knew you had it made."[14]

Until the oil boom, the population inside Kirven's corporate boundaries hovered around 500, reached 800 in 1910, fell to 300 in 1915, and was back to about 400 in 1920. By early 1922, however, it probably exceeded 1,000.[15] The town's exact population in 1922 cannot be ascertained, but one indicator of the town's growth can be gleaned from published reports of the resources of the Kirven State Bank. Between November 1919 and March 1921, the bank's deposits swelled from $49,325.59 to $155,260.78.[16]

Most of the citizens who lived within the town's corporate limits were businessmen and their families, but Kirven was the focal point for shopping for a much larger population. Citizens of three counties, mostly farm families who lived beside their fields, flocked to Kirven on weekends. As Bertha Williams, a black woman who resided in Kirven in 1922, recalled, "On Saturdays you'd think Jesus was talking down there on the main street. There were so many people, you didn't have room to sit or stumble."[17]

The 1920 census indicates that in that year 55 blacks lived inside the corporate limits of Kirven, and that another 200–300 lived within five miles of town. Witness interviews indicate that relations between the races were good. Whites and blacks were accustomed to living together. They had worked out traditional Southern codes and understandings, and did not make trouble for each other, as long as the traditions were maintained.

One of the most respected men in town was Jenkins Carter, a black man to whom everyone, regardless of color, went for advice. Each day he picked up his subscription issue of a Dallas newspaper when it was delivered by the southbound train, and then remained at the depot and read it aloud to a group of men, both blacks and whites, who gathered to hear him.[18]

Nonetheless, most of the traditions of Jim Crow were, of course, alive and healthy. Blacks living inside Kirven were relegated to an area on the west side of the railroad tracks called "Niggertown." The only work available to them was manual labor, primarily sharecropping, for which they hired themselves out as field hands, or, for women, domestic housework. A precious few were given jobs on the railroad.

Still, blacks in Kirven in the twenties did not complain. Bertha Williams declared in 1987, "We all just got along fine, like two birds in a nest." Foreman Carter, another black resident and stepson of the respected Jenkins Carter, declared adamantly in 1995, "Black and white got along good, gambled together. Whites would visit black churches. . . . Black men would shop in the same stores as the whites, would walk the same sidewalks. There weren't any rules about using the back door, like in private homes. Everybody got along good."[19]

Most of the people who lived in Kirven in 1922 had moved there during one of two local boom times, the first immediately after the railroad was constructed, and the second between 1920 and 1922. Some came because of what was happening in Kirven; others because they were weary of what was not happening in the rest of the county. The towns in Freestone County not touched by the railroad or the oil boom became dormant, or more dormant than they had been since the end of the Civil War.

Once, years earlier, all of Freestone County had been as attractive to new settlement as Teague and Kirven were in the early 1920s, and the patterns of that settlement were a significant factor in what would happen after May 4, 1922.

Founded in 1850, carved out of Limestone County, Freestone County began as a microcosm of the Old South. The soil was perfect for cotton-raising, and the Trinity River, on the county's eastern boundary, was navigable to the Gulf of Mexico during parts of the year. The vast majority of the region's settlers were from cotton-growing slave states, and they brought their culture with them.[20]

Forests were cleared and turned into cotton fields through the labor of slaves. The 1860 census revealed a population of 3,268 whites and 3,613 blacks. Not one of the latter, whether man, woman, or child, was free.[21] By comparison, the population of the mother county of Limestone was 4,537, of which only 1,072 were slaves.[22]

During the Civil War, the black population grew. Slave owners in Arkansas and Louisiana, anxious to remove their property from the advancing and liberating Union armies, sent their human chattels to Texas. In 1864 the slave population of the county was 5,614, valued at $4,153,500.[23]

After emancipation came to Texas on June 19, 1865, most Freestone County blacks stayed in the region. Some continued to work for former masters, some formed black communities in isolated parts of the county, and some obtained their own land. Eventually, most became sharecroppers, working land belonging to whites on terms of "seconds," "thirds," or "fourths," meaning that, depending upon custom and agreement, the landowner received every second, third, or fourth part of a crop raised by the tenants.[24]

The shortcoming of this reasonable-sounding system, for the tenants, was that the landowner also loaned credit to the sharecropper, or arranged to have money loaned, sometimes sold the tenants their food, clothing, and supplies, and usually weighed the harvest on his own scales. The tenant found he could never quite get out of debt. He was trapped in the system, usually sinking deeper and deeper into obligation to the white landowners, storekeepers, and bankers. Slavery had simply taken a different name.[25]

During the four decades following the Civil War, the black population in Freestone County was politically active, the county being recognized as part of the state's black belt. Republicans were the party of choice, but the Greenback Party, or Greenbackers, came on the scene in the mid-to-late 1870s. They made a play for the black vote, and rivaled the Republican party for a few years.

Greenbackers were agrarian malcontents who advocated the issuance of more paper money to redeem treasury notes and reduce debt. In the election of 1878, Galveston, Brazos, Freestone, Falls, and Bastrop counties went solidly for the Greenback ticket. In 1880, the Greenbackers elected five blacks to the Texas Legislature.[26]

But events at the turn of the century had the same effect in Freestone County as they had elsewhere in the South. In 1896, the U.S. Supreme Court upheld the doctrine of "separate but equal" in the case of Plessy vs. Ferguson, and Jim Crowism was born. Segregation of school facilities was legal, although the facilities were far from equal, and segregation on all other fronts followed.

Quickly thereafter, the imposition of the poll tax in Southern states effectively disenfranchised the black population. In Louisiana, which adopted the tax in 1898, the number of black people registering to vote in 1900 dropped by ninety-six percent from what it had been in 1896. Texas, which adopted the tax in 1902, experienced a similar result, although the state did not keep voter registration records by race, as was done in Louisiana.[27] Most Southern states had a handful of African

American legislators before the turn of the century, but thereafter there were none.

The poll tax put an end to effective African American political strength in Freestone County, but whites were still economically dependent upon black labor. Chopping, "busting middles" (removing weeds between rows of cotton), picking, and plowing in the cotton fields was back-breaking work. Some white farmers performed the labor themselves, but most relied upon black families.

Thus, there existed in Freestone County traditions and fears that were common in the deep South, and uncommon in many parts of Texas. Blacks outnumbered or nearly outnumbered whites, but were kept in submission by well-understood codes. Whites were dependent upon blacks for their livelihoods, while blacks were held dependent and in poverty through economic and social constraints. Many whites could see the fallacies and injustices of the system, but were either powerless or uninterested in changing it. Deep down, many whites were terrified of what might occur if blacks finally decided for themselves that the traditions should change.

Shortly after the turn of the century, while the railroad was bringing prosperity to some parts of the county, a boll-weevil blight hit the area and put hundreds of cotton farmers out of business. The soil and markets would not support other profitable row crops, and a man who could not raise cotton did not have many options. Citizens of non-railroad communities had greater reason to move to Kirven or Teague. The plight of Fairfield, the county seat, was particularly notable.

The town had seen boom days in the 1850s and 1860s, when it rivaled surrounding counties and even Dallas in terms of property values and growth.[28] By 1917, however, the town had declined to the point that citizens of Teague initiated a drive to take the county seat away.[29] Fairfield barely held on to its courthouse, and the county even built a new one there in 1919, but as late as February 1920, the town's citizens were still waiting for their first electric plant.[30]

Life in Fairfield and the rest of Freestone County changed dramatically in 1920, however. The oil boom was one reason. The other was Prohibition.

The Volstead Act of 1919, commonly known as Prohibition, was voted in as the Eighteenth Amendment, effective January 16, 1920. Manufacturing, selling, and supplying liquor, or providing transportation to sell it, became illegal throughout the United States, although merely possessing it was still legal.[31]

Prohibition dramatically changed the poorest sections of Freestone County. In many isolated regions, particularly east of Fairfield and along the Trinity River bottoms, moonshine stills burgeoned like wild-flowers in backwoods hollows. At first, the clear, oily corn liquor was only sold and consumed locally. The county was ideally located for exporting liquor north to Dallas/Fort Worth, south to Houston, or west to Waco, but before long-range bootlegging became common, the oil boom created a huge, profitable market right next door.

Thousands of oil-field roughnecks from across the country flocked to Limestone County derricks after the news of the Rogers well was announced. Housing became so short around Mexia that some families lived in shacks made of cardboard.[32] With the workers came prosti-tutes, gamblers, professional criminals, and bootleggers. The bootleg-gers found plenty of demand for liquor, and plenty of local supply. More stills popped up in the woods, the brakes, and the bottoms. Moonshine became a better cash crop than cotton.

Most of the stills were located east of Fairfield, but most of the mar-ketplaces were close to the Limestone County line on the west. Wor-tham, west of Kirven and north of Mexia, became the site of the Winter Garden, a fabulous roadhouse which supplied liquor, gambling, danc-ing, and women to newly moneyed roughnecks. Other "resorts" sprang up closer to Mexia and just outside of Teague.[33]

The problems of moonshining and bootlegging around Mexia and Fairfield became so acute, in fact, that in the first two months of 1922, Governor Pat Neff declared martial law, first in all of Limestone and the western part of Freestone counties, and then in the entire region of both counties. The National Guard and the Texas Rangers were sent in to assist federal prohibition agents. Huge raids were conducted in both counties, in which resorts and roadhouses were shut down, moon-shiners were rounded up, and stills were destroyed.[34]

During the martial-law period, the county received national atten-tion for its moonshining problem and the accompanying crime wave, but the town of Kirven was not mentioned in any of the reports. The town did have a bootlegger—an Italian named John Degetto who sup-plied local needs.[35] Occasionally, too, a farmer in the area would be discovered "keeping batch" along a creek bottom. However, serious moonshining and bootlegging were not nearly as prevalent around Kirven as they were in other parts of the county.

Other forces, national and local, large and subtle, were also at work, and would help alter the societal landscape of Kirven and the county after May 4, 1922.

Nationally, the country was still recovering from the Great War and America's flirtation with international politics. Even though credited with helping win the war and furthering democracy, Americans concluded after 1919 that they had gained little from the experience. One response was withdrawal, or isolationism. Another was Prohibition. A third was increased racial tension.

Blacks had served with distinction during the war, albeit under French rather than American commanders, but the notion that armed black men had efficiently and consistently killed and defeated armed white men sent a wave of alarm through the South and other parts of the nation.

This, in turn, rekindled the debate about lynching. Lynching was as controversial following World War I as abortion and gun control have been in the last few decades of the twentieth century. Northerners condemned the practice as the antithesis of all America stood for, a barbarous, heinous, racist act. Southerners defended it as a necessary tool of the American justice system. They pointed to the increased lawlessness brought on by Prohibition as support for their position. Southerners did not have adequate resources to maintain the peace, they argued, unless citizens were occasionally allowed to take the law into their own hands.

Today, the arguments on both sides seem unreal, and filled with dark comedy, but they were very real in 1921 and 1922. Particularly prominent spokespersons against lynching were James Cutler, who published *Lynch-Law* in 1905, Frank Tannenbaum, who would publish *Darker Phases of the South* in 1924, and Walter White, who would publish *Rope and Faggot: A Biography of Judge Lynch* in 1929.

The South had equally staunch defenders. Southern newspapers stood up for their own, vilifying the crimes of lynching victims and lauding the bravery of the mob. Winfield Collins published *The Truth About Lynching* in 1918, and passionately defended slavery and lynching. John Powell, of Richmond, Virginia, campaigned strenuously for racial purity through a series of articles in the *Richmond Times-Dispatch* in the early twenties, adding to the national hysteria. Scientists such as Robert Bennett Bean of the University of Virginia sought to prove Negroid brain weight was significantly lower than Caucasian brain weight in order to physiologically support theories of basic racial inferiority.

Freestone County natives were influenced by what was happening on the national scene, perhaps more than they knew, but their focus was upon local events, particularly upon looking out for each other and

standing united against outside threats. They were bound together by
blood, history, religion, custom, and interdependence. Allegiance to
community often took precedence over state and federal law. Perhaps
no case illustrated this better than the 1922 murder trial of two Kirven
residents, Carter and J. R. Sessions, which ended only a few weeks
before Eula's last ride.

The men, father and son, were patriarchs of one of the most respected "old families" in the county. Carter's father had come to Texas
from Alabama in 1849, and to Freestone County in 1853. He had served
in the Confederate infantry during the Civil War, and had built up large
land holdings thereafter. Carter had expanded the Sessions estate, and
was largely responsible for introducing cattle ranching to the region.
Besides being wealthy, the Sessions men were considered to be wise,
benevolent, and extremely trustworthy. When Carter's father died in
1902, he was eulogized as "a nobleman of the old school; who fathered
the fatherless; helped the helpless; succored the needy; befriended the
friendless."[36]

Carter and J. R. Sessions were pillars of the county, but on December 10, 1921, they were arrested and charged with murder.

The victims were two brothers, Elliot and F. F. "Fox" Miller, 34 and
36 years old, respectively, who were mortally wounded in a shooting
that day at the law offices of Bryan and Ricker, which were located in
the First State Bank Building in Wortham.

The newspapers described the relationship between the Sessions
and the Millers as a business arrangement.[37] Outside the jail and the
courtroom, however, locals viewed the Millers as mere representatives
of a Dallas bank that had accused Carter Sessions of being in default
on loans secured by land. The bank had sent the Miller brothers to deliver the foreclosure instruments. They were literally messengers who
had been shot.

The newspapers said there were four eyewitnesses to the crime, but
the exact details of what happened are not clear. One report that spread
among the locals was that J. R. Sessions, the son, was totally innocent,
but was claiming culpability in order to protect his father. Because Carter Sessions, 67, was regarded by whites and blacks alike as one of the
most honest, upstanding citizens of the county, his son's noble gesture
helped enhance the younger man's reputation, and helped set the stage
for a classic hometown court decision.[38]

According to another version of the shooting, possibly an eyewitness
account, J.R. was less noble, and completely culpable. This rendition

of the events portrayed the Miller brothers and the Sessions men as coming together in the law office in order for the latter to execute deeds, and thereby avoid the expense and exposure of a formal foreclosure proceeding. Carter Sessions signed, and when J.R. was to take his turn, one of the Miller brothers offered him the pencil Carter had used.

"No thanks," J.R. supposedly said, "I have my own right here in my pocket." His "own" held a different kind of lead.[39] He reached into his jacket, drew out a .22 pistol, and shot Elliot Miller once and Fox Miller twice, both of them in the head.[40]

According to a newspaper, one bullet went wild and took off one of Carter Sessions's fingers, a fact that seemed to undermine the version of the crime that portrayed J.R. as noble and innocent.[41]

The Miller brothers' wounds were fatal. Elliot died between Wortham and Corsicana, en route to Dallas by train. Fox died about one hour after arriving at a Dallas hospital.[42]

The Sessions were arrested, held in jail for nineteen days, and released on $5,000 bail apiece on December 30, 1921.[43] Two trials were held, one for each brother. At the first one, on February 22, 1922, for the killing of Fox Miller, the state offered the testimony of one of the eyewitnesses, Wortham banker T. B. Poindexter, followed by that of a surviving brother, Amp Miller, and finally that of the widows of the two slain brothers. The defense offered the testimony of the two defendants, and rested its case.

For closing argument, the defense paraded four local attorneys before the jury and portrayed the defendants as men "hounded to desperation" by the underhanded dealings of wily Dallas bankers.

District Judge A. M. Blackmon delivered a long charge to the jury, explaining the law, and advising them they could find the defendants guilty of murder, assault to murder, manslaughter, or aggravated assault. In regard to Carter Sessions, he instructed the jury that if they found the deceased had "unjustly and wrongfully taken advantage of him to his financial loss," and if Sessions believed the deceased were about to cause him greater financial loss, he could not be found guilty of any offense greater than manslaughter.

The jury deliberated for forty minutes and found both men innocent of all charges.[44]

The second trial was held two days later, but was not reported by the local newspapers. Whatever tactics the prosecution and defense employed, the result was the same. The second jury needed little more time than the first in order to acquit the two defendants.[45]

The Sessions walked free, thinking, perhaps, how nice hometown decisions are when you can get them. If anything, the event enhanced rather than damaged their reputation. Eight years later, J.R. would be elected sheriff of the county.

There may have been evidence in the defendants' favor that was not reported in the newspapers. The Millers and the Dallas bank may have been involved in questionable, or shady, business practices. The story illustrates, however, that Freestone County people would rally around and defend members of their community who were threatened from the outside, particularly if they were from the right families, no matter what crime they were accused of committing. This same tendency would play a significant role in the events that occurred after May 4, 1922.

The Sessions were not the only powerful, well-respected family near Kirven who could attract and hold the loyalty of their neighbors. Another was John King, of Shanks, one of the largest landowners in the area.

He and his wife, Permelia, had five sons and one daughter. The sons, Bob, John T., Drew, Otis, and Alva, were tall, stocky, good-looking, and natural leaders, with the kind of fierce, stubborn pride which made Southerners famous.

They are remembered today as having been "a very prominent family who had the best of everything, a big house, and acres and acres of land"; people who "had money . . . and moved in there with their money . . . to make it a wonderful place. They could just see the bright future for it [the town of Kirven]."[46] Grandfather King, like Carter Sessions, was 67 years old in 1922, and was described then as "one of the county's grand old men, possessing the esteem of a large circle of acquaintances."[47] He was also described as "an honored citizen of Freestone County for many years [who] enjoys the confidence, respect and friendship of hundreds of our citizens. A rugged man of simple habits, strong in his friendships, honest and upright in his dealings with men."[48] The boys were described as "men of sturdy character who are towers of strength in their community."[49] In describing the sons years later, however, some who knew them used other terms, such as "domineering," "outrageous," and "hard."

John and Permelia King had lived in Shanks since the 1870s. Three of their five boys had farms between there and downtown Kirven. Drew King, the middle boy, lived in Wortham,[50] while Alva, the youngest, may have been married and living out of state by 1922.[51]

John T., the second son, was the only one who lived inside the city limits of Kirven. He was particularly fortunate, particularly proud. At 34, his principal occupation was raising cotton with the help of hired black men. Additionally, he served as a deputy sheriff, which allowed him to wear a pistol on his hip or in his pocket, a habit which predated and survived his law-enforcement career.[52]

John T., his wife, and their son, "Happy," lived in a large colonial-style mansion, picturesque enough to be considered the showplace of the town. To complete the perfect picture, Mrs. King, formerly Hallie Green, had been one of the prettiest, most popular women in Kirven.[53]

The couple was much in demand at parties and social events in Kirven among those who, as Willie Mae Beaver said, "had it made." J. C. Whatley, a 23 year-old Kirven bachelor in 1922, recalled sixty-five years later that John T. was often the life of a party, but would stand at the table of hors d'oeuvres and eat every ripe olive there.

"It was mostly light stuff, eggs and such," Whatley said, "but if you wanted ripe olives, you had to put them in your pocket, and he'd probably find those, too."[54]

Hallie King's father, John Green, supplied the stately house for his only daughter and her husband. It is said that Mr. Green, a druggist and well-to-do landowner, arranged to have the house constructed, after which he refused to pay the builder. Evidently, he had learned the contractor failed to secure a valid mechanic's lien, and all attempts to collect what was due from Green were to no avail.[55]

Assuming the story is true, and Green acquired the mansion for the cost of the materials only, the trick did not damage his reputation in the community. On the contrary, he was a deacon in the Baptist Church and was well-known and respected for his business acumen. He would also play a minor, but important, role in the events about to unfold.

As proud, powerful, and respected as the Kings were, they might also be described as a family whose tragedy was daughters.

Eula Ausley, for whom John T. saddled the horse on May 4, was the daughter of John T.'s sister, Eunice, the only daughter of John and Permelia King. Eunice had been their second child, but she had not followed the traditional path laid out for Southern ladies.

Perhaps because she was surrounded by willful, boisterous boys, perhaps because her father's strictness invited rebellion, she broke her parents' hearts early, becoming pregnant out of wedlock at sixteen.

She gave birth to a boy and named him Nathan Dowell. The family called the little boy Dowell.

Two years later she married L. C. Ausley, who was sixteen years older than she. A year after that, she gave birth again, to a little girl this time, and died two days thereafter, on November 16, 1904.[56]

There is no available record of how Eunice's death affected the King family, but the impact is not hard to imagine. She was the only daughter, a young mother, and the first to die in a close-knit clan. The love her parents felt for her, despite whatever heartache she had caused, was demonstrated by the fact that they, rather than L. C. Ausley, took on the job of raising the two babies.[57]

Carrying on a first-syllable tradition for little girls in the King family, the baby was named Eula. Her mother had been Eunice, and her grandmother, who went by Permelia, was Eubeza.[58]

Eula quickly became the sun around which the family orbited. The only little girl and an instant, demanding diversion from their grief, she naturally became the center of everyone's attention. For her grandparents she was a second chance, and she was said to look exactly like her mother.[59] To her uncles, she was more sister than niece. Alva was only five, Otis ten, Drew fourteen, and John T. seventeen when Eula came to live with them. Only Bob, at twenty-one, was out of the house and married by then.

When Eula was two, the railroad came to Freestone County and Kirven was born. When she was five, her father was committed to the North Texas State Hospital for the Mentally Ill in Terrell, Texas.[60]

There is no record of the reasons for L. C. Ausley's breakdown. He had lived alone since Eunice's death, and may have become the victim of alcohol or the rigors of trying to extract life from the unsympathetic Freestone County soil. The loss of his young wife and two children surely helped drive him over some ragged edge.

When she was seven, Eula started school in Shanks's two-room schoolhouse. When she was fifteen, on January 16, 1920, her father died of influenza. He was 52, and had not been out of the asylum since he was committed. He was buried in Teague on January 21.[61]

As Eula grew, she steadily became more precious to her grandparents and uncles. Despite being the only girl and everyone's sweetheart, she did not develop a self-centered personality. Whatever faults she possessed, whatever and however many selfish, thoughtless deeds she committed, that has all been lost to memory. She was warm-hearted, happy, and sincerely concerned about the comfort and feelings of those around her, and that side of her personality, as much as can be recovered after seventy-five years, seems etched in marble. One eulogy described her as being the "life and sunshine in the home of her grandparents."[62] A classmate described her as having "just the sweetest personality," and as being adored by everyone who knew her.[63]

The boys eventually left the nest and most took brides. In addition to Maggie, who was Bob's wife, there was John T.'s wife, Hallie, Drew's wife, Corrie, and Otis's wife, Rena. Eula's brother, Dowell, moved in with Otis and Rena. The departure of each boy must have increased Grandfather and Permelia's awareness of their own mortality as well as their attachment to Eula. Perhaps her sweetness expanded to fill voids left by the sons, and perhaps the departed uncles, in turn, were comforted to know their parents still had Eula at home.

The year her father died, Eula completed the eighth grade at Shanks. Texas had a statewide district school system, but fifty-three of the state's counties, including Freestone, were exempted, having either community-supported or independent district schools instead. Thus, the number of grades a town's school offered depended on the number of teachers and the size of the facilities it could afford. There were 110 small schools, segregated white and colored, scattered over the county, but no uniformity in the number of grades offered. While some had only six grades, Shanks had eight, Fairfield had nine, and Streetman and Kirven offered ten.[64]

Neither a twelve-year high school education nor college was considered necessary for young ladies. Although Fairfield had boasted a female college during the Civil War and for several years thereafter, in Freestone County in the 1910s and 1920s, girls rarely were raised to believe they needed either.

Only one young lady from Kirven, Lura Bess Mayo, had left the county to go to college prior to 1920. The event was so noteworthy that the entire town turned out to see her leave for Fort Worth to attend Texas Women's College.[65]

Like Lura Bess, who returned to Kirven to teach school in 1921, Eula wanted more education, and her grandfather was not known for denying her what she wanted. In the fall of 1920, she began riding her horse the three miles to and from school in Kirven.

In March 1922, with graduation approaching, Eula began thinking about what she would do next. Grandfather and Grandmother King were surely thinking about the same subject. There had been children in the house for thirty-eight years, and the prospect of an empty nest must have weighed heavily on their minds. Perhaps it was to entice her to stay as long as possible after graduation that Grandfather King bought Eula the unheard-of gift of her own automobile.[66]

During the first week of March, Dr. William H. Andrew, the minister of Kirven's Baptist Church, arranged for a Waco evangelist, V. B. Starnes, to bring his traveling tent revival to Kirven.[67]

Starnes was accompanied by a gospel singer and a pianist, and the vacant lot downtown where their tent was pitched was approximately equidistant between the Methodist and Baptist churches.[68] An account of the revival was published in the Kirven, Teague, and Fairfield newspapers, in an identical press release, which read, in part, as follows:

> Kirven is afire with the preaching of V. B. Starnes, Evangelist, who is conducting a big tent revival in that place. The crowds are stupendous. Ever since the first sermon Sunday morning, the citizenship has known that "some one was in town." Even the old folks, who have seen many revivals, say that this is as effective preaching as they ever heard. . . .
>
> The citizenship of the surrounding country has been invited with special invitation to attend these services. They show they appreciate the invitation for they come, come from the kitchen, come from the store, come from the school, come from the farm, come from all over the country. Starnes pleases them all.[69]

The King family came. They normally attended church in Shanks, but the revival was the biggest celebration of faith, as well as the largest social event, since Christmas. Its timing, on the heels of martial law, seemed particularly fitting, and Eula's public and formal embracing of Christianity in response to Starnes's invitation was yet another example of her ideal nature, which may have seemed remarkably unlike her mother's.

Standing before her radiant grandparents and beaming aunts and uncles, enraptured by the booming voice of the Reverend Starnes, filled with the love of God and the joy of living, she could not know, nobody could know, what evil would take place on the very same spot in two short months' time.

For beneath the brightness and light which seemed to shine around Eula, the county, Kirven, and the Kings, beneath the facade of respectability and self-perceived elitism, there lurked an elastic flame of anger, the makings of a force that would take Kirven from brightness to gray, from gray to black, and to whatever lay beyond black.

In the King family, much of the dark anger was harbored by the next-to-youngest son, Otis. Twenty-seven in 1922, Otis lived with his wife, Rena, their daughter, Oleta, and his nephew, Dowell, in a brick house on the outskirts of Kirven.[70] Like John T., Otis liked to carry a revolver, and whether by popular election or general understanding, he acted as town marshal.

Otis was not as popular or sociable as John T., however. His personality was more volatile, somber, and brooding. He also possessed a particularly strong dislike of blacks. Perhaps all of the Kings did. Certainly they are remembered today for violent racism.

Blacks living in the nearby community of Simsboro in 1922 said the Kings—not just Otis, but all of them—"were ugly people who didn't believe in being fair to black people."[71] Some whites who knew them said they were "awfully overbearing" and "always doing outrageous things."[72]

Of the few specific anecdotes that exist pertaining to the Kings' racism, the following one was told by Kirven resident Whitfield Beaver to his daughter-in-law, Willie Mae.

A neighbor of Otis and the father of the telegrapher who sent first word of the discovery of the Mexia oil field to the world, Whit Beaver was home with his wife Emma one night in 1921, when they heard a loud thump, followed by a cry, from the road in front of their house. They went outside and found a black man lying in the road. Over him stood Otis King, cursing and threatening the man with extinction. Behind Otis was his car, idling, its headlights out.

After calming Otis and helping the hapless man to his feet, Beaver pieced together the story. Apparently the black man had been in the road, walking home, when Otis drove up from behind with his lights out and ran into him. The young King then cursed the man for walking in the road, and threatened to kill him if he caught him doing the same thing again.[73]

The King brothers depended upon blacks to cultivate their fields. Each brother, except Alva, employed four full-time workers and a handful of seasonal laborers. Later, and also perhaps contemporaneously, people said that the brothers were exceptionally cruel to their hired hands. If a black worker failed to plow either straight or enough, or did not hoe or pick enough in a day, Otis, John T., Bob, or Drew, it was said, would beat or pistol-whip him.[74]

Grandfather King also employed blacks, including Ben Gibson and Ben's son, Leroy, but there are no credible anecdotes about his being cruel to them. He was also said to have been overbearing, and correctly or not, his sons' strong tempers and attitudes were credited to his example. As a great-grandson recalled, "He ruled the roost, and all the boys wanted to be just like him." [75] Grandfather King was from Georgia and from an earlier generation than his sons, however. He may have been more tolerant.

At the end of March, martial law, the Starnes revival, and the Sessions trial were over, and the weather became springlike. On March 24, the *Teague Chronicle* ran a short article on page three entitled "More Prosperous Times Ahead." It began: "The opening of spring finds Freestone county people with great things in prospect and volumes to be thankful for, in spite of some seemingly unfavorable circumstances."

The three-paragraph story mentioned how agreeable the weather was for preparing farm crops, and how oil development in the county showed encouraging signs for future prosperity. It concluded: "There is nothing to mar the hopes of those interested in farming and no reason why peace and plenty should not prevail at the close of the incoming season. . . . the chances are ten to one that before many moons 'there will be something doing in the old town tonight.'"

There would be something doing all right, but not peace and plenty. There was neither reason nor expectation of anything else, but as prosperous and promising as life seemed, other forces and personalities, some as large as history, some as local as a town's leading family, were about to change things forever for Kirven, the county, the country, and the Kings.

3 The Instant when Music Shatters Glass

When Eula was not home by four-thirty, Grandmother King and Aunt Rena began worrying. Eula's new dress was finished and spread out on her bed, waiting to be fitted. Eula was exceptionally prompt, and always had been.[1] When she had not arrived by five o'clock, Permelia and Rena put out an alarm.[2]

Grandmother King went to the telephone, cranked the handle, and told the operator to ring John T.'s house. Hallie King answered, listened to her mother-in-law's hurried questions, and replied that Eula rode away from their house at four. Grandmother King asked her to send John T. to look for the girl and rang off.

As soon as she hung up the phone, she summoned Grandfather King.

"She must have fallen off her horse. She might have been in a hurry to get home and started galloping," Permelia told him. "Maybe the saddle turned, or she hit a tree limb. She may be lying out there hurt."

Grandfather King listened, but heard the details of his wife's hypothesis only vaguely. He appeared calm, but internally he was in the grip of sinister terror. Eula's disappearance was something he had feared for two years. He did not voice his worries, did not want to further alarm Grandmother King, but he already suspected their granddaughter was the victim of foul play.[3]

Mr. King telephoned the home of their neighbors, Whitfield and Emma Beaver. Eula rode by their house every day, and the call confirmed that she had passed by a few minutes after four. A call to another neighbor along the route yielded a similar report.[4]

His panic growing, Grandfather King summoned Ben Gibson, a black man in his early fifties who worked on the King farm, and told him to ride out and find the girl.[5] After Ben left, Mr. King returned to the phone and called sons Bob and Drew. Neither were home, but their wives, Maggie and Corrie, promised to send their husbands to help look for their niece as soon as they returned.

In a few minutes Ben came back, leading Eula's horse. He had found the animal with its reins tied to a bush near the bridge over Grindstone Creek.[6]

The news of the horse being tied and Eula not being nearby sent a new wave of coldness vibrating through Grandfather King's heart. Grimly, he asked Ben to get his son, Leroy, to help look for the girl. Then he told Permelia to call Dr. Whiteside. Next he saddled his own horse and rode toward the creek.[7] He feared something more menacing than a turned saddle or a low tree limb.

Forty-two-year-old William Whiteside was one of two physicians in Kirven and the King's family doctor. His services might be needed.

When Permelia called, J. C. Whatley answered the phone. J.C. was Whiteside's 23-year-old clerk, the son of the owner of the Kirven cotton gin. He worked in the drug store below the doctor's office, selling medicines, sundries, sweets, and soft drinks. In response to Mrs. King's inquiry, he put the doctor on the phone.

Whiteside listened, told her there had been no word of Eula being injured, but said he would be happy to close the office and store, take Whatley, and join the search.

A few minutes later, Dr. Whiteside bounded down the stairs from his office to the drug store and called out to Whatley, "Come on, Jaybird, let's go see if we can find that girl." Sixty-five years and one day later, Whatley recalled the incident and added, "He always called me Jaybird."[8]

Whatley recalled a lot more, perhaps the most of any witness who had survived so long, but his account rings rather dully against the bell of truth. He described being at or near each major incident of May 4, 5, and 6, and while that is possible, his placing of himself or his father center stage at some of the incidents is questionable. According to him, they were not merely witnesses, but participants and instigators. In addition to telling about seeing important events occur, he described how they actually caused some to happen.

J.C. was basking in the limelight, or lemon-limelight, when he told his tale in May 1987. He was certain he was one of the last surviving participants of the events of 1922, perhaps the very last. Who was going to challenge him?

There were, however, twenty or thirty newspaper accounts, none of which mentioned either of the Whatley men. Some, in fact, described incidents completely differently than J.C. described them. There were also more than twenty other witnesses to one aspect of the events or another, and while none may have been as near center stage as Whatley, none even mentioned seeing him in the theater. As a nephew of Whatley's recalled later, "J.C. always added to the story. Too bad you didn't get to talk to him while his wife was alive. She'd always break in and say 'Oh J.C., it didn't happen that way!' Between the two of them, you could usually figure out the real story."[9]

Still, his version deserves to be considered. If not the complete truth, it is the diagnostic truth. Even if neither of the Whatleys were as intimately involved as J.C. described, they were nearby, and he probably based his story, or embellishment, on details he either witnessed or heard about from someone who was.

He did not describe closing the store or climbing into Dr. Whiteside's car and driving along the route Eula rode each day to the creek. He simply said they went "down there and got out where the fence was broken down."

When asked if he and Dr. Whiteside were the first on the scene, he said, "There were plenty of them looking, but they weren't looking in this place, see." He did not name the other searchers, but they included Drew and John T. King, and probably Otis King and Dowell Ausley.

There were others, too. After Grandfather King contacted his sons or their wives, he or they apparently summoned help from neighbors, and word spread quickly.

Eula's friend, Mary, who narrowly missed the same fate as Eula, remembered that on the afternoon of May 4, the entire town heard she was missing, and turned out to help search:

> Her horse came home. Its bridle was dragging the ground, you know, and they put out the alarm and John T. and Otis and Alva and Drew, all the King men, they got together and they got the word out, the alarm went out, and so everybody was kind of getting together in little groups down on the street corners and little children, of course, were hanging onto their mamas' skirts, and were becoming alarmed about this terrible thing that had happened and so they were searching everywhere in the woods for her because she had to go through the woods to get home, and the thing that happened, they said that if you hear a gun shoot three times, you'll know that we found her, because everybody was so alarmed, because it had gotten dark by now, and I remember exactly where I was, up across from the church. That house is still sitting there, the old Walker House, on that street

there. . . . We sat on the old porch that came all
around the house and waited for those three shots.[10]

Ben Gibson, Grandfather King's black hired hand, and his son
Leroy may have been there, although one account puts Ben at home;
perhaps he had gone there to fetch Leroy. Some nearby neighbors,
possibly those who heard the screams, may have come forth. There
had not been time for word to spread far, but everyone who was interviewed described the summoning of help by the King family as an
alarm.

When Whatley and Whiteside stepped out of the doctor's car, their attention was drawn away from the broken fence to a patch of bare, sandy
ground nearby. Hoof prints of a horse, mixed with shoe prints of two or
more men, were plainly visible. There were signs of a struggle.

The men who made the prints were wearing brogans—work
shoes—and one pair left a distinctive mark. Nails protruding from the
sole of the worn shoes scratched the ground and left a telltale track.
Whatley was very certain of this, and mentioned seeing the tracks more
than once.

"We started in where the fence had broke down," he said, "where
they'd taken her to this place, see, and we just started out, up through
them woods, kind of spread out." There may have been a faint trail
where the men carrying Eula forced their way to the creek; Whatley
said, "[Soon] we saw something over there, and we pulled in together,
and there she lay."

Whether it was Whatley and Whiteside or someone else who first
saw her—one of the newspapers said Drew King found her—the sight
of Eula was shocking. She was in a clearing beside the creek. The initial
impression was that she had been decapitated.

She was naked, mutilated, and her head was not visible. "Her head
was beat in the ground," Whatley explained, "until it was just flat
across, in a hole in the ground that big around." He held up both hands
in a circle the size of a basketball to demonstrate the size of the hole.
Eula's murderers had stomped her face, driving her head into the soft
creek bank. The surface of the earth was even with her ruined countenance.[11] Her pretty features were wrecked, her eyes staring and vacu-
ous, her nose broken and split, her mouth blasted. Those who found
her would later comb teeth from her hair.[12]

Her throat was cut from ear to ear.[13] Her tongue had been sliced
out and was lying near her body.[14] Her chest was covered with
lacerations.[15]

Newspapers reported that she had been stabbed in the chest more than thirty times, but J. C. Whatley denied there were any knife wounds. He swore the marks on her chest and throat were the same as those in the bare patch of ground, made by nails protruding from a pair of heavy work brogans.

Lower on her body was greater horror. She lay in a pool of blood, most of which flowed from her vagina.

Dr. Whiteside found a cedar stick near the body. It was covered with blood, spongy flesh, and coarse, curly hair.

"They'd taken an old knotted stick about that long, see," Whatley explained, holding the index finger of his left hand against the inside crook of his right elbow and cupping his right fingers to indicate its length. "There was knots all over it, and they just jobbed her with it 'til they tore her all to pieces inside." [16]

Whiteside directed Whatley back to the car to get a rope and a lantern. The sun was nearly down. The day was donning its mourning wear.

When Whatley returned, Whiteside directed him to string the rope around the body and to let no one inside except the girl's favorite uncle, John T. King.

Whatley did not describe the approach of the other searchers, except to confirm that John T. was the only one allowed inside the rope. If anyone fired three shots into the air, as they promised the townspeople they would do, Whatley did not mention their doing so. The sight and condition of Eula's body may have caused them to forget.

Such outrage and horror can only be imagined, but must have been tremendous. For the Kings, the shock was nearly insurmountable.

The proud men of the King family, the uncles, older brothers, and grandfather, finding the flower of the family, their north, south, east, and west, so terribly misused, so cruelly violated, was more than they could bear.

Some of them lost an essential grip on sanity that darkling spring evening. Death was no stranger, but Eula's death, her murder and violation, was something their hearts could not absorb, their minds could not assimilate. They experienced in their consciousness that instant when music shatters glass. The shards would fly wide and cut deep.

Whatley said that John T., Whiteside, and he picked up Eula's body and carried it to an abandoned house some two hundred yards away. There was an empty house nearby that may have belonged to a family named Fainter. Another account reported that six men took turns carrying her across their locked arms, and that they carried her to the Kings' house.[17] Whatley said they laid her on the porch, and while he held the lamp, Whiteside examined her wounds.

"They didn't rape the girl," Whiteside reported. She had been mutilated with the stick, but not raped, although how he could have been certain under such conditions is difficult to comprehend. There may have been an attempt in his diagnosis to avoid some degree of grief, to ward off some element of reprisal.

The sheriff and an ambulance were summoned by members of the search party, and from the little knot of men on the porch of the house, the dark news spread to three counties. It spread by mouth, by telephone, and by automobile, stretching out from Kirven to the far corners of the region like strands of a web, awakening a dark keeper, loosing a secret horror.

As the news spread, the men on the porch tried to clean Eula's body as best they could, to restore a vestige of her beauty, to restore familiarity to the ruin.

"We finally got as much blood out of her hair and stuff as that," J. C. Whatley said. "[We] cleaned her up so much as we could with no water there or nothing, and then we turned her over to the sheriff's department, see, and they brought the ambulance to pick her up."

Whatley paused and considered for a moment. The day was May 5, 1987, and it was a gentle spring evening very similar to the one sixty-five years and a day earlier, when Eula was murdered. A meadowlark sang somewhere nearby, and cicadas hummed in the trees. The moment seemed ripe for vivid observation, keen understanding, closure— for a statement that would capture the essence of the time and emotion of the event.

Instead, he cleared his throat and continued.

"And as far as I know, for three or four years after that, well, that hole was still in the ground out there."[18]

4 Sheriff Mayo

The sheriff who received the call to retrieve Eula's body, Horace Milton Mayo, is part of the mystery of this tale. He was a man of two minds, capable of great sensitivity and insensitivity, wisdom and stupidity, bravery and cowardice.

Faced with terrible challenges that few people will ever encounter, he tried desperately to do what he believed was right, and sometimes succeeded magnificently. Yet other things he did defy explanation, and he can be viewed as a villain as easily as he can be viewed a hero in this tale. The passage of time has made two facts certain, however. On May 4, 1922, he was five months into the worst year he had ever experienced, and his life would not get any better.

The 42-year-old Mayo was a former cotton gin operator, farmer, and contractor who built houses, schools, and roads, including portions of the road from Kirven to Fairfield, before becoming sheriff. He was from Kirven, having moved there from Ward's Prairie in 1905, just before the railroad arrived. He operated his father's cotton gin—which was later sold to Walter Whatley, the father of Dr. Whiteside's clerk, J.C.—and tried cotton farming, but thought he had found his niche after turning to law enforcement. He was one-hundred-percent mistaken.

Like John T. King, Mayo had served as Kirven's deputy sheriff. He was a crack pistol shot, but unlike John T., he did not habitually wear a pistol. In 1918 he ran for sheriff against incumbent J. F. Roper and lost.[1] In November 1920, Roper became county judge, Mayo ran again, and this time was successful.[2]

Mayo campaigned on four claims—that he would wipe out moonshining; that he was a church-going Christian man; that he was the best pistol shot in the county; and that he was well-liked by all who knew him.[3] The four points assured his election, but three of them immediately conspired to do him in.

The oil boom in Limestone County, and with it, the moonshining industry, exploded the month he was elected. Dozens, perhaps hundreds, of Freestone County citizens saw serious money to be made violating a law they did not support.

Mayo pitched in and began working to fulfill his campaign promise. On December 10, after being in office only ten days, he and his chief deputy arrested their first moonshiner.[4] Another was captured on Christmas eve, another in early February 1921, another on March 15, and two more in August.[5]

During this time, he was enjoying his new office and enhanced reputation. Shortly after being sworn in, he purchased a new automobile and moved his family—his wife, Bess, and their three daughters, Lura Bess, Grace, and Ruth—into living quarters on the first floor of the new jail in Fairfield.[6] In July 1921, accompanied by Bess, he attended the State Sheriff's Convention in distant Amarillo, while the older daughters, Lura Bess and Grace, visited an aunt in Austin, and the youngest girl, Ruth, visited relatives in Oklahoma.[7]

On September 3, 1921, however, Mayo committed an act that cannot be explained, and which would taint his reputation for decades. A man named Jerry Winchester was living in a wooden frame house two miles east of Kirven with a girl who was the daughter of Winchester's half-brother. Armed with a warrant charging Winchester with incest and accompanied by John T. and Otis King, Mayo went to arrest the man.

The newspaper reported that Winchester was standing on his gallery, or porch, when the officers approached, but made a run for the house when the lawmen told him he was under arrest.[8] Another version of the story, passed down orally to later generations, said that Mayo became intoxicated, worked himself up imagining what might be going on inside Winchester's house, went there, called him out, and shot him dead.[9]

An eyewitness account was entirely different. Twelve-year-old Sarah Goolsby was playing with her younger brother in the front yard of the house across the road when Mayo drove up, parked at Winchester's, and went inside without knocking. She thought later that he was alone, but admitted that he may have had one or more deputies with him. The two children did not pay much attention until shots rang out.

Within moments, cars and people were converging on the scene, and the news was passing from person to person for the children to hear—Mayo had walked into Winchester's bedroom, where the unarmed man was lying sick in bed, and had summarily shot him to death.[10]

Whatever the true facts, more than one shot was fired, Winchester died, and the young lady was taken into custody.

Other tongues passed the story to later generations, and painted a still darker picture. They added that the Winchester girl was not jailed, nor freed, but was provided with another place to live, courtesy of Horace Mayo, who became her frequent visitor, and her lover.

Considering what occurred later, and how controversial Mayo was to become, the latter story is probably nothing but vicious defamation, spread by men, possibly members of the Ku Klux Klan, who grew to hate him. On the other hand, something did seem to take the drive out of Mayo's Prohibition enforcement campaign at that time. Only one more arrest of a moonshiner was reported during the next five months, or, in other words, until the governor declared martial law in Freestone County in February 1922.[11]

Prohibition violations were so widespread in Freestone County during 1921 that mass meetings of citizens were called "to build sentiment for the enforcement of all laws." A "League to Enforce Prohibition" was formed in April of that year, and its members vowed to take action to put an end to the "spirit of lawlessness that prevails in our country."[12]

If Mayo was caught up in the movement, it escaped the notice of the local press. On the contrary, despite the arrests he had made, insinuations began to flow that Mayo was becoming soft on moonshining, or worse, that he was taking bribes.

Friends of the Jekyll-headed Mayo might not have been surprised by such reports. They knew the sheriff was no teetotaler. Before Prohibition he had downed more than a few while swapping stories with his friends, the Hogan boys, the Teers, and others. A mere amendment to the U.S. Constitution was not likely to change his habits. Doubts about Mayo's dedication to the Eighteenth Amendment were bolstered by a prank he pulled sometime in 1921.

Mayo purchased a new car, a Nash, after being elected.[13] The practice of a county supplying its sheriff with a patrol car was a concept for the future. The notion of a sheriff traveling around the county by any other means than on horseback, in fact, was a pretty novel idea.

So Mayo was immediately recognized one afternoon when he drove slowly into a small community in the county—perhaps Streetman or Cotton Gin. He drifted back and forth across the center of the main street, parked erratically, opened the door with difficulty, and lurched, squinting, onto the sunny sidewalk. He staggered when he walked, slurred when he talked, and smelled of moonshine. A few moments after he arrived, he was challenged to a shootout.

The gunplay was not violent and the challengers were not criminals.

They were local youths who had spied a rare opportunity to best the finest marksman in the county.

They dared him to some competitive target shooting; Mayo agreed, and bets were made. The sheriff allowed his opponents to fire first, then dropped all pretense of intoxication.

Straightening, he drew a steady bead on the targets, shot each dead center, collected his winnings, and drove merrily out of town.[14]

The stunt may have enhanced his standing among the county's good old boys, but it gained him no votes from the Sunday School, abstinence, or temperance crowds. That was unfortunate for Mayo, because he was an exceptionally conscientious churchgoer and family man. All of his three daughters were adamant about their father's Christianity and gentle nature. Each recalled how he took the family to church Sunday mornings and evenings and to Wednesday prayer meetings, and how he directed the choir.[15]

Horace Mayo had a rich tenor voice, and singing was one of his greatest joys. Before becoming sheriff, he taught singing lessons throughout the county. His students were adults and children, men and women, and the only songs he taught were hymns.[16]

He also held neighborhood singing fests on Sunday afternoons, bringing friends together and serenading anyone who cared to listen. Bess, his wife, would play the guitar, and the two oldest daughters sang as a duet. Lura Bess, born in 1902, sang soprano, and Grace, born in 1904, sang alto.[17]

Mayo took the two girls to churches, banquets, parties, festivals, and reunions throughout the county. They were cute and talented, and Freestone folks were grateful for the entertainment. The Mayo sisters were popular celebrities within a limited realm.

When Lura Bess was old enough, her mother took organ lessons by mail so she could teach the girl to play the piano. Thereafter, until she went away to college in 1918, Lura Bess played the piano for her father during the lessons he taught, as well as at song fests and church. Eighty years later she recalled fondly how, perched between his knees, she would share a little piano stool with her father, playing while he sang.[18]

Mayo reveled in his family, and his daughters were his pride. He delighted in teasing them, hugging them, perching them on his knees or lap, and telling them tall tales. The day Lura Bess joined the church in Kirven, he met her at its front door, picked her up, threw her into the air, and caught her.[19]

The man the daughters saw, however, made up only half of their father's personality. Among his peers or in his cups, he was often very different.

To complete this unlikely array of qualities in a sheriff, and possibly explaining some of what happened to him, Mayo was an exceptionally sensitive man.[20] He hurt easily and carried the scars of slights and perceived slights for months and years after they were inflicted.

He may have come by his sensitivity honestly. He might have inherited it. As Lura Bess recalled, other members of the family were also delicate, and reacted strongly to disappointment.

Horace's sister, Mary Bell Mayo, for instance, did not recover after her father forbade her to see the young man she had fallen in love with in her teens or early twenties. Lura Bess described what happened:

> She had taught school. She had graduated from college there at Fairfield, and she taught school for a year or two, and I was her favorite, and she was the prettiest thing, oh my. My granddaddy, her daddy, owned this real nice place close to the cotton gin in Fairfield. It was called the Sandbed Place, because it was in the sand, and it was THE place. When he bought it, my mother and daddy, and I was a baby, four or five years old, we moved there with Aunt Mary . . . but then she seemed to lose her ability to take care of herself, and would just wander around and not know what she was doing.[21]

Mary's father and mother decided she had suffered a mental breakdown, and that she needed to be sent to a mental hospital. Like L. C. Ausley, she was taken to Terrell, in Kaufman County.

"And when they drove off with her," Lura Bess recalled, "it just nearly killed me. I just cried and cried. I wanted Aunt Mary, you know."

Mary never recovered. Like L. C. Ausley again, she died in the asylum, on June 23, 1928.[22]

Sheriff Mayo was carrying at least two wounds on his sensitive soul the night he received the news about Eula.

One was inflicted by the Ku Klux Klan, members of which had appeared in Freestone County on September 22, 1921, less than three weeks after the shooting of Jerry Winchester.[23] Initially, they did no more than leave mysterious envelopes of money at the office of the *Teague Chronicle* newspaper, with directions for them to be delivered to needy women in the community.

Additional envelopes contained letters defending the secret society, which, their writers claimed, had been "maligned by the prejudiced and misrepresented by the ignorant." One letter declared:

> Some misguided good citizens have criticized the Klan, but many bad citizens are alert to the danger that threatens their criminal purposes. The members of the Klan comprise the truest and best citizens of this Republic. They are against every evil influence everywhere in society and in government. They are against immoralities in our national life and will cleanse it. They are sick of the loopholes in our laws and will close them. They are tired of unfaithful officers and will supplant them.[24]

Mayo was the principal officer of the law whom the local members of the Klan considered unfaithful. Whether it was because of his record against moonshiners, or whether it was because of the Winchester shooting, the shooting-contest prank, a kindly attitude toward blacks, or because he had crossed the Ku Kluxers somewhere else, feelings on both sides were decidedly fixed. Months after the publication of their first letter, the Klan would be openly hostile to Mayo, but the sheriff would stand up to them, writing a statement that was published in the newspaper in which he declared:

> I will be perfectly plain here and now and leave no room for doubt. I am unable to see how any officer of the law can subscribe to anything as lawless as the Klan. Instead of being for law and order, it is the very opposite. Instead of an orderly enforcement of the law, they would inaugurate mob law. A law that requires men going about with hidden faces and robed in disguise is hardly worth enforcing. Law enforcement first of all should be open, above-board, fair and impartial. The Klan is the very antithesis of the spirit of law enforcement. Do I make myself clear?[25]

The second, deeper, more recent, and more worrisome wound on Mayo's soul that day was inflicted on him by Pat Neff, the governor of Texas.

Neff was from Waco, only sixty miles from Fairfield. He had been elected in the same election as Mayo. He had campaigned in Freestone

County, promising, like Mayo, to enforce Prohibition and put an end to moonshining.[26] Both men were Democrats, and Mayo assumed he had the faith, trust, and support of the governor's office.

On February 3, 1922, however, without even notifying Mayo, Neff sent seven cars, one airplane, and two truckloads of federal agents, Texas Rangers, and the Texas National Guard to raid Freestone County in the wee hours of a Friday morning.

They came from Mexia, in Limestone County, passed through Fairfield shortly before 5 A.M., and stopped in the pre-dawn darkness on the eastern edge of town.[27] Precisely at five, a private from Brenham shinnied up a pole and cut all telephone wires servicing the countryside east of Fairfield. When the young soldier was down and back in his truck, his captain and a Texas Ranger gave the signal for the raid to begin.

At almost the same instant, Mayo was awakened by the office telephone in his family's living quarters on the lower floor of the county jail. The call was from Austin, 160 miles southwest of Fairfield, from the governor's office. Mayo was told that Neff was extending martial law, effective immediately, to all of Freestone County.

The eastern half of the county was being raided by state and federal authorities, and the sheriff—the chief law-enforcement officer of the county—had been given no advance warning. There were apparently doubts about Mayo's loyalty to Prohibition even at the highest levels of state government.

The raiders had a map, thanks to the work of Lieutenant Taylor of the Texas National Guard air service. Taylor had piloted a biplane over the area on January 27, marking isolated camps in ravines and along creek banks. The sight of an airplane was rare in 1922, and his flight had raised the curiosity of Freestone County citizens, who optimistically assumed, as one local newspaper reported, that the pilot was looking for a location for a new oil well.[28]

Taylor was in the air that morning, also, appearing with the dawn and circling as the raiders moved from still to still, rounding up prisoners and moving quickly on to the next site. The only shot fired by moonshiners was directed at his airplane. It missed.

By 11 A.M., the Rangers and the National Guard soldiers had seized nine stills and rounded up fifty-four prisoners. A chagrined Sheriff Mayo and his three deputies joined the raid late. Most of the work was done by then, but they managed to corner three prisoners.[29]

On February 7, the Teague Klan offered its support to the governor.

A lengthy letter published in the *Teague Chronicle* criticized local law-enforcement officers for their failure to enforce Prohibition, and proclaimed it the duty of the public to give courage and support to the efforts of the federal officers, state troops, and Texas Rangers sent in by the governor.[30]

Immediately adjacent to the story in the *Chronicle* was one about the Teague Preachers Association's call for "drastic measures" to put an end to the lawlessness in the county.[31] The good reverends seemed to be glaring squarely at Mayo from their pulpits.

Mayo may have been the victim of guilt by association. Before declaring martial law in the eastern half of Freestone County, Governor Neff had, in January, declared martial law in Limestone County and a portion of western Freestone County. Officers had raided large, impressive "roadhouses"—the Winter Garden, between Mexia and Teague, and the Chicken Farm, near Wortham. These elaborate clubs contained not only bars with great quantities of illegal liquor, but roulette wheels, crap tables, poker tables, blackjack tables, "chuck-a-luck," cafes, cabarets, armed guards, and secret trap doors for escape.[32]

The Chicken Farm turned out to be located within 200 yards of the home of one of Mayo's deputies, Jim Wasson, who had sold the land to the operators of the roadhouse for $750 an acre, reserving the mineral rights. That was an unheard-of high price for land in the county in 1922, but Wasson claimed that he had no idea what was going on in the building, and that he had been told it was a dance hall and restaurant.[33]

To make matters worse for the image of law enforcement in the area, five of the deputy sheriffs of Limestone County were found to have been frequenting the Derrick Hotel in Mexia, another establishment of questionable repute, where they regularly partied with a foursome of young ladies who were rooming together. One of the girls, who called herself Roxie Page, testified on January 15, 1922, that the officers brought "white mule whiskey," corn whiskey, red whiskey, and "Jamaica ginger" to the girls' room in fruit jars, half-gallon jars, bottles, and cases.

The woman who ran the hotel, Mrs. Elizabeth K. Taylor, gave a deposition the day before, saying that the previous Sunday the officers had brought a "talking machine" to the girls' room, where they had partied, and that the next morning she found one of the officers in bed with Roxie Page. She added that the deputy and Roxie were not married.[34]

With such dubious reputations among local deputies to contend with, it is no wonder that Mayo was regarded with suspicion. Perhaps it was justified, perhaps not, but everything about martial law being instituted in his jurisdiction made Mayo miserable. He had not been informed about the raid before it started, and having state and federal law-enforcement agents invade his county was tantamount to being overrun by Sherman's army. Now the great state of Texas, the Ku Klux Klan, and even local preachers were lining up on the same side, against him.

He could not hope to be re-elected unless he reversed the impression being planted in people's minds—that he could not do his job. So he launched his own moonshining raids. On March 11, accompanied by deputies Henry Jay Marcus Childs, John T. King, W. H. Robinson, and Kirven City Marshall Otis King, he rounded up three stills, three white men, and twenty-five gallons of corn whiskey near Winkler, in the northern part of the county. The posse also destroyed thirty-five barrels of mash.[35]

The little victory lifted Mayo's spirits, and a couple of weeks later he sent a defensive letter to the local newspapers, stating his case and trying to put things back on track.[36] The letter may have made him feel better, but his problems continued, and for weeks thereafter he dwelled on his misfortunes and what he should do about them. His sensitive mind was still swirling with such thoughts when the news of Eula Ausley's murder came the evening of May 4.

He was in his home at the jailhouse at the time. The news filled him with apprehension, and he left immediately for Kirven in the Nash, accompanied by Chief Deputy Childs, the son of a former sheriff.

Whatever his thoughts that night had been, they became dominated by the scene that greeted him on his arrival at the site of the murder outside of Kirven.

Armed men were rushing to the scene. A mob was gathering, both in town and at the house to which Eula's body had been carried. Townspeople and strangers were everywhere, excited, shocked, and alarmed.

Details of the crime, mixed with wild speculation and rumor, were running rampant. The farmers between Shanks and Kirven who heard Eula's cries were telling everyone that the screams came twice from the direction of the attack, once at around four-thirty and again at about five. Eula must have been held captive and tortured for thirty minutes before she was killed.[37] Their shame and discomfort at not having investigated the source of the screams must have been enormous.

A bloody club, credited with being the instrument used to bludgeon her face, was reportedly found near the body.[38] It may have been the knotty cedar stick, used for other purposes.

According to another account, a rusty, blood-drenched ax was found stuck in a tree three hundred yards from the murder scene, and was the murder weapon.[39] A third report said that a large rock found near the murder scene had been dropped on Eula's head.[40]

A Mexican woodcutter was reported to have been seen chopping firewood in the creek bottom earlier in the day. He became the first reported suspect.[41] Still other tales described gangs of black men armed with knives and axes who were roaming the countryside, plotting to kill other innocent women and children.[42]

The ambulance arrived and carried Eula's body to the hospital in Teague. Mayo met with the distraught King family, heard their accounts, and interviewed Grandfather King in private. He listened intently to the old man's theory concerning the murder of his granddaughter, and promised to investigate it thoroughly.

The hour was late when Mayo returned to Fairfield.

5 Manhunt

The night passed. Darkness prevented the Kings, their friends, and anyone else who might have been inclined to do so from searching for the killer or killers of Eula Ausley. Instead, dozens of armed men stood watch in doorways around Kirven, and knots of people remained vigilant, telling and re-telling the details of the day's outrage.

Mayo was on the scene early in the morning, arriving before the crowds he knew would soon appear. Following leads supplied by Grandfather King, he examined the scene of the murder and found clues supporting the old man's suppositions. Within two hours of sunrise, he had two suspects targeted for arrest, but neither was home.[1] Employing the technological sophistication of the day, he telegraphed the Texas State Penitentiary in Huntsville and requested bloodhounds be sent to Kirven.[2]

In the meantime, Kirven was filling with armed men from three counties. Wives and children watched from windows or joined the throngs on the wooden sidewalks and unpaved streets. Dozens of automobiles competed for parking places with buckboards and carriages.

The town's two cafes were filled to overflowing. Knots of townsfolk gathered, some angry and gesticulating, others fearful and whispering, while around them a current of newcomers and darting children ebbed and flowed.[3]

Another stream of visitors drove, walked, or rode from Kirven to the site of the murder. There they gazed in hushed silence at the basketball-sized hole in the ground beside Grindstone Creek, still protected by the rope strung by J. C. Whatley.

Several businesses closed so that their proprietors could participate in the morbid excitement, but those that could prosper from a crowd kept their doors open. Whiteside's drug store was one of the latter, and J. C. Whatley was busy there dispensing cold drinks. John Green's drug store and the confectionery were also bustling. Less apparent was the need to keep a cotton gin operating, but even so, J. C. Whatley's father, Walter Whatley, remained at his that day.[4]

Rumors were abundant, and Grandfather King's suspicions were surely whispered from ear to ear. The Mexican-woodcutter tale was still being repeated, and several people speculated that the killers must have been familiar with Eula's habits, which meant they were locals and likely to be nearby.

Mayo's name was on everyone's lips. What was he doing to find the killer? Had he found any clues? Had he made arrangements to protect other women from a repeat of what happened to Eula? Could he handle this outrage any better than he had handled moonshining and the imposition of martial law?

Members of the recently formed League to Enforce Prohibition may have reminded each other of the resolutions they had made the previous year to put an end to lawlessness. Brothers in the Klan may have exchanged knowing looks. When no suspect was arrested by ten o'clock, the members of the mob took matters into their own hands.

Attention and suspicion were focused on black men in the community. Where had they been when the murder took place? Could they all account for their whereabouts? Two or three blacks were questioned closely and released. One of them was afraid to go home alone afterward; he knew what could happen to a lone black man who had been thrust into the spotlight by accusatory white men. Only when the Methodist minister of Kirven agreed to accompany him was he willing to walk to his house.[5]

The sheriff's call for bloodhounds had been acknowledged but not fulfilled. The Texas Department of Corrections confirmed the availability of dogs, and H. L. Kindred, an employee of the *Mexia Daily Telegram* newspaper—probably the only pilot available—was preparing to fly from Mexia to Huntsville, ninety miles south, to pick up the animals. He would pilot the same airplane used by Lieutenant Taylor during the martial-law moonshining raid.[6]

The mob could not wait, however, and loosely organized groups spread out, shoulder to shoulder, to move through the fields and forests. A long line of volunteers began walking from Grindstone Creek toward town. Another moved from town north. Nobody knew exactly what they were looking for, but everyone was certain they would recognize it when they flushed it from hiding.

There were hundreds of men. One newspaper put the size of the mob at one thousand.[7] They carried shotguns, Winchester rifles, or bolt-action Springfield 303s, or wore revolvers in holsters high on their waists. A few wore overalls, but most were clad in shirts and dungarees, with short-brimmed hats. Some wore vests. Young men wore caps and knickers.

There were a few blacks scattered among the searchers, including Jim Foreman, Ellis Foreman, Jenkins Carter, and two of Carter's nephews, Tommy Carter and his brother.[8] The murder of a white girl was a very sensitive matter. Appearing among angry whites after such an event could focus outrage on a black man, but failing to help could do the same. Joining the posse, perhaps, would overcome any suggestion that they had something to hide.

Such thoughts must have been shared by another black searcher— McKinley "Snap" Curry. Curry, 22 or 23 years old at the time, was employed full-time by Eula's uncle, Otis King. As was the custom of the day, he lived on land farmed by King in a house supplied by King.[9]

Little is known of Curry. He is listed in the 1920 census as being black, 20 years old, and married to Agnes Curry. He may have been from Louisiana.[10]

Agnes was 26 in 1920, and the couple is listed as having two children, although they apparently were not Snap's. They were a girl named Jesse, 7, and a boy named Walter, who turned 9 that March. Both children and their mother are listed in the census as mulatto.[11]

Two witnesses interviewed, Bertha Williams and Foreman Carter, knew Snap, but not well. Snap was a field hand. Foreman worked for the T. & B. V. Railroad, and Bertha was a domestic housekeeper and cook for some of most powerful white families in the area. As Carter recalled, Snap was a "lower class Negro" with whom he would not normally associate.[12] He also said Snap was hot-headed, and liked to get into fights.[13]

Curry viewed the scene of the murder and overheard talk about what was planned for the killers when they were captured. He also heard about the bloodhounds en route from Huntsville. All of the newspaper and other accounts except one agreed that Curry returned to his home after learning this news.[14] The other report said he stayed with the mob and continued to search, first with one posse, then with another.[15] Stories also vary about what happened next.

Bertha Williams said that Agnes Curry came forward with an important revelation. The way Williams heard it after the event, Snap had come home the previous evening, May 4, covered with blood, and in response to his wife's inquiry, said the horse he had been riding had reared over backward, driving the saddle horn into his chest. He might have displayed a wound on his chest.

According to Williams, Curry's wife became suspicious of the story, but agreed to help him wash the blood from his clothes. The next morning, however, when she heard the report of Eula Ausley's murder, she contacted Thelma Sessions and told her of the blood and her doubts about Snap's truthfulness.[16]

Also according to Bertha Williams, the person who alerted the whites to focus their attention on Snap was Thelma Sessions. She was the wife of J. R. Sessions, who, with his father, had recently been acquitted of the murder of the Miller brothers, and the Curry cabin was located in a pasture bordering on their land. Thelma was also a granddaughter of Jim Rogers, a former sheriff of Freestone County who was killed by horse thieves in 1872, as well as a cousin of Hallie King, the wife of John T. King.[17]

The account that had Curry spending the morning with different posses instead of going home reported that he was with one posse while the other went to his house, and that Agnes Curry told the white men of that group that Snap came home the previous evening with blood on his shirt sleeves.

According to this version of the story, Snap told his wife on May 4 that he had been hunting rabbits with two friends, Tom Barry and Shadrick Green, and that his clothes had been stained as a result of him skinning a rabbit. Supposedly the other two men also had blood on their shirts, which they attempted to wash out. This story had it that Snap's wife was "jealous of him," and that although they lived together, they were not happy, and "there was a difference between them."[18]

The nature of any marital difference, which might have involved Agnes's mulatto children, an attraction Snap may have had for Eula Ausley, the couple's age difference, or any number of unrelated causes, can only be speculated. That Snap and Agnes did not get along, however, has become a standard ingredient of the tale, and has been reported and repeated faithfully for three-quarters of a century to explain why a black woman would betray her man to a white mob.

According to J. C. Whatley, his father, Walter F. Whatley, was at the cotton gin that morning while the posses were searching, and he saw Curry ride by, coming from the direction of the scene of the murder. Recalling that he had seen the same black man riding the same route on the same horse the evening before, when Eula was killed, the older Whatley became suspicious, and decided to drive out to Curry's house and talk to him.

According to J.C., Walter Whatley arrived at the Curry home, found Mrs. Curry alone, and asked if Snap was around.

"And my daddy asked her," J.C. claimed, "and she said, 'No, he come in just a little bit ago and turned his horse loose, and he went across that field.'"

She pointed to a pasture west of the Curry home. "'Never said a word to me.' So he said, 'Well, did he change clothes last night when he come in?' and she said, 'Yes, they're around there in the old wash pot, see, for me to wash and I haven't done it.'"

J.C. recounted that his father "went around there and she went around there and there was his old shoes that had them old hobnails in them, and everything that they had stomped her with and all that, and blood all over them, and his pants and everything, and all, and he was just give away. So Poppa come back to town and got a bunch on his trail, see." [19]

Other newspapers reported still another version, saying the posses began sweeping the countryside around 10 A.M., and found Curry's freshly washed clothes hanging from a clothesline in back of the Curry cabin. The members of the mob then put Mrs. Curry "through the third degree" and learned of the bloodstains she had seen the previous evening. [20]

The *Dallas News* reported that the clothes were still bloody when they were found. The *Houston Chronicle* took the story one step further, reporting that posses passing through the yard "behind the shack of 'Snap' Curry, 26 year old negro," found a freshly washed set of clothes hanging on the line, questioned Curry's wife, and she admitted that Curry told her he *murdered* Eula. According to the *Chronicle*'s reporter, Agnes said Snap threatened her with death if she did not help wash the blood from his clothes, or if she told on him. The *Chronicle* said she was then taken to the Kirven jail for safe-keeping. [21]

According to the *Kirven Commercial Record*, the "posses began scouring the country for him, after his wife had reported he had come in late the night before and had washed his bloodstained clothes. His shoes were found caked with blood where he had evidently stamped the life from the girl's body." [22]

However it happened, word spread through town before noon that Snap Curry was the murderer and that he was fleeing west on foot into the woods and creek bottoms. The chase began.

The men in the mob scattered in different directions. Some sped for

Wortham by automobile, the nearest town to the west, to set up road-
blocks and patrol the back roads. Others headed for the Curry home,
from which they spread out in long lines and moved west, beating the
brush. Still others took off on horseback and on foot, across country,
hoping to overtake the quarry.

H. L. Kindred, meanwhile, was busy flying the biplane. The ninety-
mile trip to Huntsville took an hour and fifteen minutes, and when he
landed near the Texas State Penitentiary, he found news of his arrival
had preceded him. A crowd, reported to contain the entire population
of Huntsville, was at the airport to witness his arrival and departure.
All had heard of the crime in Kirven and of the airplane used in the
martial-law raid, and all were curious.

Thirty minutes later, Kindred taxied off again, accompanied by
Dog Sergeant Simmons, of the penitentiary, and two of its best bloodhounds. Their flight was the first in Texas' history in which bloodhounds were transported to a crime scene in an airplane, and the image
of the two sad-faced dogs in a biplane, tongues lolling and wind blow-
ing their long ears, is irresistible. By the time the men flew to Mexia,
landed, drove to Kirven, and set the dogs on Curry's trail, however,
they were too late to be of any assistance.[23]

While the mob focused its attention on Curry, and the bloodhounds
were in flight, Mayo was proceeding in another direction. According to
several newspaper accounts, he arrested two white men in connection
with Eula's murder on the afternoon of May 5.[24]

Newspaper reports in the big cities of Texas described the manhunt
with dramatic overtone:

> Outraged men grabbed the weapon closest at hand
> and rushed to head off the assailants. From Mexia,
> Waco, Teague, Corsicana and a dozen other towns,
> cordons of men in automobiles were thrown out to
> block the roads and search the countryside.
>
> Farmers and business men of three counties joined
> together to comb every inch of the territory. Creek
> bottoms were beaten all day and acres of grassland
> were flattened.[25]

And:

> Scores of men scoured the bushes and creeks. . . . It is
> freely predicted here that should an arrest be made the

> slayer will never be taken to a jail as the citizenship is
> worked up to a frenzy and the prediction is made that
> shortshrift will be made of the murderer. . . .
> Airplanes and blood hounds are being used in the
> search for the slayer and officers here are confident
> that the murderer will be apprehended before the day
> is over.[26]

Curry surely suspected the kind of fate that would await him if he was captured, and one can imagine his feelings of panic, mingled, perhaps, with guilt, as he fled across country. He must have run from cover to cover, bush to bush, tree to tree, through water when he could, steering clear of open spaces and roads, wondering when he would hear the baying of bloodhounds in the distance behind him.

Adrenaline may have given him super-human strength at first, but exhaustion and terror must, like drunkenness, have finally reduced his thoughts to a narrow funnel of focus, seemingly clear, around which all circumstance except hope of survival was blurred. The need to escape must have become the most complex concept he could grasp, and his mind and body must have ached, flagging, until even the likelihood of destruction might have ceased to seem dreadful.

Still, he was lucky, or wily, to the end, and despite the number of pursuers, their frenzy and their confidence, Snap Curry managed to elude them all for over six hours. When he finally was captured, it was only after being betrayed by another black man.

At about 4 P.M., a black farm worker named Richard Spence, mistakenly identified as Harry Spence in some newspapers, was riding a horse down a dirt road near the home of his employer, Homer Miller.[27] Millerville, as the locals referred to the area, was approximately five miles west of Kirven.

According to J. C. Whatley, Spence knew nothing about the murder, and was "going down to the creek to maybe fish a little, something like that, maybe run a trot line. He was just a pure-dee nigger who worked for the Millers."

Topping a hill, Spence was greeted with a curious sight. Ahead was another black man, lying prone, rolling from one side of the road to the other.[28]

The man rose as Spence approached, and Richard recognized Snap Curry.

"What are you doing?" Spence asked.

"I'm in trouble," Curry said. "A bunch of white men are chasing me. I was trying not to make any tracks. I been staying on the grass, rolling when I couldn't. Can you help me get out of here?"

Spence pondered the question for a minute and came to a decision. "Climb up on this horse," he told Curry.

According to the *Houston Chronicle*, contrary to Whatley's version of the events, Spence recognized Curry, knew why he was being pursued, and rode with him to Homer Miller's house, where "Spence alighted, saying he wanted a drink of water. He disappeared in the farm house. A moment later, Miller appeared on the porch and covered Curry with a gun."

Whatley, who knew Spence and heard his version of the story in later years, said "when he got the mule [*sic*] turned around and everything to go back up the road, well he just bearhugged that damned nigger and began to kick that mule and run him on up to Millers', see, and just turned him over to the Millers."[29]

Bertha Williams, who was in Midlothian visiting family on May 5, said it was not Spence, but one of the Millers who captured Curry.[30]

Whatever the details, Snap Curry was captured, and there was no question of his guilt in the minds of his pursuers. There may have been no question in Snap's mind, either. Regardless, the only viable questions remaining were how he would pay for the crime, and when.

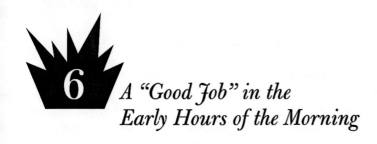

6 A "Good Job" in the
Early Hours of the Morning

The Miller family took Curry to Wortham, six miles from Millerville. There he was locked in the vault of the Wortham Bank at around 6:00 or 7:00 P.M. Sheriff Mayo was contacted in Kirven.[1]

When Mayo and Deputy Childs arrived, they found a mob milling about in the street. After parking the car in an alley behind the bank, Mayo and Childs entered the bank through the front door while the mob watched. Inside, the vault was opened and before the mob was any wiser, the two lawmen had slipped their prisoner through a rear window and into their waiting automobile.[2]

Mayo was afraid Curry would be lynched if he remained in Freestone County, so the sheriff sped south, toward Mexia, planning to turn west and drive to Waco. News of their flight was telephoned ahead, however, and cars were parked across the road to stop them.

When Mayo saw the roadblock, he backtracked, turned east, and headed for Fairfield. He arrived at the county seat without further incident, and locked Curry in a cell on the second floor of the jailhouse.[3]

Darkness had set in, but Curry was in jail only a few moments before a mob began to form outside. As men streamed in from Kirven, Wortham, and elsewhere, the size of the crowd swelled to more than five hundred.

Mayo had three deputies with him. Their identity is not recorded, but Jay Childs, Ed Foreman, and Luke Marberry are likely candidates. Mayo's wife and three daughters were also present, in their home in the first-floor living quarters of the jail.

The *Kirven Commercial Record* reported that Curry made a statement while he was still in Wortham, implicating two other blacks, John Cornish and Mose Jones, who were immediately arrested and taken to Fairfield. The *Houston Chronicle* said that Curry made the statement while he was in the Fairfield jail, and that Mayo ordered authorities in Kirven to bring the other two men to the county seat.

More likely, Cornish and Jones were picked up and brought to the jail before the mob had a chance to form. Mayo wrote a week later that all three were simply "landed in jail" before the mob gathered.[4] At some point, fifteen dollars was found in the pocket of one of the three men, probably Curry.[5]

J. C. Whatley, who was in the mob, said, "Well, they carried that nigger on, and he implemented [sic] these others, see, and they went and got 'em down in jail in Fairfield, and a bunch of us went down there to get 'em and the sheriff said 'no.'"[6]

Johnny Cornish was mistakenly identified by the Associated Press as J. H. Varney, and several newspapers across the country repeated the error.[7] Cornish was a 19-year-old farmhand who, until recently, had lived with his mother, Nettie, outside of Kirven near the site of Eula's murder.[8] The proximity of his former home to the crime scene may have been a factor in his becoming a suspect. A few weeks earlier, he had married, and he and his new bride were living in Kirven.[9]

Bertha Williams, who had known Johnny since he was a baby, said he worked occasionally for Otis King, chopping cotton or moving cattle, but was not a steady hired hand of the Kings. Johnny's family remembered him as a loner who never had many friends, and who spent a lot of time by himself in the woods or fishing. Oddly, one of the few close friends he did have was a white physician, Dr. William Sneed, who lived in Fairfield.[10]

Johnny was the oldest of six children. Their mother, Nettie, was black, but all her children were listed in the census records as mulatto.[11]

Their father was a white man named Bud Thompson. Thompson had not lived with Nettie and their children, but he had taken care of the family and had openly acknowledged the relationship.[12] According to the recollections of natives, Thompson had been a businessman and a respected member of the community, which is some testament to the relaxed nature of race relations around Kirven prior to May 1922.[13]

Thompson had passed away a year or two previously, however, and his black family was relegated to living in a tent near Hinds Lake. Quite recently they had begun moving to Fairfield, where Nettie had family, and were still in the process of doing so on May 5, driving back and forth between Kirven and Fairfield in a wagon.[14]

Mose Jones, at 46, was the oldest of the three arrested men. Like Cornish, he worked part-time for Otis King. His wife, Louise, was twenty years younger than he, and the couple shared their home with Mose's parents, 75-year old Lige Jones and 63-year-old Melissa Jones.

Mose and Louise had three children, the oldest a six-year-old daughter named Nattie. The names of the other children were a stinging irony in light of what was about to happen. Otis Jones was five. Kirven Jones was three.[15]

Sometime between 10:00 P.M. and midnight, a committee of the mob approached the jail and asked the sheriff's permission to interview the prisoners. Mayo agreed.[16]

Supposedly, Curry confessed to the committee in the jail, although no written version is known to exist and if he confessed at all, he may have done so an hour or more later. Whether the confession occurred in the jail or not at all, newspapers provided several particulars of Curry's alleged statement.

The *Kirven Commercial Record* reported Curry's words in the following way:

> . . . he made a full and frank confession of the crime, stating that he and the other two negroes under arrest had planned the same several days before. He stated that another lady was to have been served in the same manner. According to the statement of Curry, who said that he knew he was to be killed at once and that he believed he deserved death, he joined the other two negroes at the lonely spot where a creek crossed the road traveled by the girl on her way to and from school. When the girl came up, riding horseback, Curry seized the horse's bridle while the other two negroes dragged her from the saddle. He stated that the girl was so strong it took the utmost efforts of the three of them to carry her the several hundred yards to where the body was found. Miss King screamed a number of times while being carried to the thicket, according to Curry. Arriving at the bank of a small running branch covered with dense growth of small timber, Curry said that both of the other negroes committed a criminal assault upon the young girl, after which Cornish stabbed her 25 times with a pocket knife. Both Jones and Cornish then beat her head and face into the ground with a large club found nearby, according to Curry's statement, and that Cornish also mutilated the body with a stick in a most horrible manner. After the crime was committed, Curry said the negroes separated and that he at once returned to his home.[17]

The *Dallas Times Herald* reported on May 6 that Curry said the trio planned to assault not one, but two other women from the Kirven vicinity at the same time, and that Jones alone beat Eula's head into the ground, after Cornish stabbed her twenty-five times. On May 7, the same paper declared Eula was first dragged into the woods and assaulted, or raped, after which one of the three blacks searched the creek for a hole deep enough to drown her. Spared such a death by a shortage of water, she was killed by stabbing and having her throat slashed, after which "her head and face were beaten and stamped to pulp to prevent recognition." Another account said the men cut out Eula's tongue so she would not tell on them, after which they realized she could still write, so they killed her.[18]

The *Austin Statesman* said the three men had planned the crime since January.

The committee came out of Curry's cell and told Mayo they "had decided to wait until two more negroes suspected of being implicated in the matter were caught and examined before any further action against the three prisoners was taken."[19] They left the jail and reported their findings to the rest of the mob.

Whether Curry actually confessed or not, and if he did, whether he did so in the detail reported, the mob was certain of the guilt of the trio, and spent little time debating the legal and philosophical considerations of its next step.

As Mayo wrote later, "I was again requested to parley with the crowd, and when I opened the door, was seized and held while men rushed the jail and took all three negroes. Resistance to the determined citizens would have been folly as well as suicide on the part of myself and three deputies. The men had formed and carried out their preparations too calmly and thoroughly to brook opposition, and I feel certain they would have torn the jail down stone by stone if it had been necessary to take the negroes."[20]

J. C. Whatley, who was outside the jail with the rest of the mob, said, "When Mayo opened the door the second time, the old ex-sheriff just knocked the hell out of him and knocked him out."[21] He did not identify the ex-sheriff, but Mayo's three daughters, who were in the jail, were certain that their father was not knocked unconscious, or even hit.

The three girls remembered the mob taking the prisoners, and said that they were not loud or boisterous. Instead, the mob moved with silent, deadly purpose, speaking, if at all, in vesper voices.

"Daddy told us to go and stay in our rooms," Lura Bess recalled, "and don't get out and don't turn our lights on or anything, and just be real quiet because there were some men coming to take some of the prisoners upstairs, and they had an outside entrance to the thing there, and he just said to stay in there, and, 'I'm going to be in here with you, so don't be afraid.'"

The entrance to which she referred was outside the first-floor living quarters, but inside the front door. A stairway ascended directly to the jail at a right angle from the outside entrance, while another door—locked—stood between the family and the entryway.

"We never heard a thing," Lura Bess continued, "and we were scared to death. They took those men out of their cells and down the stairs, and we never even heard them go. . . . It was just the slickest thing you ever saw. You wouldn't have known a thing was happening. . . . There wasn't any yelling or screaming. It was just as silent as could be, and we didn't, we were right there, and we couldn't hear them coming down the steps, even. They didn't make any noise or anything."

Then, contemplating, she added, "I don't know why it never made a mark on us kids that we didn't get over, but it made a mark on my daddy, one he never could get over." [22]

The three terrified prisoners were placed in two automobiles, Curry in one and Cornish and Jones in another. Members of "the committee" crowded in around them and others in the mob dashed to their own cars. [23] Soon a funeral-like caravan of at least 165 vehicles was winding along the dirt backroad between Fairfield and Kirven. [24] Along the way, the cars crossed concrete bridges built years before by Mayo.

According to the Kirven newspaper, Curry was in the back seat of one of the lead cars, where he was "between two members of the committee who had questioned him without much success in the jail, and he made a full and frank confession of the crime. . . ." One can imagine him sitting between two furious members of the mob, immobile, enduring scathing verbal abuse and promises of terrible punishment, any hope of survival blasted.

It was past midnight when the cavalcade filed into Kirven, which, despite the excitement of the day, was dark and asleep. According to a report in the *Houston Chronicle,* though, "as the procession advanced to the town square, windows were thrown open, lights appeared, and a few minutes later, practically every man, woman and child gathered around the little square." [25]

The place where the procession stopped was often described in newspapers as the town square, or even as the courthouse square, but the site was neither. The place was a large vacant lot located immediately south of the downtown business district, between the Methodist and Baptist churches, the same place where V. B. Starnes had pitched his revival tent and Eula Ausley had accepted Christ into her heart two months earlier.[26]

Some of the cars following the leading vehicles parked on the north side of the open lot, across from the Methodist church. Some may have left their engines idling and their headlights on. The rest pulled into whatever parking spaces the drivers could find, and their occupants hurried to join the circle forming in the lot. The members of the mob, together with the populace of Kirven that had turned out, brought the number in the crowd to somewhere between 500 and 1,000 people.[27] While the crowd gathered, the King brothers held council. The Kirven newspaper said that "at the request of one of the uncles of the dead girl, the crowd discussed the matter quietly," but such democratic deliberation was cursory at best. The members of the mob knew their purpose, and "soon probably fifty men began carrying wood and other inflammable material."[28]

The source of the wood was reported later to have been the T. & B. V. Railroad. The local railroad section chief, Cap Spurgeon, was said to have generously donated a stack of cross ties, as a kind of civic contribution from local industry, to the project.[29] If so, however, the cross ties were not the initial fuel supply.

John Green—Hallie King's father and John T.'s father-in-law—had ten cords of firewood piled against the side of his drug store, immediately next door to the vacant lot, and he contributed the logs freely. The wood had been cut on Green's land outside of town by an elderly black man and his wife who could not have dreamed how the fruit of their labor would be utilized.[30]

The hideous intention of the mob was apparent, but some of the participants were not content with the punishment about to be inflicted. "Out from the cars the blacks were dragged to the ground. A curtain of men screened them from the onlookers. A knife flashed . . . , and the negroes lay upon the ground, horribly mutilated."[31]

J. C. Whatley, who was present, but did not claim any credit, described the act of the mob more simply: "They castrated one or two of them, or something like that."[32] Another contemporary said "they cut off everything the negroes had."[33] Another commentator was artfully euphemistic, reporting that "no organ of the negroes was allowed to remain protruding."[34]

More likely, only Curry was unsexed. The men in the mob, particularly Grandfather King, had reservations about the guilt of Jones and Cornish. Also, anecdotal information, which follows, suggests the latter two victims were unharmed, even spirited, prior to being put on the fire.

A sulky riding plow, often referred to in newspaper accounts as a cultivator, and locally as a breaking or turning plow, was either in the vacant lot or nearby, and was dragged into the center of the lot. The farming implement was relatively small, but heavy, designed to be pulled by a mule, with cast-iron wheels, a single large blade, and a metal seat.[35]

According to one newspaper report of the event, "an old plow was obtained from somewhere—kerosene and crude oil appeared as if by magic. From the cowering trio, the mob dragged 'Snap' Curry, the only one of the three who had confessed. With a rope he was strapped to the seat of the plow. He was apparently unafraid, although he must have suffered horribly from the mutilation." [36]

At approximately this time, the preachers from Kirven's two churches, the Methodist minister and Dr. Andrew of the Baptist Church, "came forward and prayed for the salvation of the blacks' souls." [37]

J. C. Whatley said he opened Dr. Whiteside's drug store, and was serving cold drinks to members of the crowd while everyone else was doing the dirty work.[38] Perhaps he was. Mobbing and lynching could be thirsty work, and Dr. Whiteside may have sanctioned the serving of refreshments. On the other hand, it seems unlikely that members of the mob would suddenly decide to leave the excitement and take a break for a cold soda pop. Whatley may have told the story in order to distance himself from as much guilt as possible, but without taking himself out of the picture, or he may have served drinks later, before the crowd dispersed, and conveniently changed the timing of his activities.

Wood was stacked around the plow and doused with gasoline, kerosene, and oil. A match was applied, and flames leaped up and crawled toward the doomed man. The crowd was silent, staring.

Someone asked Curry if the other two men were guilty, and he replied loudly enough for all to hear, "Burn those other Negroes too. They are just as guilty as me." [39] Another version of his statement was, "You can't do no more to me than you're doing, but nothing you do will make me suffer as much as she [Eula] did." [40]

One newspaper claimed that "a lick of flame ignited the oil-soaked clothes of the black" but he "continued to answer questions from the crowd by giving more details of the crime, his answers checking exactly with his previous statements."[41]

A less credulity-straining version of Curry's last words was printed in several papers. Apparently, he began to sing. The song was an old hymn, "O Lord I Am Coming."[42]

Not every citizen of Kirven was on the scene. B. J. Ausley, Eula's nephew, was certain his mother's parents, the Hudsons, would not have come out of the house. "Mrs. Hudson was one of those old types who never did anything but sit and look at the Good Book," he said. "They wouldn't have participated."[43]

Walter Whatley forbade his youngest daughter, 11-year-old Ruby Kate, to leave the house, and the Beavers, Whit and Emma, locked their doors and stayed at home. For years thereafter they remembered "hearing the screams."[44]

Other parents made a point of calling their children out to witness what was about to happen. James Claude Goolsby, a barber and part owner of the town's confectionery, called his young son, Jim, out of the house to watch. He thought witnessing the punishment would be "a good lesson" for the boy. Instead, what the boy saw haunted him for the rest of his life.[45]

Still other parents had responsibilities to tend to, and were too busy or distracted to keep track of their offspring. One such couple consisted of a man who attempted to lend calm to the event and a woman with two infants to care for. Their older sons, aged 12 and 10, were asleep on a pallet in their parents' bedroom—they had been too frightened by the events of the day to stay in their own bedroom—when their next-door neighbor pounded on the bedroom window and shouted, "Wake up. They're bringing the Negroes back. They're going to burn them out here."[46]

The parents and boys got out of bed quickly. The father, a religious man, had already attempted to calm the emotion-charged environment during the day. After the report of the arrest of the three men, he had hoped tensions would subside. Now they had reached a towering new zenith. He rushed out as soon as he was dressed after hearing the neighbor's report, but found he could do nothing except talk to the members of the mob and pray for the three men's souls.

The two brothers threw on their clothes and went outside after their father. The boys' mother stayed at home to care for her two babies, the youngest of whom was only six months old.

The boys saw the crowd gathered in the vacant lot, and went to the steps of the Methodist church to watch. The event was under way when the brothers arrived. Curry was already burning. The younger of the two boys said the mob was in a circle with a center about the size of a typical living room, and that the people stood in rows ten to twenty persons deep. He could not see Curry, but said he assumed "the Negro wasn't in much of an upright position anyway."

Both brothers remembered the members of the mob being serious and intent upon their work.

"It was quite a good-sized crowd," the younger one said. " . . . there wasn't a lot of noise. It was a fairly silent crowd for that many people." The older brother agreed, saying, "The crowd wasn't particularly loud."[47]

Neither of the boys mentioned what Curry was saying, if anything. He may have been silenced before they arrived on the scene, but one report stated that "as the flames mounted about Curry's body, his chant rose higher and higher until he could be heard throughout the downtown part of town."[48]

Curry lost consciousness in ten minutes and died.[49] The smell of burning flesh filled the air. The wind took on a taste.

"A few moments later, the bonds were burned through and he dropped, face first, into the flames."[50]

The crowd hesitated at this point. Neither Cornish nor Jones had confessed, despite "third degree methods" having been administered to them.[51] They were still denying their guilt, and displayed a degree of confidence. Cornish was heard to ask Jones while Curry was burning, "Will we get that too?" "No," Jones replied, "what have we done?"[52]

"A slight delay occurred as the leaders debated the fate of Jones and Cornish, who reiterated their innocence," the Kirven newspaper reported. John King, "the gray haired old grandfather, a patriarch in appearance," supposedly came forward at this moment "and a most affecting scene took place. In a shaking voice the old man questioned the two remaining negroes and told the crowd he was convinced they were guilty."[53]

Later revelations, as well as Cornish and Jones's steadfast denials of guilt, make this detail seem unlikely.

More likely is that "it was decided that Curry's confession was proof enough" and Jones was brought forward. A traditional version of his death was that the fire was too hot at this point to tie or chain him to the plow, so a rope soaked in water was tied to his wrists and members of the crowd proceeded to drag him back and forth through the flames until he died.[54]

Sitting in a lawn chair in front of his trailer house in Kirven on May 5, 1987, two hundred yards from the scene of the burning, J. C. Whatley scoffed at this anecdote.

The day of his interview was a pleasant spring day in a quiet place, significantly different from the turmoil sixty-five years earlier. The meadowlark was still calling, and a silver needle of a jet was pulling a white thread of vapor beneath the sun. Whatley was drinking iced tea and holding court.

"They was all tied to the plow, soaked with gasoline and set afire all together," he declared. "I wouldn't know how many gallons of gasoline they used, see," he stated, "but I stood right there in the front door of that drug store and stared just as straight and level as I'm looking at your car right here, and that's the way they died."

Pausing a moment, he repeated a claim he made twice that day, and that he had probably made numerous times over the years. "Yeah, well, I saw it. I was there, but I never went across the street to it, see, and I never threw a damned stick of wood on them."[55]

By his own admission, however, Whatley was in the drug store serving drinks most of the time, or at least he was across the street, and there were a lot of people between him and the fire. His is the only account that suggests all three were burned together. Every newspaper said they were burned one at a time, and the youngest of the two brothers who were watching said, "When one man burned up, they pitched another on the fire, and when that one burned they threw the third one in the fire."[56]

What may have happened is that Whatley did not see the three bodies until after all were dead, and had been raked together on the pyre for final cremation, and he assumed all three were burned simultaneously.

Another traditional anecdote was that members of the mob stood around the fire, and if one of the victims tried to crawl out, they kicked him and hit him and drove him back into the flames. The older of the two brothers who watched the men being burned said, "One would wriggle out every once in a while and get thrown back in."[57]

More specifically, Mose Jones was said to have made a dash out of the flames immediately after being thrown in, despite being secured with a rope, only to run directly into Otis King. The namesake of Mose Jones's infant son was armed with a radius rod from a Model T Ford, and he swung the heavy piece of iron like a club, smashing his former hired hand in the face and knocking one of the doomed man's eyes from its socket.

Jones supposedly reached up and wiped the eyeball from his cheek, stared at the carnage on the back of his hand with his remaining eye, and was jerked backward into the flames by the members of the crowd who were holding the rope.[58]

Jones died in about six minutes,[59] and the mob turned to Cornish. The details of his death are better substantiated, and even more bizarre.

As he was brought into the light from the fire, several Kirven men recognized him. Foreman Carter, who knew both Johnny and the boy's white father, Bud Thompson, and who heard the story from his step-father, Jenkins Carter, described what happened next.

> Some of the guys, some of the Whites, said, "That's Bud Thompson's boy, get him out of there, that's Bud Thompson's boy." So they got him out, but he had such a nasty mouth . . . you see, your mouth can get you in a lot of trouble. Well, he didn't know no better. He was raised that way. His mother had a filthy mouth, and he used four letter words all the time, and he cussed at the guys, and so they said, "Throw him back in there. Hell, put him back in." They got him out, but he had such a nasty mouth, they said put him back in.[60]

Roped, bound, having seen the agony of his companions, but too stubborn to be docile, Cornish tossed away his last chance for redemption.

His death might be viewed as a microcosm of early-twentieth-century Southern racism. A black man with the right connections would be protected, even when associated with heinous crime, but only so long as he respected the codes, acted docile, and "kept his place." Johnny Cornish did not. He reacted angrily, and bravely. Your mouth, as Foreman Carter observed, can get you in a lot of trouble.

He was pulled into the fire, pulled back, pulled forward. Then he fell quickly to the ground, "clasped his arms around the plow," thrust his face into the flames, and inhaled deeply, meeting death in the quickest manner available.[61]

"After the third negro had been burned to a crisp, all three bodies were piled together and a mass of fuel and oil flung over them. This

was ignited, the flames soaring 25 or 30 feet in the air." More wood
and fuel was piled on them, and the bodies were cremated.[62]

Daylight was breaking, gray as crematorium ash, and the crowd began to disperse. According to the younger of the two brothers, they
had been there nearly two hours, and, according to the *Kirven Commercial Record,* "after forty-eight hours of sleeplessness and without
paying much attention to meals, the citizens of three counties who had
worked unceasingly in the effort to solve the most dastardly crime in
the history of Freestone County returned to their homes believing that
the three negroes had met the fate they deserved, and that they alone
were guilty of the crime."[63]

The *Houston Chronicle* carried a similar summary: "The blackest
entry in Texas' history of crime had been chalked down on the records
against the negro trio—and the general feeling here was that the mob
of 600 did a 'good job' in the early hours of the morning."[64]

The shameful entries in Texas' history, the horror and the cruel
irony were over . . . for about a day.

7 This Cold World of Care

News of the murder of Eula Ausley, the manhunt, and the burning of Curry, Cornish, and Jones spread rapidly. The Associated Press and newspapers in Dallas, Austin, and Houston picked up the story of Eula's murder on May 5. On May 6, as smoke was still curling into the sky over Kirven, papers in Brooklyn, Chicago, Dallas, Houston, and Austin carried front-page reports of the burnings. By May 7, at least a dozen papers in cities in the south, the midwest, and the northeast, including New York City, Little Rock, and St. Louis, made Kirven their top news story. Some of these newspapers catered only to a black or socialist readership, but others were part of the mainstream press.

Banner headlines startled their readers. "Triple Lynching Follows Thrilling Texas Man-Hunt."[1] "Negroes Burned at Stake at Kirven, Texas."[2] "Texas Mob Burns Three Negroes."[3] "Texas Mob Roasts Men Alive at Stake."[4]

In Kirven, the members of the crowd dispersed to their homes while the fire was still burning, leaving only "little knots of people conferring in whispers."[5] The youngest of the two brothers who had witnessed the burnings stayed on the front steps of the church and watched until the flames died out, then went to the pile of ashes and poked at them with a stick.

"I walked out to where it all happened, to where the plow was and the ashes were still smoking," he said. "There was just the plow and a bed of ashes, probably twelve or fifteen feet in diameter." He saw small pieces of bone among the coals.[6]

About 10 A.M., curious outsiders began to arrive. At first they only looked and asked questions. Some visited the scene of Eula's murder and stared at the gaping hole in the creekbank. Others, reporters, interviewed natives, looking for details for their next edition. Around noon, as more people arrived and the embers cooled, a new phenomenon emerged.

Folks began investigating the ashes, and an interesting discovery was made. Three black, charcoal-like lumps were raked from the dying coals, but they were not charcoal. Larger, about the size of a man's fist, with the consistency of incinerated meat, they were soon identified as something else entirely—in J. C. Whatley's words, "the niggers' hearts!"[7]

The symbolism was irresistible. The murderers' hearts were so hard, so evil, they were impervious to fire.

Folding knives were pulled from the frayed pockets of overalls. The roasted organs were sliced into pieces and distributed, tangible evidence of the stoniness of the perpetrators' souls, something to display to grandchildren, a lasting souvenir.

Whatley tried to invert the culpability for this latest atrocity, saying, first, "Niggers come here and would pick up them hearts and cut out a chunk of that heart and take it with them," then shifted blame to "tourists that done it. It wasn't people from here that done it."[8]

The likelihood of any black person making an appearance at the scene of the pyre and competing for pieces of the bodies is too remote for consideration. Furthermore, while the souvenir hunters may have been outsiders, their prizes were almost certainly not Cornish, Jones, and Curry's hearts, but their livers.

The mistake was not original. After the poet Percy Bysshe Shelley drowned in the sea off the Italian coast near Leghorn, his decomposing body washed ashore on a nearby beach and authorities, fearing disease, ordered it burned rather than removed. Shelley's friend and biographer, Edward Trelawney, witnessed the cremation, and extracted what he thought was the poet's overly large, indestructible heart from the ashes.[9]

The organ turned out to be his liver.[10] As the largest, densest, most blood-gorged mass in the human body, the liver is often the most resistant to flame, and the mementos claimed in Kirven on May 6 were surely pieces of those organs.

The younger of the two witness brothers said he knew of only two local people who kept souvenirs; one of them kept a piece of the plow, and the other some "residue" of the bodies. He said he heard of "the hearts and livers being cut up and distributed," but he did not see anyone doing it.[11]

When all the slices of the organs were claimed, if indeed they were, the members of the crowd contented themselves with the other available trophies. The pieces of bone were picked out and pocketed. Bits of chain and removable parts of the sulky riding plow were raked out of the ashes or pried off the implement.[12]

A young man who lived in Corsicana did not visit Kirven that day, but his girlfriend accompanied a carload of friends to the scene of the burnings. When she returned, she triumphantly displayed a piece of bone she had taken from the pyre to the young man. He never called on her again.[13]

Bertha Williams, Dr. Whiteside's black housekeeper, returned from Midlothian late that Saturday afternoon. Most of the visitors were gone, and she described the scene as "just as quiet as if somebody'd been burning dirt."[14]

Nettie Cornish and her other children were returning to Kirven after taking a load of belongings to their new home in Fairfield, riding in a wagon drawn by a jenny named Kit, when they received word of Johnny's death. A friend, Uncle Charley, met the family on the road, stopped the wagon, and said, "Nettie, somebody done killed your child."

"What child?" Nettie demanded, looking around.

"Johnny," Uncle Charley told her.[15]

Later in the day, Nettie was visited by Johnny's friend, William N. Sneed, Jr., a white physician from Fairfield known as "Dr. Billy." Dr. Billy's parents had taken in an orphaned black boy during the Civil War, had given him their name, and reared him as their own, an older brother to the Sneed children. Dr. Billy was always a friend to Freestone County blacks.[16] He was particularly angry when he visited the dead boy's mother.

"I know where Johnny was," Dr. Billy told Nettie decisively. "He wasn't anywhere near where that girl was killed. He was with me, down in the bottoms. He didn't do anything wrong. I know where he was."

Dr. Billy probably knew more, had probably heard the horrifying details of his young friend's death, but he spared Nettie's feelings. "He didn't suffer any," Dr. Billy told her. "They hit him in the head and knocked him out before they put him in that fire. He never felt any pain."[17] Nettie and her children believed everything Dr. Billy said, and remembered his words for life.

Newspapers reported calm on Saturday "for the first time since the greatest manhunt in the history of Texas started last Thursday."[18] Articles speculated about whether any members of the mob would be arrested for the lynching. None were.

At Fairfield, the brother of a white man arrested on Friday turned himself in to Sheriff Mayo and revealed why the brothers' actions on Thursday might have appeared suspicious. The explanation was accepted and both men were released.

In Mexia, a black man mentioned by one of the "lynched Negroes in his alleged confession" was told to leave the county by law-
enforcement officers.[19]

At the King house in Kirven, "hushed voices retold the tale of the
murder"[20] and plans were made for Eula's funeral.

She was buried on Sunday, wearing the white dress her Aunt Rena
had sewed for her graduation. The Reverend V. B. Starnes, the traveling evangelist who had preached at Eula's conversion, was conducting
a revival in Fairfield, and was summoned to Shanks from Waco to preside over the ceremony.[21] Hundreds of people crowded into the church
in Shanks and followed the girl's coffin to the little community cemetery, where a grave was open next to her mother's.[22]

That day or shortly thereafter, a monument was erected over the
grave, larger than Eula was in life. The name carved on it was not Eula
Ausley, but Eula King. Her grandparents apparently wanted to show
the world that she was a thoroughly adopted daughter, in spirit if not
by law. There also may have been a lingering desire to erase the memory of the unfortunate L. C. Ausley.

The monument carried four simple lines of poetry as her epitaph:

> Eula King
> Nov. 14, 1904–May 4, 1922
> She was too good
> too gentle and fair
> to dwell in this
> cold world of care

The time for mourning and healing should have begun when the last
shovelful of dirt was placed on her grave. Violence should have been
over in Freestone County.

It was not.

Rumors began Saturday afternoon about blacks in Limestone County
and Dallas who were planning to revenge the deaths of the three men,
and Sunday afternoon, reports began vibrating through the county that
armed mobs of black men were rising up to retaliate.[23]

Afternoon and evening church services were canceled when it was
reported that a race riot was under way in Corsicana, less than thirty
miles north of Kirven, and soon thereafter, a self-appointed "Paul Re-
vere" ran from house to house in Kirven, shouting, "Women and children go to the school! The Niggers are rising up!"[24]

The two brothers who witnessed the burnings went to the house of a family friend instead of to the school. Black mobs marching on Freestone County were expected any minute. Texas Rangers were supposedly on the way also, ready to erect a machine gun brought from the National Guard arsenal in Waco on top of Kirven's tallest office building to repel the blacks.[25] A Kirven resident named Batchelor Nettle later told his son, Doug, that a freight train was stopped on the tracks and he saw a machine gun placed on top of a boxcar where it could rake downtown Kirven.[26]

Willie Mae Beaver was in Kirven visiting her in-laws, Whit and Emma Beaver, when the town began filling with carloads of armed men. Soon, one of the automobiles skidded to a halt in front of the Beavers' house. Willie Mae's father, W. J. Keeling, was driving. He was accompanied by three friends from Mexia, all carrying rifles. They had received the news of the approaching mob, and knowing Willie Mae was in the line of fire, had raced to her rescue.[27]

The day passed without the appearance of armies of blacks, however. The younger of the two brothers heard later that a large group of people had been seen attending an African American church east of town, and someone had mistaken them for an armed mob.[28]

No mob came that evening, either, but armed men patrolled the streets, discussing what had happened Friday and Saturday, and what might happen the next day. At some point, a group of them decided to take the law into their own hands again.

Some of the men had heard that Cornish and Jones had claimed their innocence by saying they were fishing with Shadrick Green while Eula was being murdered. Others recalled hearing that Mrs. Curry had said that Green had showed up at the Curry home with Snap and Tom Barry on Thursday evening, supposedly after hunting rabbits, and that all of them had blood on their shirts. This was evidence too damning to ignore.

Green, about 25 years old, worked occasionally for Bob King. He had been taken into custody on Friday, and had told Sheriff Mayo he had last seen Cornish and Jones at 4:00 or 4:30 P.M. on Thursday. After questioning, he had been released.

On Monday morning, a farmer on the way to his field found Green hanging from a tree along the road from Kirven to Fairfield. He was naked, his neck was broken, and his body was riddled with bullets. He had apparently been killed first and then hung from the tree, according

to the *Dallas Times Herald*, "as a warning to other negroes." Bertha
Williams said, "They took him down in the Caney bottoms and broke
his neck—Caney bottoms about six miles east of here."[29]

Among the first people to come down the road after the discovery
of Green's body, but before he was cut down, were the unfortunate
Nettie Cornish and her family. She and her children were leaving
Kirven for good, taking the last of their belongings to their new home
in Fairfield, when suddenly they were confronted with the gruesome
sight, a terrifying reminder of the horror that had touched their family
so recently.[30]

The immediate effect on the Cornishes of the discovery of a fourth
lynching victim was confirmation of the wisdom of moving away. The
immediate effect on other blacks was not recorded, but can be imagined. The effect on whites was both recorded and dramatic. Once
again, feverish rumors flashed through the region about vengeful mobs
of black men descending on Freestone County.

Mayo's office was notified of the discovery, and he sent deputies to
cut Green down and take his body to an undertaker. He was also ad-
vised that a mob of whites was pursuing a fifth black, while a mob of
blacks was approaching from Dallas, or possibly Mexia.[31]

Mayo had at least seven deputies scattered around the county, but
probably could not muster all of them. One, Ruffin Bain, had been
seriously wounded in a shootout in nearby Jewett the previous year.[32]
Another, John T. King, was surely preoccupied with his family. Another was Jim Wasson, who had been discredited by selling his land to
the builders of the Chicken Farm roadhouse. The remaining four, Jay
Childs, Ed Foreman, Luke Marberry, and John Hagley, were not force
enough to contend with what appeared to be a race war in the making.

Swallowing some enmity, he telephoned the governor's office in
Austin to request aid, and followed the phone call with a telegram to
the governor, asking, "Please send me as many as ten rangers to Fairfield at once."[33]

Considering that the total force of Texas Rangers in the state only
numbered fifty,[34] Mayo's request for ten of them was ambitious, but
Neff responded in full, ordering two detachments to Freestone County.
One was ordered to Kirven from Austin, and was commanded by Captain Frank Hamer. Hamer would gain national fame twelve years later
by engineering the ambush in which the notorious outlaws Clyde Bar-
row and Bonnie Parker were killed.

The other detachment, under Captain Tom Hickman, was ordered to move south from Fort Worth. Both Ranger captains were familiar with the county, having participated in the moonshining raids during the martial-law period the previous February.

The Fort Worth detachment moved by car while the Austin-based Rangers were told to travel by train, or, if that means of transportation appeared to be too slow, they were also to travel by automobile.[35]

Next, Mayo contacted John T. and Otis King to request that they join him in a public announcement stating that no further violence would be tolerated, and that any persons bringing firearms into Kirven would be arrested and disarmed. The King brothers agreed, and added that the family of their dead niece believed all the guilty parties had been punished.[36]

In Austin, Secretary Walthal of the governor's office issued a statement to the effect that the Rangers would work under Mayo to suppress any uprising of blacks, and assured the press they were not being sent to investigate the lynchings. The Austin newspaper observed that feuding between blacks and whites was intense, and said that a race war was feared.[37]

By Monday afternoon, these latest rumors of a mob of avenging blacks, like those that had circulated previously, had proved unfounded. Sheriff Mayo sent another telegram to Austin advising the governor that he "had the situation well in hand" and requested cancellation of the order for Texas Rangers. The governor obliged and called back his men.[38]

Once again, there was opportunity for both calm and recovery. Once again, neither occurred.

8 Terror

Between May 9 and June 2, 1922, terror reigned around Kirven. Any black people living within five miles of the town were in danger. They were threatened, stalked, and in several cases, murdered.

Rumors, as well as facts, concerning fresh outbreaks of violence and lynchings surfaced on a daily basis. Some black families were informed, summarily, that a son or husband would be killed when the sun went down.[1] In response they moved, or went to the homes of distant friends or relatives, or, at a minimum, slept in the fields at night. Those who did stay in their homes were careful to avoid appearing outside during the day or in front of a lighted window at night. Those who ventured out avoided the roads and did not go to town.[2]

One black man caught in the open was chased by a mob of white men on horseback. Seeing that escape was hopeless, he sought refuge in the only available shelter, an outhouse. The mounted men surrounded the little wooden building and peppered it with pistol bullets until the man fell out the door, dead.[3]

If a white person knocked on a black person's door, there would be no answer. If a white person tried to talk to a black person, the latter would say nothing but, "You got to talk to my grandfather," believing that older black men, especially those who had lived during the slavery era, would be seen by white men as being trustworthy, and therefore safe from harm.[4]

Fresh tales of black bodies found hanging from Freestone County trees—strange fruit—made the rounds. Several young black men were supposedly taken from their homes at night and required to dig their own graves before being shot.

A farmer east of Kirven smelled an unpleasant odor in one of his fields and tracked it to the corpse of a black man, fully clothed, lying in a shallow grave. He had been shot in the back.[5]

The family of the two brothers who witnessed the burnings heard a similar tale, probably the same one, which described a black man found kneeling in a grave in a field, shot in the head. Buzzards seen circling the woods where Eula's body had been found two weeks previously were said to be feeding on the body of Tom Barry, who had disappeared.

Batchelor Nettle, the young white man from Kirven, was traveling on the Fairfield–Mexia road when he came upon a mob of white men who had tied a black man to a tree, and were proceeding to shoot away his ears and nose with revolvers. As Nettle watched, Sheriff Mayo drove up in his Nash automobile and parked. Mayo walked through the tormentors to the doomed man, removed a pistol from one of the white men's hands, shot the black man in the head, handed the firearm back, and said, "Now he's over his misery."[6]

No one will ever know exactly how many blacks were killed during those twenty-five days. The local newspapers reported only two in addition to the four who died on May 6 and May 8. The younger of the two brothers who witnessed the burnings placed the number at eleven or twelve. Foreman Carter, the stepson of one of the few blacks to weather the storm without leaving Kirven, authoritatively declared that there were twenty-seven, although he could provide no names.

Many people in Freestone County blamed the King brothers for the reign of terror. As J. C. Whatley recalled, "The King brothers an' all were just goin' down, and if they saw a damned nigger, well they just shut him down. All the way from Streetman back down into this country, here."

Despite the newspaper assurances of John T. and Otis that the family was satisfied the guilty had been punished, and despite their plea, or command, to commit no more violence, four of the brothers were apparently a long way from being satisfied. John T., Otis, Bob, and Drew King—all the brothers but Alva—were said to have been the ringleaders of an avenging gang of whites who committed murder after murder after murder.

So it is said.

Foreman Carter declared there were lots of different people committing the murders. Lura Bess Mayo said, "They were sort of like professionals. They came from up at Streetman, and over at Corsicana and Mexia," and carried out the crimes. Bertha Williams defended the Kings, saying they were not cruel to blacks, and that they did not commit the murders. She said the killings were done by "just men, men here from seven or eight different towns."

The local newspapers linked the Kings with only two killings after the burnings—those of Leroy and Allie Gibson—but an out-of-state paper implied the Kings were not present, reporting that the men who killed the Gibsons were friends of the Kings who were trying to do them a favor.[7]

There were also, undoubtedly, the "heroes" of the Ku Klux Klan, who probably went boldly in disguise into the dark nights, to kidnap, gang up on, gun down, or otherwise dispatch single, unarmed, terrified black men in the name of one-hundred-percent Americanism and the principles of their organization. Certainly the Kings should not be given any credit the Klan is due.

Ironically, white people around Kirven were nearly as frightened as the black population during May and June of 1922. Eula's friend Mary recalled that children would not enter an empty room without someone accompanying them. While scared black people sat in the dark, knowing they might be targets in a lighted room, fear among whites led them to insist on having lights left on all over the house at night.

Willie Mae Beaver recalled how her in-laws, Whit and Emma Beaver—white folks—stayed in their house and would not even answer the telephone. Rumors about lynchings were everywhere. Strangers in cars, the purpose of their business around Kirven unknown, were seen in town every day. Murder and mayhem were in the air. Everyone, black and white, was nervous.

The oldest of the two brothers who witnessed the burnings recalled hearing one of the tales that caused white fright. Supposedly, a mob of blacks surrounded the home of a white family just outside of Kirven a week or two after the burnings. Carrying clubs and torches, they were reported to have marched around the besieged family's house before attacking a wagon load of cottonseed, ripping open sacks, and scattering the seed to the winds. The brother said he saw the house, but his story strains credibility. Freestone County blacks may have felt outrage, but their predominant reaction to what had happened was one of terror.

Newspapers, meanwhile, were looking at Freestone County from a variety of angles. The burning of Curry, Cornish, and Jones was still receiving publicity in places far removed from Kirven, but as shocking as the truth was, papers in some cities painted a tale even more outrageous.

The *St. Louis Argus,* an African American newspaper, reported the lynchings in an article on May 12, saying that "as soon as the news began to spread telling the death of the girl, the men in the country began to drink their bad whiskey and gather in little groups here and there looking for fun." In describing how the three black men were taken by the mob, the paper reported that "Curry was 'turned over' to the mob for 'safe keeping' while the sheriff and the other part of the mob went to get Varner [*sic*] and Jones."

The *Chicago Defender*, another African American paper, reported on May 13 that before burning the men,

> the mob indulged itself in imposing the most horrid mutilations on the bodies of the victims. Ears were clipped off, feet were mangled and eyes punched out. No independent organ of the body was left untouched, the men being stripped in front of the female members of the mob, some of whom stayed in automobiles, and the frenzy of the crowd being allowed to run its course.

The acts of the two Kirven ministers were described in the Chicago paper as being more satanic than Christian: "White preachers in the crowd encouraged its actions and indulged in a mock ceremony for the souls of the burning. The pyre was built between two white churches."

Grandfather King and a cousin were reported to have "held the living bodies over the fire until life was gone." Sheriff Mayo was said to have made no effort to protect Curry or the others.

The local spin on the Kirven incident was entirely different. Freestone County editors and citizens stepped forward to defend the acts of the mob. On May 12, the *Fairfield Recorder* ran an editorial in which it said:

> Naturally, our people will be criticized for the mobbing of the guilty, yet so long as our women are attacked so long will the people of the nation mete swift and terrible punishment. Had the perpetrators of this crime been of another color, the punishment would have been the same. Had the innocent victim been of another race, her people would have clamored for swift punishment just the same.[8]

The *Teague Chronicle* carried stronger sentiments the same day. A county resident named T. L. Childs, perhaps a member of the mob, wrote a ringing defense of his neighbors:

> The crime was committed in such a brutal and diabolical manner and the young girl mutilated in such

a way as to stamp the crime of such fiendish character that the strongest of men were nauseated. When
brutes capable of such revolting acts are caught,
human nature cannot be expected to stand up to the
high tests of every day life, and the punishment of
the negroes at Kirven did not even in a small way pay
them their just desserts [*sic*]. We resent insinuations
from the outside world that Freestone County citizens
are savages . . . they are just ordinary red-blooded
American citizens who are always ready to defend
their womanhood with their lives and when their loved
ones have had the hand of the rape fiend on their
throat, be that hand black or white . . . [9]

The *Dallas Times Herald* ran a completely different report on
May 12, summarizing the contents of a strange note mailed to the Dallas
Police Department from Mexia. Written on tissue paper and sealed in
a bottle, the missive declared: "I guess the people are satisfied now.
They have lynched four innocent men for a murder I myself committed. I am the man who killed Eula Ausley." Whoever sent the message claimed that jealousy was his motive, and that he had escaped
while the mob was burning the three men, but the police dismissed the
report as "a practical joke, or the work of a demented man." [10]

The possibility of the four men being innocent was scarcely entertained around Kirven. Instead, a motive that fully explained the murder
of Eula was circulated, and the story would be accepted in the county
as the ultimate truth for three-quarters of a century.

The motive was revenge, people said, revenge by the three black
men for the treatment the King brothers had dished out to them, their
hired hands, prior to the murder. As J. C. Whatley explained:

> Otis and John T. and the others was big farmers, and
> they worked them niggers. And they would set their
> niggers, it was all done with mules and cultivators,
> things like that, and they'd raise a lot of cotton, but
> when they come in in the afternoon, if they hadn't
> plowed so many rows that he thought they ought to,
> well he'd just take out his six-shooter and beat him
> over the head a few licks and send him on home,
> see. And well, they paid 'em for working for 'em,
> see. It wasn't a great deal but they paid 'em some

> money, and they had to get their own stuff to eat and
> ever'thing, and ever'thing else, and they had to go back
> to work the next morning with that face beat up with
> a six-shooter, see. And it wasn't just them but it was all,
> John T. done the same thing, and Otis and the other
> one. They all three [sic] done it. . . . The Kings all
> had the same number of niggers around them all the
> time. . . . It leads down to this one thing, that a nigger
> lives for revenge, . . . and they were getting revenge
> for the way John T. and Otis had treated them.

The depth of the black murderers' fiendishness was enhanced by tidbits of information that got out about their motives. It was said, and accepted as gospel, that they had murdered Eula when they did because they knew she had been converted during the Starnes revival, but believed she had not yet been baptized. The black men, the gossip ran, wanted to murder her quickly in order to ensure that her unbaptized soul would be denied entry into the kingdom of heaven.[11]

The King brothers' great-nephew, B. J. Ausley, was born after the lynchings, but he heard the traditional story about the motive for the crime from his maternal grandmother:

> The Kings beat their blacks. My momma and grand-
> mother [Hudson] said, "that was the cause of it. If
> those niggers didn't do right, they'd take a trace chain
> and whip the hell out of them." But of course my
> daddy was a little prejudiced. They [the blacks who
> were lynched] couldn't get back at none of the boys
> because in those days they carried guns, and if they
> had a nigger out there plowing cotton, they'd just
> whip the hell out them if they plowed up a little cotton
> or didn't plow right.[12]

Sheriff Mayo's oldest daughter, Lura Bess, said the Kings did not have a reputation for being mean or violent before the troubles, only afterward. "Nobody knew before that happened, I guess, and then people started saying that's the reason, because they whipped them so."

Bertha Williams, of all the witnesses interviewed, was in the best position to know and report factually about the King family's treatment of their black hired help: she was one of them. She cooked and cleaned for Grandfather, John T., and Otis King and their wives. She was also the most opinionated on the subject. When asked if Otis and John T.

would beat or pistol-whip their hired hands, she replied, "Well I never knew them to do one thing, and I used to work for them. I never knew one thing. . . . Never! John T. was married to Mr. Green's daughter, and I used to work for her in her beautiful home and it was cultured, like the rest of her life. Everybody just got along like two birds in a nest, until this happened."

The King brothers may not have known what people were saying, may not have known they were credited with being the catalyst for the murder of their beloved Eula. People were not likely to casually raise the subject in their presence, but the revenge story made sense to citizens of the South. Fear of revenge by blacks was as old a bugaboo as Nat Turner's Rebellion. The white Southern psyche was constantly straining to rationalize the treatment of blacks by whites, during slavery, Reconstruction, and Jim Crow days. Whites under the same conditions would have wanted revenge, and, indeed, were astonishingly quick to wreak revenge when they believed the occasion warranted it, and so the nagging psyche yammered, Why not blacks as well?

The phenomenon is interesting. The white penchant for taking revenge, a custom Southerners of the period staunchly defended, was turned back upon the black race, not as a normal human reaction to loathsome conditions, but as a failing of people of color. As J. C. Whatley, a stereotypical 1920s white Southerner, confidently declared in 1987, "It leads down to this one thing, that a nigger lives for revenge."

On May 13, one week after the triple burning, Sheriff Mayo wrote a letter to the editor of the *Houston Chronicle*. While some of what he wrote, which was published in the local papers, shed light on his role in the recent violence, other statements he made were notably curious.[13]

He began by referring to the newspaper's account of the execution of the three blacks published in its May 7 edition, saying the article was inaccurate and "very far apart" from what he had actually furnished to the newspaper. He then set about correcting the account, first by defending his protection of the black prisoners, whom he said he took to the jail because all of the roads out of the county were guarded by members of a mob. He made it clear that he was not sympathetic with mob law, and then fumed that the *Chronicle* had said there were only two prisoners in the jail, instead of three. He explained how he tried to protect them, and why he could not resist the determination of the mob.

Next he said something nobody had said before—that "these negroes all confessed to taking part in the murder of Miss Ausley, and no doubt is entertained in any quarter of their guilt." No one else, not even the highly biased local newspaper editorialists, had contended that Cornish or Jones had confessed. Mayo's statement was particularly odd in light of later revelations.

He went on to talk about how horrible the murder of Eula Ausley was, and how "it would be a poor man who could have viewed the body or heard these negroes describe the manner in which they committed the crime, and then say that burning them was out of place."

His grand finale, however—nearly 500 of the 866 words in the letter—was directed not at the recent lynchings, but at events associated with the period of martial law four months earlier. He complained that it was not just for a great paper to "hark back to other incidents in order to condemn the people of a county or community." He complained about "advertising stunts" that occurred then, such as using an airplane, and chided the *Chronicle* for stating in the May 7 article that there were numerous "notorious" roadhouses in the county, and for calling the citizens of Freestone County "backwoods people."

He rallied to his electorate's defense, compared them favorably with the residents of any county in the state, and shamed the paper for casting slurs upon them. He ended by demanding an apology from the *Chronicle*, and promised there would be no more mob law in his county.

What makes the letter from Mayo particularly curious is the fact that the *Chronicle* actually printed *none* of the statements Mayo accused it of printing in his letter. Neither the May 7 issue nor any previous or subsequent issue of a Houston newspaper contained *any* of the errors Mayo "corrected" in his letter.

A small portion of what prompted his complaint may have appeared in the *Dallas Times Herald* on May 6, where it is mentioned that Curry was taken from officers *before* he was placed in the jail, and that the mob took two men—one of whom was misidentified as J. H. Varney—out of the jail. That story also casually refers to Kirven as a "backwoods community."

The Dallas story did not, however, as Mayo's protestations suggest, imply that Mayo failed to make any effort to protect the blacks, nor that he was sympathetic with mob law, and the article did not even mention the martial-law period or "notorious roadhouses." The story did not, as Mayo accused it of doing, "hark back to other incidents" or condemn the people of either Freestone County or Kirven.

So what was Mayo talking about? Was he simply careless? Did he read the Dallas paper, get angry, think about what was said, conjure up more than was there, get the Dallas paper confused with the Houston paper, fire off a missive to the wrong editor, and supply all of the local newspapers with copies of his letter?

Perhaps that is what happened, but there is evidence that suggests that Mayo's letter was carefully crafted and purposely aimed at the wrong newspaper in order that it would be read solely by Freestone County residents.

If so, two tempting conclusions can be drawn about Mayo's motives for writing the letter. The first is that he was simply anxious to tell his side of recent events, including his still-smoldering version of the moonshining raids, and, knowing he would have an audience, he exaggerated the inaccuracy of the Houston newspaper article in order to wave the flag and beat the drum in defense of local voters. He knew he needed the votes.

The alternative conclusion is that Mayo, and perhaps other leaders of the county, desperately wanted the readers and voters of Freestone County to believe that the mob had executed the genuine killers of Eula Ausley, and that Mayo and others had done all they could possibly do, both to protect the killers from the mob, and to see that justice was carried out. In other words, this conclusion is that Mayo was under pressure to say things, including lies, to cover up actions even more horrible than the burning alive of untried murderers. Subsequent events, still to be described, make this very likely.

There is no evidence that the *Houston Chronicle* published, or that it even received, Mayo's letter.

On May 26, the Freestone County papers printed another communication to another major Texas newspaper, the *Dallas News,* which, this time, was printed in the big city newspaper. Under the heading "Kirven Negroes are for Peace," a petition signed by 103 black men from Kirven conveyed a tone of dignified terror, stating, in part:

> This is to certify that the law-abiding negro citizens of Kirven, Freestone County, Texas, desire that the world should know that they are in perfect peace and harmony with the good white people of this place. And we further desire that the world should know that when the interests of our good white friends are disturbed, ours are disturbed. We also desire that the world should know that there has not been one word of dissatisfaction as to the punishment of the desper-

ate murderers. We sincerely hope that all such characters have been cleaned up from among us not only in
Kirven but in the entire race. The negro citizens of
this place gave every assistance possible in helping
to capture the murderers. If we only knew we had
other such characters among us we would be perfectly
willing to see them go in the same like manner, as we
feel that death in its severest form would be too good
for any individual of this character. We desire the
good white people to know that it is the desire of the
negroes of this place to live here for their interest as
well as ours.[14]

Black citizens of Kirven had reason to petition and promise. The
continuing stories of killings of local blacks were followed in the latter
half of May by reports of mob lynchings and burnings in other parts of
Texas. While to many citizens, black and white, the stories must have
suggested that the fabric of civilization was coming apart, the editor of
the *Fairfield Recorder* saw them as further vindication of the deeds done
in Freestone County. On May 26, he printed a summary of four lynchings that had taken place elsewhere in Texas since those in Kirven and
declared: "No one favors mob law. It is a terrible thing and a dangerous
thing, yet so long as Southern womanhood is the victim of the rapist
and the murderer, just that long will Southern manhood mete swift and
awful punishment to the perpetrators."

The same edition contained other, happier news—that four new oil
wells were going down, three within seven miles of Fairfield and one
eight miles southeast.

On June 2, the *Fairfield Recorder* reported another lynching, in
nearby Waco. After briefly, and inaccurately, describing the horrible
crime supposedly committed by the black victim, who was said to have
killed a white man and assaulted his white female companion, the editor
stepped up on a soapbox to give absolution to members of the Kirven
mob for their recent conduct:

No safety for our women even when protected by an
escort! How long can such a state of affairs exist? The
leading paper of the State is growing alarmed over the
"growing tendency of mob law," the Governor is
shocked over the frequency of mob law, but not a
word about the growing tendency of the black brutes

to ravish and murder the womanhood of the south; and not a word about the conditions existing that are bringing about a breakdown of law and order. It is time for the daily papers and the politicians to wake up and see "whither we are drifting."

Whither the county was drifting, in fact, was toward ultimate sanity, but more acts of violence would have to occur before a stable shore would come in sight. And as the county was drifting, the truth was sinking deeper and deeper beneath the waves.

PART TWO

The South is memories, memories—it cannot help believing that yesterday was better than tomorrow can possibly be. Some of the memories are extraordinarily well-packaged, it is true, but when a place has been reduced in its own estimation no amount of artful packaging can hide the gloom.

— LARRY MCMURTRY,
In a Narrow Grave: Essays on Texas

The scene of the burnings of the three men accused of Eula's murder, taken on May 6, 1922, approximately six hours after the burnings, depicting the plow around which the three men died.

Portrait of murder victim Eula Ausley, heavily retouched in the 1920s. Almost certainly the "cheap enlargement" described by Dan Kelly as being on the wall in her grandfather's home and "worshipped like a shrine." Used by permission of B. J. Ausley.

The grave of Eula (Ausley) King.

Horace M. Mayo and wife, Bessie Kelly Mayo, circa 1900.
Mayo served as Freestone County sheriff from 1920 through
1922. Photo courtesy of Dr. Michael Ditto.

The ruins of the bridge across Grindstone Creek where Eula was seized by her murderers on May 4, 1922, and near which her body was found.

Kirven (or Kirvin) Methodist Church, in front of which the three men were burned alive, and from which the two brothers witnessed the burnings.

Prologue to Part Two

The foregoing account, together with additional events and details told in subsequent chapters, makes up the standard and universally accepted version of the Kirven burnings, at least as far as the story is understood and believed in the county today. The most critical element of that version, however, is utterly false.

In the spring of 1990, I accepted a job with a law firm in Austin and moved away from Freestone County. The Kirven story, like half a dozen other interests, hobbies, and writing projects, was something I sporadically dusted off, tinkered with, and put away again. I could not abandon my interest in the story, but I had no clear direction to go with the research, and months sometimes passed between efforts.

I tried to find other witnesses, and was moderately successful, but most of the stories they told merely repeated what I had already heard.

Not sure of the next step, I began transcribing the tape-recorded statements of people I had interviewed, beginning with those of J. C. Whatley. The job took days. Whatley had relished the opportunity to reminisce, and had done so for hours, frequently traipsing down utterly unrelated bunny trails of memory. For every paragraph of usable information, I ended up with dozens of typed pages. When I finished, I turned to the interview of Bertha Williams. By then, it was 1993.

I had talked to Miss Williams on the front porch of her home in Kirven on June 5, 1987. She was over ninety years of age, missing both legs, and confined to a wheelchair. Her mind was absolutely clear, but she was not an easy witness to interview.

Unlike Whatley, who was happy to bore me with hours of unrelated detail, Miss Williams volunteered very little, preferring to respond to direct questions. She was also difficult to understand, because she mumbled, and had an elderly, black, Southern accent.

She was also impatient. Because I could not understand all she said, I sometimes asked a question she had already answered. When I did, her tone took on a distinct edge of irritation as she repeated herself.

Finally, she had relatives visiting from out of state who were suspicious of my motives. Twice they interrupted us to question my purpose and credentials. It was the most tense of all the witness interviews I conducted. I was anxious to conclude the visit and leave. I was recording the interview, so instead of continuing to irritate Miss Williams by asking her to repeat or clarify her statements, I decided to simply ask questions once and let her talk, figuring I would determine what she said later.

We ranged over several topics besides "the troubles," as she called them, but initially, all the information she gave me about Eula's murder and the subsequent violence only repeated what I had heard elsewhere. I egotistically believed I knew all the vitals about the burnings, but nobody knows less than a person who thinks he knows everything.

Besides reading the newspaper accounts and interviewing some witnesses, I had talked to members of the county historical commission who knew the story. Most members of the commission were too young to have been there at the time of the events, but they had talked to old-timers, most of whom were by now gone, and they confirmed or added to what I had heard and read elsewhere. In addition, there was Harry Hughes, a co-worker at Dow Chemical, who had grown up in Kirven, and who shared with me what he had heard about the burnings.

All the explanations were the same. Every version described how Snap Curry, John Cornish, and Mose Jones, in order to exact revenge for the cruel treatment they had received at the hands of the King brothers, raped and murdered Eula Ausley, or Eula King, but were found out, arrested, taken from the jail, and burned alive. There were inconsistent details, but there was no doubt in any white Freestone County native's mind, or in mine, about the basic facts.

Miss Williams had known the men who were lynched, so she could provide information about them that I had not been able to find elsewhere. I thought this would be the most significant contribution she could make, so I tried to think of different questions to ask her about them. After inquiring about their physical appearance, I asked her why she believed they had killed Eula. I expected to hear the standard tale about beatings and mistreatment by the King brothers, followed by revenge by Snap, Johnny, and Mose. Instead, she began explaining that the real murderers were white men.

I listened and asked a few more questions, but she was difficult to understand. Besides, in my ignorance, I believed she was merely repeating some myth about the event that had grown up in the black community to exculpate the lynching victims. I paid lip service to what she was saying, but promptly returned to my original line of questions about the men who were killed.

Six years passed before I tried to decipher all she had said. The transcription process was slow, and more tedious than slogging up and down Whatley's bunny trails. I had to play and replay the recording, concentrating on one word at a time, never retrieving some of them, but finally piecing most of it together. What finally emerged startled me.

Me: Did any of those men have a bad reputation before this happened?

Bertha: No, everything was quiet. Everybody just got along fine.

Me: What was the opinion of the people to explain why the girl got killed and why all of it happened?

Bertha: Nine years to the day, a white man came here that Otis had cut nearly to death with a butcher knife. He and his sons and Snap is the ones that murdered the girl. See, the man got Snap to help he and his sons kill the girl. Nine years prior to that Otis had cut him nearly to death with a butcher knife, and he got revenge by killing Otis's niece.

Me: Are you saying a man hired Snap to do it?

Bertha: I guess so.

Me: Well that's interesting. That I hadn't . . . All I had to go on was talking to some of the other old-timers and then there's an old newspaper account of it, and the explanation I'd heard before was just that Otis and John T. were real . . . would beat them, would pistol-whip them and . . .

Bertha: Well I never knew them to do one thing, and I used to work for them. I never knew one thing. Never!

Me: You never knew anything that Otis or John T. did . . . is that what you're saying?

Bertha: Never! John T. was married to Mr. Green's daughter, and I used to work for her in her beautiful home and it was cultured, like the rest of her life. Everybody just got along like two birds in a nest, until this happened.

Me: Hmm, that's a whole new insight for me, that somebody from outside . . . you say that nine years after it happened . . .

Bertha: Before it happened.

Me: Is when he cut him up, but then how . . .

Bertha: He was seen in Kirven that day, and from this day

	to then he's never been seen, then one night he and Thelma moved away. Nobody ever knew where they went to.
Me:	Okay, but, and that was a white man?
Bertha:	Yes.
Me:	Did Snap or somebody say that man had hired him, or how did it get out that he'd . . .
Bertha:	Hired him.
Me:	Hired him?
Bertha:	I don't know. He was working for him. I don't know if he give him some money or not.
Me:	Let's see, Mose was the oldest, what about Shad Green [the black man hanged after the burnings], how old was he?
Bertha:	He was 'bout as long as me in it. He was older than Snap. He was killed right along the same time.
Me:	Uh-huh. He was lynched that very night, the same night as the burnings [*sic*—actually Green was lynched the next night].
Bertha:	Yeah, they took him down in the Caney bottoms and broke his neck, Caney bottoms about six miles east of here . . . and they got so mad after that they just went right on killing and running everybody off.

Reading it now, I want to scream "Thelma! Who the hell was Thelma? You fool! Why did you change the subject and start asking about ages? She was ready to name names, did name a name, and you ignored her. Why didn't you ask her the name of the white man who killed Eula? Why, why, why?"

Mostly, my failure to do so was because I could not understand a lot of what she said. I was struggling to hold up my end of the interview, wracking my brain to ask relevant questions, and I did not hear her mention Thelma. I also did not consider this part of her story to be credible, did not expect her to reveal sensitive details about an old murder, was too polite to ask her to name a white man she was accusing of murder, and did not expect her to tell me if I did ask. Also, I was a dim bulb.

All I had to do was ask the right questions. She would have been perfectly willing to reveal more. She obviously knew the man and the family who she believed committed Eula's murder—who they were, and what they were like. Perhaps I would not have believed her, but

I could have preserved her version of the tale, researched the name, found out what I could, and might have tracked down some new species of facts, might have learned a truth. As it turned out, there was a lot to learn.

Yet I did not bother to ask the questions! The magnitude of my carelessness was astounding.

I called a friend in Freestone County to try to contact Bertha Williams again, but as I feared, she was dead. More of her story than the amount I had obtained, including the name of Thelma's husband, was lost forever.

I shook my head in sad disbelief. How could I have been so stupid?

In fact, I had already been even more stupid than I yet knew. I had been in possession of the clues that would lead to solving Miss Williams's mysterious statements, and much more, for five years.

There was in my trove of research tapes and notes a crumbling paperback entitled *100 Years of Lynching*, by Ralph Ginzburg. I had either acquired the book at a library sale in Fairfield or retrieved it from the library trash in 1988. I was a member of the Fairfield library board of directors, and when they had a sale, or discarded used books, the head librarian would tell me if any were historical in nature and I would buy them or retrieve them from a stack next to the dumpster.

I had picked up the Ginzburg book because of its relationship to the subject matter of the Kirven story, and had thumbed through and read some of the newspaper stories of lynchings and burnings. Many accounts went beyond the bounds of violence and cruelty, and into the realms of the ghastly and barbaric.

The excerpts and summaries were in chronological order from 1861 to 1961, but when I first obtained the book, I turned to May 1922 and found nothing about the Kirven incident. I put the book in a box and forgot about it.

Several weeks after transcribing the Williams and Whatley tapes, I returned to the story and decided to look for non-Texas newspaper accounts. At that point in my research, I had found stories about the Kirven events in the Dallas, Houston, and Austin papers, but most of the accounts were similar and cited the Associated Press as their source. I assumed that out-of-state papers that printed the story, if there were any, would contain the same information and would credit the same source. I did not expect to find new information by moving far away from the scene of events, but lacking other directions to go, I decided to give it a try.

I thought of the Ginzburg book, remembering that many of the articles about lynchings were taken from the same newspapers, but from editions printed in different years. Certain papers apparently catered to stories of lynchings. Even though the Kirven incident was not mentioned in the ragged paperback, it might serve as a useful tool by providing the names of target newspapers from different parts of the country.

I found the book and began jotting down the names of the newspapers quoted most often. I came to May 1922, moved two pages further on, and, to my surprise, found an account of the Kirven incident, printed out of chronological order.

The newspaper quoted was the *Brooklyn Citizen*, dated May 6, 1922, and the story was a harshly biased version of the tale, depicting the members of the Freestone County mob as brutes who snipped toes, fingers, and ears from the lynching victims before they were burned. Except for those embellishments, however, the facts of the story were the same as those in Texas newspapers.

Still, I was excited to learn that the story was reported from a different perspective, and in Brooklyn! Where else might it have made the news?

The next day I dashed to the Austin city library and fired off interlibrary loan requests for articles from twenty-one newspapers around the country that might have carried the Kirven story. The same evening, feeling like I was making progress, I picked up the Ginzburg book again, re-read the Brooklyn story, and, for the first time, read the article which followed it.

This one was from the *New York Call*, dated May 7, 1922, and thus also out of place, but the location given for the story was Fairfield, Texas. It had the tantalizing headline, "Sheriff Holds 2 Whites in Crime That 3 Burned For."

The excerpt identified "Cliff and Arnie Powell" as white suspects in the crime. Sheriff Mayo was quoted to have said the Powells and the Kings were feuding because one of the King sons was cut in a fight with them years earlier.

I was elated. Surely I had found the elusive "Mr. Thelma." Sheriff Mayo's quote about one of the Kings being "cut" was the same language Bertha used, even if she had identified the opposite party as the one who was injured. This was surely Bertha's story! Perhaps there was something to it after all.

The next day I galloped to the State Archives to review the microfilmed census records for 1920. I was certain I would find a family of Powells with sons Cliff and Arnie, as well as a mother, wife, or daughter-in-law named Thelma.

I did not. I found a few Powells in the county, but no Cliffs, Arnies, or Thelmas. I did, however, find a family of "Prowells" living near the Kings, with sons Claud and Audey. There was no Thelma, but the sons were not married in 1920, so the names of any wives added to the family by 1922 would not have been included. Perhaps the New York newspaper merely got the names slightly wrong. I decided to track down the Prowells to see what I could find.

That evening, still enthusiastic over my recent discoveries, I picked up the Ginzburg book again, and turned the page. Perhaps what really happened is that the Good Lord, tired of handing me clues and evidence on a silver platter, literally giving me witnesses who knew the story and a book with the story in it, shouted, "TURN THE PAGE! TURN . . . THE . . . PAGE!" loudly enough for my subconscious to hear.

There, on page 164, the next page after the *New York Call* story, dated not May 1922, but January 2, 1923, and with no source location named, was a report from the *New York World* entitled "Finds Triple-Lynch Victims Were Probably Innocent."

The article was about the work of a white man named Dan Kelly who was sent to Kirven by the National Association for the Advancement of Colored People (NAACP) to investigate the lynching incident and learn the truth. No Powells or Prowells were mentioned, but the story was based upon "records made public today" by the NAACP.

I was truly stunned, genuinely excited, pretty embarrassed. There was a report somewhere by a secret agent!

I had been carrying the story around with me in a box for something like six years. I had had the necessary information all along for more research, but had never bothered to read it, never bothered to turn the page.

The next day I called the NAACP's headquarters in Baltimore and asked where they archived their records. "The Library of Congress," I was told.

Great, I thought, the largest library in the world. Although I figured I was chasing a long shot at best, I obtained the library's number from directory assistance in Washington, D.C., and called.

The call was answered with a recorded message that provided a lengthy introduction and offered an electronic menu of seven options.

"For Congressional research, press one; for visitor information and directions, press two; for copyright and book publishing, press three," and so forth.

I pressed four, to hear about conducting research, and got another electronic menu, with five choices this time. None sounded like what I wanted and I hesitated too long. Another electronic voice came on and said, "Your call is being disconnected from the system, and will be transferred to a reference librarian."

Okay, fine, that was what I wanted anyway.

A few seconds later, a live person answered. I told her I was looking for an NAACP report. "That will be in documents," she said. "I'll transfer you."

Jeff Flannery answered. I told him I was looking for an NAACP report from 1922.

"We have over a hundred thousand NAACP papers," he replied, "but they aren't indexed."

My heart sank.

"There is a company that microfilmed some of our collection, though," Jeff continued. "If you contact them, they may be able to help you."

I thanked him and asked for the name of the company. He put me on hold while he retrieved their catalog.

When he came back, he said there was an index to microfilms in the back of the catalog. "What's the subject of the report? I'll look and see if it might be in here."

Thinking how lucky I was to find such a helpful bureaucrat, I told him, "Lynching."

Jeff rustled some pages and said, "There's a whole section on lynching, and two sections on the anti-lynching campaign, several pages of listings. It will take a while to look through it. Tell you what I'll do. Give me as much information as you know, and when I get a chance, I'll check and see if I see it. If I do, I'll write you. Maybe I can narrow your search a little."

Really appreciative now, I told him, "It's a report dated January 1923, by a man named Dan Kelly about an incident that occurred in Kirven, or Freestone County, Texas."

He wrote down the information and asked for my name, address, and telephone number. "When I get time, I'll see what I can find, but it will be a few weeks," Jeff said. I thanked him, told him I really appreciated it, and started to hang up. Just before I did, he said, "Oh, here it is."

I caught my breath.

"'Report of Dan Kelly on Investigation of Lynchings at Kirven, Texas,'" he read, "but it's dated May 6, 1922. Could that be it?"

"Y-yes," I stammered. "May 6 is when it happened. That's it." My mind was racing. I could not believe my good fortune.

"Look," I said slowly, "I've been researching this story for over six years, and I just learned about the report last night. What do I have to do to get a copy of it?"

If he had said I needed to do so, I would have been on a plane for Washington the next day. Instead, he said, "It's just thirteen pages—I'll mail a copy to you."

He did, bless his heart, and it was better than I had dreamed.

I now know what any knowledgeable scholar about the history of lynching could have told me: that the NAACP papers, as well as numerous books, articles, microfilm, and the records of the Commission on Interracial Cooperation Papers at Atlanta University, are readily available for research, but I was not a knowledgeable scholar, and knew none who studied lynching. I was simply floundering for clues.

But as if I had finally found the hidden switch in a computer adventure game, the doors opened and witnesses began to appear. Shortly thereafter, I located the youngest of the three daughters of Horace Mayo, living in Arlington, Texas. She told me her two older sisters were still living; the elder of the two had been teaching school in Kirven when the lynchings occurred. A good friend of mine, David McCartney, of Tehuacana, Texas, in Limestone County, located other witnesses, including Lutisia Foreman, née Gibson, and Foster Foreman, whose stories remain to be told, as well as one of two brothers who, as boys, witnessed the burnings from the steps of the Kirven Methodist church. Harry Hughes interviewed Mary, the last friend of Eula to see her alive, and suggested I talk to another woman, who turned out to be a classmate of Eula. Finally, he pointed me toward B. J. "Bill" Ausley, Eula's last surviving nephew.

The last link in the chain was finding Foreman Carter. Doing so turned out to be only slightly less fortuitous than finding the Dan Kelly report.

On January 8, 1995, I went to Freestone County to interview Lutisia and Foster Foreman. Lutisia had witnessed the killings of Leroy and

Allie Gibson. Her husband, Foster, had witnessed the confrontation between blacks and whites that followed.

The interview went well, and afterward, I met with Harry Hughes in Kirven and told him the status of my research. He had been interested in the story of the troubles since he was a boy, and was intrigued, though not convinced, by the Kelly report. He also suggested other witnesses to interview. One of them was Foreman Carter.

The reason Harry had waited until 1995 to suggest I talk to Mr. Carter was because the latter had spent the last seventy years of his life living in New York and New Jersey. He had moved back "home," to Kirven, a few months earlier. As it turned out, he had moved home to die.

I told Harry I would like to talk to Mr. Carter, and the following April I came back to Kirven and went with Harry to the old man's mobile home.

I had recently had some bad luck with witness interviews. Two ladies who had known Eula and lived through the troubles had agreed to talk to me, only to change their minds and cancel the interview before I arrived. At the beginning of my talk with Mr. Carter, I was afraid a wave of trepidation in the community might be developing, and might infect him as well.

Mr. Carter was reserved at first. Like Bertha Williams, he did not know me or my motives, and I was prodding old wounds that were not completely healed. His answers were noncommittal, and provided minimal information. I pressed on, however, determined not to repeat the mistakes I had made with Bertha Williams. I hoped to find a key to unlock his trust.

As will be described later, I found the key, and more. Mr. Carter not only confirmed the Prowell story, he revealed information probably known by no other living person.

Other events followed. A visit to the Shanks Cemetery the following January revealed another startling irony, and the following year, I was privileged to be able to locate and talk to a surviving sibling of Johnny Cornish.

But what of Thelma? Was there a Prowell woman named Thelma whom Bertha Williams saw for the last time shortly after Eula was murdered?

That is a question I still cannot answer. The story of the Prowells follows, but my research has not revealed a Thelma in the family. The name of Audey Prowell's ex-wife is missing, and she might have been the elusive Thelma, but I doubt it. Audey was only eighteen in 1922, pretty young to be married, and pretty young to have a wife so well known that Bertha Williams would remember her name after seventy years, particularly if the Prowell family was absent from the county between 1920 and 1922, which was evidently the case.

Bertha may have been mistaken about the name. She was, after all, mistaken about Otis King cutting one of the Prowells nine years to the day before Eula was murdered. The incident actually occurred two years earlier, not to the day; further, it was not Otis King who did the cutting, but a Prowell, and it was not Otis who was cut, but one of his brothers.

Again, however, I doubt it. I believe that in telling me that name, Bertha Williams was revealing a fact she had kept filed away for many years, a detail she had pondered over, a tidbit of information she knew too well to mangle. I believe she was referring to Thelma Prowell.

I cannot prove it, not yet. All I have right now is one other clue.

The death certificates of Audey Prowell and his little brother, J.L., both include the name of their mother. Annie Prowell, the wife of Thomas Prowell, was a Gibson before she married. Her maiden name is on both certificates, as is her middle initial—Annie *T.* Gibson.

So far I have not discovered Annie's complete middle name, but someday I shall.

 *A Visitor from Waco*

Among the many visitors to Freestone County during the weeks following the lynchings of Curry, Cornish, Jones, and Green was a white man named Dan Kelly. He said he was a newspaper reporter from Waco, and he was about half honest.

Kelly was from Waco and he was there to make a report, but not for a newspaper. He was an undercover agent, dispatched to Freestone County by the NAACP, then headquartered in New York City.

The NAACP, founded in 1909 and chartered in 1911, kept records of lynchings and other atrocities committed against blacks, and the Kirven case was of special interest. There had not been, according to its reports, a triple burning before. Kelly was sent to find out as much as he could about what had happened and to file a report in time for the thirteenth annual conference of the NAACP, which would be held in Newark, New Jersey, at the end of June 1922.

He made, filed, and explained his report. His account did not read or sound like the typical newspaper stories of the day, whether Northern or Southern.

Kelly's full name was Dan Kezer Kelly. He was born in Taylor, Texas, on July 31, 1896, attended Waco High School from 1912 to 1915, enrolled at Baylor, in Waco, and then attended the University of Texas in Austin in 1917 and 1918.[1] How the 25-year-old became an agent for the NAACP and accepted the assignment to investigate the Kirven burnings, as well as what became of him afterward, are some of the minor mysteries of this story.

Kelly began his report by going out of his way to establish his credentials as an understanding Southerner, and to avoid coming across as a crusader against lynching. He added personal opinion, but avoided vitriolic judgment of the people who participated in the lynchings. Instead, he concluded, forty years before the civil rights movement became organized, that it would have to be the blacks who must take the initiative to achieve the physical, civil, and personal rights they were being denied, by some method other than petitioning and legislation, for, he argued, the race problem "is not going to be solved by white people." The result is that Kelly's report rings with both credibility and prophecy.

Kelly summarized his report in a presentation at the NAACP Convention, and his speech received minor publicity.[2] Thereafter, the report was filed with the association's papers in New York City. Later, along with other NAACP documents, it wound up in the Library of Congress in Washington, D.C. There is no evidence that any citizen of Freestone County heard of the report in 1922, or, indeed, at any time prior to the publication of this book. If they did, they probably chose not to believe it, because Kelly's report turns the traditionally accepted account of Eula's murder on its ear.

Kelly made some factual errors, but the sincere attempt of the author to present his story in an objective manner is clear. The report follows in its entirety.

THIRTEENTH ANNUAL CONFERENCE, N.A.A.C.P.
REPORT OF DAN KELLY ON INVESTIGATION OF LYNCHINGS AT KIRVIN, TEXAS, MAY 6, 1922

At the request of the National Association for the Advancement of Colored People I undertook to investigate as clearly, as candidly and as thoroughly as I could the actual facts and circumstances surrounding the lynching of three Negroes at Kirvin, Texas, on May 6, and later the hanging of a fourth and the unexplained disappearance of a fifth, all growing out of the alleged attack and murder of a seventeen-year-old girl.

I believe I can say that the things I say to you are based upon a candid examination of the evidence that I was able to secure by speaking to more than a hundred people, talking to the sheriff and many of those who proudly proclaimed that they had taken part in the burning; and I think if I were prejudiced, my prejudice, from my birth, education and training, would rather lay against the facts that I shall present.

It may be of some value to you to know that my grandfather served in the Confederate Army. A great uncle was wounded in a battle shower, and a third died from privations in a Federal prison during the

Civil War. I was born within thirty miles of Kirvin,
and educated in the city schools and University
of Texas.

I left Waco a week after the burning of the three
first men. Four days after, the fourth was lynched, and
the fifth disappeared a day or two after I got there.

Kirvin, Texas, is a town of about a dozen stores.
A railroad runs through it. One train goes north and
another south each day. Those of you from the South
know what type of town it is. It is just at the beginning
of the backwoods section of Texas. Few of the people
of the community have been out of the county; some
speak of having once visited the Dallas Fair.

It is interesting to know that this little seventeen-
year-old girl who was foully and brutally murdered
was riding home from a beautiful, brick, slated school.
I was informed that there was no Negro school in that
section of the country. As I was able to ascertain these
facts, the story I would summarize is this:

This community consists of white landlords and
Negro tenants in the greater part. There are, of
course, some of that variety which commonly are
called the poor whites who undertake to work for
themselves on their own farms, but most of the work
is done under the tenant system, the share-crop
system, by which the owner furnishes the tools, the
house, the land and the equipment; the tenant does
the work and they share up half and half on the produce; but it is weighed on the owner's scales; the cotton is classified by the owner, and often the tenant
ends up by being in debt to the owner at the end of
the year.

When I arrived in Kirvin, I came there in the guise
of a newspaper man from Waco, because I was going
to ask questions, and you had to have a very good
reason for asking questions there. I first went to
Mr. John King, who is the grandfather of the girl who
was murdered, and he told me his story. Briefly his
story is this:

On Friday afternoon about four o'clock his daugh-

ter should have been home from school. She rode a
pony from school to her home every day, about a three-
mile ride along the edge of the Grindstone Bottom.
As she did not get in at the usual time, the old man
became nervous and called up his neighbors. She had
been seen passing this house and that house, but no
further could they trace her. Although there is great
prejudice in the community, there is also a certain
softening influence. The old man King, about seventy years old, one of the wealthiest landlords in the
community, when his granddaughter failed to appear, became frightened. He called out Ben Gibson,
a Negro about fifty years old and said: "I want you to
go down and find my granddaughter." The old Negro
got on his horse and went to look for the girl, and
although later they accused Negroes of this act, it is
interesting to know that in his agony this old farmer
depended upon and called upon a Negro to go down
for and safeguard his granddaughter.

I said, "Mr. King, did you suspect at that time that
something had happened to your granddaughter?"
He said, "I knew something had happened to my
granddaughter." I inquired why. He said, "Because
I have been afraid of something for two years." I
asked "Why have you been particularly afraid for
two years?" Then he told me of a feud that existed
between his family and the neighboring family for two
years, the Prowl family. They were also landlords of
that community, proud, although they were mostly
uneducated—proud and high-tempered just as was
the King family. Just two years previous to that the
Prowls and Mr. King's son engaged in an argument
in which he accused the Prowls of cheating in a cattle
deal. Two of the Prowls jumped on King's son and cut
him with knives so that he had to be taken to the hospital. He recovered but was maimed for life.

The Prowls left the county and have never been
back since and they had threatened when they left,
"We will make you feel it and will make it hurt you
where it hurts most."

Now, the old man's children had grown up and
settled down in that community and his whole life was
centered around this beautiful granddaughter of his.
He purchased for her an automobile, her own pony,
and everything she could wish. So he said, "The minute she did not come I thought then that those Prowls
had done something foul." Then we know that this
Ben Gibson found the horse she had rode tied near a
thicket along the road. He brought the horse home
and left it. Then old man King got on a horse and
went to his nearest son and asked that son to go out
and hunt for the granddaughter. While Ben Gibson
was in his home, immediately after he had brought
the horse home, the wife of one of the Prowl sons
came to this Negro and asked him what business was
it of his to go down and get that horse; and she has
never explained to this day how she knew that horse
was tied there.

They went to the thicket and found the girl's body
horribly mutilated. Then they organized a posse to
find the murderers. They sent for bloodhounds.
While they were organizing the posse, old man John
King, broken as he was with the news, told me, "I
went down there and got on a wagon and I talked with
them and pleaded with them to go slow because at
that time I felt those Prowls had done it and I did
not want them to lynch any innocent Negroes. I knew
they would suspect Negroes and I went there and told
them to be sure they got the right man before they did
anything."

It is interesting to note that immediately after the
word spread that his girl had been murdered the two
Prowl boys, Audley and Claude, disappeared. Then
the mob gathered and they went to the Prowl boys'
home to ask them to explain their part in the act,
because they suspected them both—that is, the King
faction did. The mob separated into groups and went
from one part of the community to the other waiting
for the bloodhounds to come. In one of these groups
was a Negro named Snap Curry. Negroes and whites

both were searching. Following every clue was Snap Curry. One of the stories is that Snap Curry disappeared when the bloodhounds came, but that I heard from one man and from one man only. The others give the indication that he was with some group at all times; and Snap Curry was the first one they burned, although he had followed one of the groups all day.

After the groups had gone over the community, the first thing they did was to check up on all the Negroes to explain where they had been and what they had been doing. When they went to Snap Curry's house his wife, after they had put her through the third degree, told them that Snap Curry came home with some blood on his shirt sleeves and that another Negro, Tom Barry, and Shad Green also had blood on their shirts which they attempted to wash out. It is interesting also to know that the wife of Snap Curry was very jealous of him and that they were not living happily together. Although they stayed in the same house, there was a difference between them.

As far as the evidence goes, Snap Curry explained that he had been hunting rabbits and in skinning them had gotten blood on his sleeves. There was no investigation of his story, no test made of the blood, no analysis whatsoever was ever made about that blood, so about that story we can never know the exact facts.

So, with this evidence, Sheriff Mayo started out with his deputies to search for these three and some others. They found three, Snap Curry, Mose Jones and one named Smith [*sic;* it was actually Johnny Cornish]. They took them to the old court house, to the county jail. On the way, Snap Curry, under threats and beating and other cruel treatment, named some others who had been with them that day and all those who were actually present at the time state that his only statement was that "Those others are as guilty as I," but he never admitted that he actually committed the crime. On the way to Teague they were overtaken and finally taken away from the sheriff in a bank building where he was trying to hide them.

The mob took the Negroes back to Kirvin and on a little square between the Methodist and Baptist churches, there was an old plow, a single disk plow with a seat on it, and one after another the mob made them sit in the seat while they piled on wood, threw on gasoline and burned them one after another. The last two who were burned declared their innocence while they had any breath of life in them, the only confession being from Snap Curry in which he said, "The others are as guilty as I, and if I burn, they deserve the same treatment."

It is interesting also if you will listen to some of the details, harrowing as they are. As they sat around that burning flame and saw Snap Curry, the other two, Mose Jones and Smith, stood by and watched him burn without any apparent excitement. One said to the other, "Will we get that too?" and Mose Jones answered, "No; what have we done?" Standing there watching, it seems that if they were guilty, if they were at any time to confess or feel a sense of guilt, they would have done so at that time; but the opinion of those who stood by was that they were surprised when they were called upon to go on the fire next.

Two of them burned rapidly. The third one the mob was not satisfied to burn in this way. So they tied a big rope, which had been soaked in water, around his neck and another around his feet. Then they threw him in the flame for a moment and pulled him out, threw him in again and pulled him out, and continued to do that until the rope burned and he clasped his arms around the plow and refused to be dragged away, meeting his death as soon as he could.

The next morning a fourth Negro, Shad Green, was found hanging to a tree, and a week later a fifth disappeared. A week after that, about two weeks after his disappearance, I went back to the community, and over the trees of that thick, impassable bottom, I saw vultures flying around. I asked someone what that was. They said, "Very likely that is Tom Barry, killed and left there to rot without even a decent burial."

So we have five Negroes, burned, lynched or foully done away with for the alleged crime of murdering a seventeen-year-old white girl.

The morning after the burning the sheriff found the two Prowl boys, Audley and Claude, and they were arrested and asked to explain what their tracks were doing in the mud going from this very thicket where the girl was murdered. The tracks were fitted to the feet of these two boys going straight up to their homes. The sheriff asked them to explain the meaning of these tracks, tracks which were made the very day and previous to the murder of the girl. These two white boys then confessed that in that very thicket they were making bran mash for the purpose of distilling alcohol and they admitted that they had been to that very thicket where the murdered body of this girl was found that very day, and upon this explanation—after three Negroes had been burned and a fourth hanged—upon that explanation they were freed.

In talking to Sheriff Mayo I asked this, "Did you investigate if there was any bran mash in the thicket?" He said that he did not. I asked him, "Do you believe that they are innocent?" After asking me what the hell business it was of mine, he said that enough had been punished for the deed already. It is interesting to note that a week later the Prowls, every one of them, moved away from that community.

Sheriff Mayo himself said that he believed that Mose Jones was innocent. The evidence itself indicates that no more than three persons were engaged in the act of murdering the girl. Therefore, any way you take it, two of them were innocent. I spoke to the people of the community, many of them. They had no particular interest in the matter that two innocent Negroes had been burned. Some of them even started the story, "Well, I don't believe that Mose Jones was guilty, but Snap Curry wanted him to go on the trip with him." No one was moved by the fact that their guilt had not been established by the evidence. They did not seem concerned that none of them had been given a trial and a chance to establish by legal evidence his innocence. None of them seemed to be concerned that it was in any way a dishonor and a stain upon the community. In fact, the whole incident was one of which those who had engaged in it were seemingly proud. I asked one man if Mose Jones was related to any of the others. "Well," he said, "he was in pretty close relation to them on the night of the burning." I drove my car up in front of a gasoline station just across the street from where the burning took place. I asked, "Will five gallons take me back to Waco?" The man answered, "I guess so. Fifty gallons took three niggers to hell the other night."

And so it was. The people of that community are utterly unaware of the fact that they have done any deed for which they should be ashamed. They feel no kind of conscious scruples. It is no matter of offense to their consciences that these victims may not have been guilty. They have the idea that Negroes have paid the penalty and the matter is settled as far as they are concerned.

The last day that I was in Texas there had been a great washout. The bridges were washed out and I went on horseback. I wanted to talk to the people of the community again before I left. Three weeks from the day on which it happened I talked to some people. I asked Sheriff Mayo would there be a grand jury investigation and he seemed utterly astonished that I should ask such a question. He looked at me and said, "By God, I don't believe you are from Waco."

I went again to see old man King who in three weeks had aged ten years. His heart was broken, his spirit was broken. On the wall of his home was a cheap enlargement of his granddaughter's picture at which he worshipped as though it were a shrine. The old man told me, "I believe still, although those rascals, some of them, may have been implicated, they could not have thought of such a deed. I still believe that those Prowl boys are the ones who did it." Although five people have paid the penalty, still that

old man felt that the white men were guilty, and to
this day those tracks leading from the very scene of
the crime to the Prowls' home, white men's home,
have never been investigated or explained. The reason
the Prowls disappeared the night after the murder was
discovered has never been explained. That the wife of
one of the Prowls should know that this Negro, Ben
Gibson, had untied the horse and brought him home
before the body was discovered, how she knew that,
has not yet been explained. In the hearts of the people
of that community who know the facts, they believe
that at least two of the Negroes burned were innocent.

I rode down there three weeks later and while I
was there I got a telephone call to come back to Waco,
that there was a lynching going on there. I said to
myself, "I will do some more investigating while I am
here." I got on my horse and in two hours and a half
I had ridden forty-five miles back to Waco. I got there
just in time to see an automobile coming down the
main street dragging the corpse of a Negro, Jesse
Thomas. It seems that a night or two before that a
white girl was assaulted and she gave a description
of a Negro who was tall, black and had a gold tooth.
They arrested a Negro with a gold tooth and put him
in the county jail, and a mob of five hundred gathered
outside to take his life, but the sheriff and some rangers stood there with their guns and defended him. In
the meanwhile a deputy sheriff had found another
Negro who was tall, black, with a gold tooth, at Corsicana and was on his way to Waco. The mob was waiting for him.

A third Negro was also found. The sheriff took him
in his car to the home of the girl, who was still nervous and utterly beside herself after her experience.
This man with the gold tooth was brought into her
room and she screamed. The father of the girl pulled
out a gun and shot him on the spot. The mob took
him and burned him and dragged his body through
the streets of the town.

I talked to the people of that community. I never

found a single one who condemned the act. All
seemed to think it perfectly justifiable.

A week later I talked with the Governor of the State
who was from Waco. I asked him what he thought of
lynching in Texas. At first he said nothing, but the
next day he gave out a dispatch to the Associated
Press in which he said that he believed that the mob
should be tried in a county other than that in which
the lynching occurred. That was his remedy for
lynching in Texas.

These were the facts of these two investigations.
I made other investigations but not as thoroughly. It
would seem to me that the people of Texas in general are utterly unconcerned that there is a problem
involved in lynching, that there is any shame or disgrace attached to it, that any severe action must be
taken to suppress it, and further than that, the people
of the communities that I visited are utterly ignorant
and unconcerned with the fact that there is such a
thing as a race problem in these communities. They
are utterly unconcerned with the fact that half the
population is denied for all practical purposes political suffrage, the right of education, the right even to
own property, that their civil rights, their personal
rights are denied on any and every occasion, that discrimination of every kind are exercised against them.
It has always been that way, and so far as they can see,
it will probably always be that way.

So it would seem to me that whatever solution
there is of the race question in the South and in the
North, it is not going to be solved by the white people.
It has got to be taken up and handled by the Negro
himself. As far as I can see, there is no hope that the
white people of the South will even give the Negro any
assistance in solving the race problem or in securing
to himself even the physical rights of his civil liberty
and personal security; and it seems to me that more
than petitioning, even more than legislation will have
to be pursued in order to secure these rights. The
Negro in the South and in the North must be edu-

cated, agitated or in some way aroused to a willingness to maintain with whatever force is necessary his
personal dignity, his civil rights, and the defense of
his life.

While I was in Texas I wore slung in under my arm
a thirty-eight automatic, and I felt safe in that community and in all the communities because of that thirty-
eight automatic, safer than I did because of the fact
that I was a citizen of the United States, or of Texas,
or of that community. And you who live there and
you who go there will find the same to be true of you.

So there you have it. A problem which, every way
you pursue it, from whatever angle you look at it, the
solution of it, the responsibility for the solution of it,
is always forced back upon the Negro. Whatever acts
one man may do, whatever acts a political party may
do well and good; but after all, this solution rests
upon the Negro himself and my advice to the Negro
would be to show a willingness to be responsible and
to seek that solution.

Query: Was there any evidence that the granddaughter of Mr. King had been criminally assaulted?

Answer: The doctor who examined her stated that
there was not.[3]

 *Confirmation*

Standing alone, and despite its objectivity, the Kelly report is not enough to overcome the accepted, Freestone County explanation for Eula's murder and the subsequent racial violence. Lynching was a political issue in 1922. The NAACP was a special-interest group, a lobbying organization. There was mileage to be made from any story of Southern, white racism and lawlessness. Kelly might have had his own agenda. He could have invented the story.

He did not.

Although none of the Freestone County newspapers identified the Prowell brothers nor mentioned white men being arrested, the first Associated Press report published after Eula's murder, that of the *Dallas Times Herald* for May 5, the day before the lynchings, stated that two white men and one black man had been arrested. The *Austin Statesman* reported the next day that "two white men were detained today for further investigation of their actions preceding the attack on and murder of Eula Awsley [*sic*], for which three negroes were burned at Kirven this morning. No announcements of charges being filed against the men have been made, according to reports here. They were held pending investigation only." The *Houston Chronicle,* on May 7, reported that "two white men taken into custody at Fairfield were released when they proved they had no connection with the crime."[1]

Northern and northeastern newspapers, however, specifically identified the white men from the very beginning, with various versions of their number and the spelling of their names. They also contained details that were consistent with the Kelly story.

The May 6 edition of the *Brooklyn Citizen,* for instance, printed the following account:

MOB BURNS THREE NEGROES FOR BRUTAL CRIME IN WHICH TWO WHITE MEN ARE HELD

Fairfield, Texas, May 6 — Claude and Audie Crowell, white men, were in jail here to-day pending an investi-

gation in connection with [the] assault and murder
of pretty little Eula Ausley, 17, at Kirven, for which
crime three negroes were terribly mutilated and
burned to death at dawn to-day.

Tracks leading from the scene of the murder led to
the house of the brothers, Sheriff H. M. Mayo said.

"The shoes of the Crowells fit the tracks," was the
terse comment of the sheriff.

One of the brothers was arrested yesterday and the
other surrendered after the mob had taken the negroes
from the jail here.

"In the pocket of one of the negroes was $15,"
the sheriff said. "The King and Crowell families had
some kind of fight some time ago, in which one of the
Crowells was badly cut. This is just another clue we
are following."

In the *New York Call* of May 7, the report read as follows:

Fairfield, Tex. May 6 — Claude and Audie Crowell,
two white men held here pending investigation of
their connection with the murder of Eula Ausley were
released from custody here shortly before noon today
when authorities were convinced they had no connection with the crime.

John King, grandfather of the dead girl, told the
officials that he was convinced that the three Negroes
burned at the stake at Kirven today were guilty of the
crime and the Crowells had nothing to do with it.

Previous to the release of the Crowells, however,
Sheriff H. M. Mayo declared that tracks leading
from the scene of the murder led to the home of the
brothers.

"The shoes of the brothers fit the tracks," was the
terse comment of the sheriff.

One of the brothers was arrested yesterday and
the other surrendered after the mob had taken the
Negroes from the jail here.

The version in the *St. Louis Argus,* on May 12, was:

Much secrecy surrounds the holding of three white
men in connection with the girl's death, two of whom

are well known in the community. It is said that
strong evidence is against them. The real truth in this
case will probably never be known to the "outside
world." There is some talk of "doing away" with the
white men who are in custody, but who knows?

In the May 13 edition of the *Chicago Defender*, the report read:

Two white men, the Prowell brothers, were arrested
later on charges growing out of the crime for which
the innocent men paid their lives—that of the slaying
of Eula Ausley, 17-year-old white girl.

Moving backward in time, more evidence can be found in a newspaper story about the cutting incident that helped fuel the feud.

On May 26, 1920, a Thursday, the same day of the week and a little
less than two years before Eula was murdered, Drew King, one of
Grandfather King's five sons, was attacked in a restaurant in Kirven,
not by Claude and Audie Prowell, but by their father, Tom Prowell,
and Tom's brother, Rob.

Drew King, the *Fairfield Recorder* reported, "was badly cut about
the face, and had a serious stab in the side. He was dangerously
wounded, but at this writing is recovering. It is reported that there had
been ill feelings between the Kings and Tom Prowell for some time." [2]

The two older Prowell brothers escaped, and were believed to have
been heading for Mexico, where Rob Prowell had been working. A
reward of $100 was offered for their arrest.

Then, on June 30, 1920, charges of "assault to murder" against Tom
Prowell were dropped. The single sheet of paper in the dusty archives
of the Freestone County Courthouse does not provide any information
or clue about the reasons the charges were dismissed. [3]

There is other evidence concerning the feud. B. J. Ausley, Eula's
nephew, knew the Kings were having problems with a white family,
and he had heard of the Prowells, but did not know any details. [4]
He was born after the troubles, and knew only stories handed down
by non-King family relatives. He thought the fight between the Kings
and the Prowells, all of whom he described as "hard men," was over a
fence line.

And, of course, there was Bertha Williams, who had worked for the
Kings, and who said the murder was committed by a family of whites—
a father and two sons—who had been involved in a knife fight, not with
Drew, but with Otis, and not two, but nine years "to the day" before

Eula was murdered. She said, apparently, that no members of the family were seen from the day of the knife fight until the day of Eula's murder, and that they were then seen in Kirven, but they left that night and were never seen again.[5]

After seventy-five years, the Prowells' movements are difficult to reconstruct, but there is enough documentation to verify that they were in Freestone County prior to 1922, and that they left the county some time shortly after the troubles.

Census records for Freestone County show the family of Andrew Thomas Prowell and his wife, Annie, living near Shanks in 1900, 1910, and 1920. The 1920 census shows the family living on farm number 304 in Precinct 6. Grandfather John King's family is listed as occupying farm number 300 in the same precinct.[6] Thomas and Annie were both forty-two in February 1920, when the census was taken. Six children were listed, including sons Claud (21), Audey (16), and J.L. (10). About a month before the attack on Drew King, Tom Prowell rendered, or reported ownership of, 358 acres of land in the county, together with six lots in Kirven, on which he paid $69.71 in ad valorem taxes.[7]

There is no record of any of the family living in Freestone County after 1920, but rural Texas records are sparse about such information, and at the date of this writing, names of persons counted during the 1930 census have not been released for public examination. Three of the witnesses interviewed remembered something, but not very much, about the family.[8] When some of the Prowells did surface, they were living elsewhere.

Claude, whose full name was Andrew Claude Prowell, showed up in 1925, living in Fort Worth, Texas, married to a twenty-two-year-old woman named May Lavada Burch. There, on December 1, Mrs. Prowell gave birth to their second child, a son. The little boy's birth certificate verifies Claude's identity by stating that the father was born in Kirven and was a farmer. The certificate also suggests that Claude may have covered a lot of miles between 1922 and 1925: May Burch is identified as being a resident of Eltopia, Washington.[9]

On January 25, 1929, a third child was born to Claude and May Prowell. By then they were living on a farm near Elkhart, in Anderson County, Texas. Anderson County is east of, adjacent to, and just across the Trinity River from Freestone County.[10] A fourth child was evidently born between 1929 and 1934, because a fifth child, another son, was born to the Prowells on August 4, 1934.[11]

Claude stayed in Anderson County the rest of his life, dying there

of "natural causes" at the age of 62 on November 17, 1959. His death
certificate indicates that he served in World War I. He was buried in
the Rockwall Cemetery in Rockwall, Texas.[12]

While Claude was moving around, perhaps going to Washington
state, and certainly to Fort Worth and Anderson County, his brother
Audey, or Charles Audey Prowell, was also on the move. He served in
World War II, was married and divorced, and died on April 27, 1952,
at the age of 48, in San Angelo, Tom Green County, Texas, of acute
pulmonary edema, while working as a cook in a cafe. He was buried in
Fairmount Cemetery in San Angelo on April 29, 1952. An autopsy was
performed, perhaps because he died so young. His death certificate did
not provide the name of his ex-wife.[13]

The other Prowell brother, Joe Lee, or J.L., who apparently did
not participate in the murder of Eula, lived in Dallas. He died there
on June 9, 1969, arriving DOA at Methodist Hospital after suffering a
coronary occlusion at the age of 59. He was never in the military, and
was never married. At the time of his death he was the manager of Bill
Woods Salvage Yard. He was buried in Laurel Land Memorial Park in
Dallas on June 11, 1969.[14]

The foregoing is only circumstantial evidence, of course, and does
not finally verify the Kelly report. Newspaper stories can be wrong,
and the Prowell family could have moved from Freestone County for
any number of reasons. There is still more, however.

In late 1994, Foreman Carter, then 95, came back to his native
Kirven from New Jersey. He had been gone more than seventy years,
living in Dallas, New York, and New Jersey. Suffering from emphysema,
he had returned home to die.

Although his biological father was a white man named Hughes,
Foreman Carter was black, and had been raised by the locally well-
known and very respected Jenkins Carter, a black man who had been
born into slavery in 1863. Foreman took his last name from Jenkins,
and referred to him as "Poppa."

Foreman grew up in Kirven and knew all the principal actors in the
drama of "the troubles." Perhaps fortunately, he had not been in Kirven
during May and June of 1922, having taken a job shortly before in Corsicana. However, various members of the Carter family were involved
in the events. Several had joined in the posses searching for Eula's
killers, and Jenkins Carter was one of the few blacks who stayed in
Kirven, having been granted special protection by a white patron.

Carter Sessions and his son J.R. put the word out shortly after Shadrick Green's lynching that no one was to molest Jenkins Carter or his family. Anyone who did would answer to J.R., a man feared and respected, some said, because he could shoot other white men and not be convicted.[15]

Foreman visited his stepfather and other relatives after the burnings, and probably heard more accurate details of the events than those heard by blacks who did not enjoy the protection of a powerful white family, but he did not remain at home. From Corsicana, Foreman moved to Dallas. He found work, but after being hassled one evening by a Dallas policeman, he decided to move much further north, to New York City.

He found a different world in the big city, and ultimately found a prize job, as chauffeur to the attorney general of New Jersey. He loved the work, and the attorneys general, dozens of them, apparently loved him. He held onto the job for fifty years.[16]

Meanwhile, still in Kirven, many years after the troubles, Jenkins Carter, Foreman's "poppa," had an interesting experience.

The amount of respect with which he was treated in the community was shown by the fact that both blacks and whites sought his advice on personal and public matters.[17] Thus, he may not have been surprised when an old white friend approached him, and said he wanted to tell him something important, but in strictest confidence. He was surprised, however, by the information the man conveyed.

The white man, whose name is lost, said that another white man, a man named Prowell who used to live in Kirven, had recently admitted to murdering Eula Ausley. The man wanted Jenkins to know, and provided details. He thought someone in the black community needed to know.

Jenkins was not sure what he should do with the information. Decades had passed since the burnings, but race relations in Freestone County were still strained. He turned the story over and over in his mind. The past had passed, he may have thought. Spreading this story around would achieve nothing, except to get people stirred up again.

Besides, white people still had funny ideas about what should be done to blacks who made wild accusations against whites. A black who did not stay in line, did not know his place, was said to have "made a badge for himself." As Foreman explained, his poppa did not want to "make a badge for hisself."

Jenkins decided to keep the story quiet, and told no one, not even his wife or children.

Then, probably in the 1940s or 1950s, before Jenkins' death in 1956, Foreman Carter returned to Kirven from New Jersey for a rare visit, and Jenkins made a decision.

Foreman lived far away, and had a good job that would keep him far away. He was sensible and trustworthy. Jenkins decided to entrust his weighty information to his stepson.

Jenkins called the younger man out of the house, the house Jenkins had lived in since before the troubles, a shack on the edge of Kirven that still stands. He led him into the front yard to a clump of chinaberries that also still exists. There he explained what he had been told about the man named Prowell. He expressed his concern about keeping the information quiet, and Foreman understood completely. He had no interest in badges either, nor in bestowing them on any old friends or relatives. He agreed to keep the information quiet.

And he did. Perhaps he told friends in faraway New Jersey or New York. Perhaps, after moving back to Kirven in 1994, he confided the information to black friends there, but probably not. Foreman was an easy-going man who had an easy-going attitude toward race relations. He declared the secret of long life to be "clean living, taking the world as you find it, and taking Jesus as your friend." There was no point in stirring things up. As he said once about an old acquaintance, Johnny Cornish, "your mouth can get you in a lot of trouble."

Then, in 1995, a white friend of Foreman's, Harry Hughes, asked him if it would be all right for another white man to come talk to him about the old days. Harry liked to talk about the old days, was a neighbor who had known Jenkins Carter, and had always been honest and kind to Foreman, so Foreman agreed. On April 9 of that year, a man from Austin dropped by with a tape recorder.

Foreman was living in a small mobile home on the lot next to his father's little house, now empty and sagging from the weight of decades. His routine was to rise late, go to Fairfield for lunch at the Senior Center, spend some time visiting and playing dominoes with old friends, and then go home and sit in a lawn chair in front of his trailer to watch the world go by.

He still saw old acquaintances, including a few who had lived through the troubles, and he still had family in the area. Despite being 95, he had older siblings to visit. His brother, Holbert, was 98, and their sister was over 100.

Initially, Foreman was cautious in the interview. He had no way of knowing what the stranger from Austin wanted, or what he might do with the information. He answered questions as completely as he could, but volunteered little, and when the stranger steered him toward the worst of the old times, "the troubles," Foreman steered him back toward safer paths, such as baseball.

When the stranger asked Foreman what he had heard about the men who were burned, and about who killed young Eula Ausley, however, Foreman decided to tell the story Jenkins had told him. "Well," he replied slowly, "I first heard that it was the boys who was accused of it, naturally, but I heard later . . . a white friend of Poppa's told him . . . it was years later . . . this man who committed the crime, admitted to Poppa that he did it."

"A white man?" the stranger asked.

"Uh-huh." Foreman said. "He did it . . . it was, you know . . ."

"Do you remember his name?" the interviewer asked.

Foreman frowned, looked down, and shook his head.

The stranger continued. "Do you know, was his name Prowell?"

Foreman looked up. A smile spread across his face. "I believe it was," he said, chuckling, "I sure believe it was."

Foreman seemed very relieved to have found a white man who would believe his poppa's story. He opened up and told all he knew, including the story of the Cornish family, Bud Thompson [Johnny Cornish's father], and how Johnny's "filthy mouth" got him into so much trouble.

Foreman believed that the Prowell who confessed was on his deathbed at the time.[18] Considering that Claude was, at that time, just across the Trinity River in Anderson County, he would be a likely suspect, but the year of his death, 1959, coming after that of Jenkins, makes that unlikely, or at least unlikely that he was dying at the time. A more likely candidate is Tom Prowell, the father of Claude and Audey, who first knifed Drew King, then vowed revenge, and who probably orchestrated the murder of Eula, even though he may not have been present when she was killed. Tom Prowell's whereabouts after 1922, and his ultimate place and year of death, have not come to light.

The notion that innocent black men were killed for a crime they did not commit in the South during the twenties is not particularly startling. Other lynching reports are rife with proof of the innocence of black victims. The Kirven event, however, is different.

The fact that three men were burned alive, at least two of whom were completely innocent, and the third of whom may have been, together with the fact that other innocents were summarily murdered, imbues the Kirven events with particular poignancy and tragedy. And, as will soon be revealed, the Kirven lynchings had significant, long-lasting impact, both locally and nationally. More killings would be committed, a race war would be narrowly averted, a large final irony would occur, and the rest of the world would hear of, and be touched by, Kirven, Texas.

Doll Rags

On June 1, 1922, Leroy Gibson went to Kirven to visit his girlfriend and was arrested. He was black, in his early twenties, and the son of Ben Gibson. Father and son worked for Grandfather John King, and Ben was the first person old man King had turned to for help when Eula had been late getting home.

Leroy's family speculated later that the men who seized him in Kirven believed he had played a role in Eula's murder. The story they heard, or believed, was that Leroy had found Eula's body, picked her up, placed her across a horse's saddle, and led the horse to the King farm, getting blood on his clothes in the process. Thereafter, the Gibsons surmised, the story of Leroy's involvement became twisted in white people's minds, or became twisted in the story's telling, and the blood on Leroy's clothes turned him into a suspect.[1]

Leroy might have been one of the first blacks bold enough to appear on the streets of Kirven after the burnings. He may have reasoned, logically, that his employment by Grandfather King provided a mantle of protection, such that he could conduct himself in a normal manner. If so, he was mistaken.

The local papers did not say why he was arrested, but reported that he managed to escape after being wounded in the leg. The details of his adventure must have been terrifying, exciting, hair-raising, but they are lost to the ages. Leroy did not live to tell them, and none of his abductors revealed any particulars. Otis and John T. King may have been party to his arrest, but it cannot be proven.

After his escape, Leroy began walking, or limping, south. He could have stopped, if he had wished, at his father's house near Shanks after three miles, but he did not, suggesting, perhaps, that the King brothers were among his pursuers. Instead, he continued walking to Simsboro, nine miles from Kirven, where his grandparents, an uncle, an aunt, and various cousins lived.

Simsboro was one of the county's black communities that grew up after emancipation. Located a couple of miles off the Fairfield–Mexia

Road leading from Kirven to Teague, the village consisted of a scattering of houses surrounding the Pleasant Hill Church. Some of the community's inhabitants were sharecroppers, and a white-owned store located on the only road provided them with the necessities of life, but many people there owned their own land, and were not as dependent on whites as some other blacks in the county.

Simsboro had no telephones, newspapers, or electricity. The residents were so isolated that they had heard nothing of the murder of Eula Ausley or the violence that had occurred during the subsequent month. Mose Jones once lived in Simsboro, and still had friends there. Yet the people had no reason to go to Kirven, and no one had brought the news into Simsboro.[2]

Later, when the Gibsons living in Simsboro heard the story of Eula's murder, they were told she had been killed by a white boyfriend because she was pregnant. There is no evidence to support the story, although it may have been spread by people familiar with the fate of her mother. The story may also have been inspired by Eula's brutal mutilation with the stick. Why else would anyone do such a thing except to destroy evidence of a pregnancy?

More likely, the boyfriend story was speculation, an attempt in the black community around Simsboro to account for the girl's murder with something more reasonable than a desire for revenge by mistreated field hands. The black community there would have believed that the men who were burned were innocent, and would have welcomed a believable story to rally around, but did not know the story of the Prowells.

Besides, the people of Simsboro had not been terrorized for three weeks, and they were a proud, self-contained black community. They were prepared to resist oppression and restore some pride and dignity to the situation.

Leroy's 13-year-old niece, Lutisia Gibson, Lutisia's mother, Aby, the girl's 24-year-old brother, Allie, and two or three of her sisters were at home the night of June 1. They were in the house, cleaning up after supper, when they heard someone singing in the field across from their house.

After a moment they recognized the voice and the song. The singer was Leroy, whose nickname was "Dutch," and the song was the 23rd Psalm. Leroy rarely visited, certainly not at such a late hour, and the family ran to meet him.

Seventy-three years later, Lutisia was living at the same location, although in a newer, different house. She had talked about the incident rarely over the years, having learned early on that it was not a wise topic to discuss. Even her children, all grown, had not heard her tell it, and they gathered around her bed to listen to the interview. At 86, she was bedfast, but she recalled the details with clarity, as follows:

> He was shot in the leg, but not so bad he couldn't walk from Kirven. . . . "The Lord is my Shepherd and I shall not want," that's what he was singing. We could hear him singing. We said "Oh, Leroy's singing." We called him Dutch.
>
> He came here first. He came to my mother's house first. My mother said "Leroy, it's best for you to go up to Pap's." That was my grandpa, and so we helped him to get up there and they got him cleaned up and put him in the bed.[3]

Pap was Mose Gibson, Leroy's 75-year-old grandfather, Ben's father. Others in Mose's house, located up a hill and approximately 150 yards east of Lutisia's home, were Mose's wife, Jane, age 67, and their son, Floyd. Floyd, Ben's younger brother and Leroy's uncle, was 32. He had served in World War I, possibly in the 369th Colored Infantry.

A doctor, Claude Batchelor perhaps, may have been summoned to tend Leroy's wound. If so, he did not regard the location of his patient as privileged information. Bertha Williams, who worked for Dr. Whiteside, reported that "a doctor" was the one who told men in Kirven where they could find Leroy.

The morning and afternoon of the next day, Friday, passed without incident. Lutisia and her family visited Leroy after lunch, and Allie was still there that evening. Lutisia was playing in the front yard of her mother's house with her sisters, and the sun was going down, when they saw an unusual sight. Lutisia continued:

> Mmm, oh Lord . . . it was almost sundown . . . about the middle of the evening, we could see the people coming across there with guns. We could see the guns shining in the sun. And we said, Lord, they're coming after Leroy, and my mother, she, and I don't know how many children it was . . . I know I was here and some of the other children were here, and all we could

do was stand and look. They went and brought Leroy
out. . . .

Q: How many men were there?

A: It was about twelve, as far as I can remember, it was
about twelve men. And after they brought Leroy out,
they carried him across the field there [indicating
an open pasture some 50 yards from the site of her
grandfather's house], and shot him into doll rags.

Q: And just shot him?

A: Just shot him and shot him and shot him.

Q: Shot him several times?

A: Oh, more than that . . . I imagine all of them shot him,
about twelve people shot him, emptied their rifles.
They say he was shot into doll rags.

Q: What happened next?

A: Why, they came back to the house, I guess to see what
else they could find to do, and anyway, my uncle, he'd
been in the army and he was a good marksman . . .

Q: Floyd?

A: Floyd. And they wanted to kill him, but my grandmother put 'em there and said "Please don't kill my
son. Please don't kill my son." So they all left him
alone, and in fact they thought they were all gone,
and Allie, my brother, said, "I'm gonna go down to
see about mother and them."

Well, he took his rifle in his hands and started out
and got as far as the gate and there was a man standing at the corner of the house and shot him down.
And at that time Uncle Floyd said, "Oh, they done
shot Allie." Well, he went and picked up Allie's gun,
and just leveled it, and we don't know how many he
shot and how many he killed, but anyway, with that
rifle he just laid down and just began to shoot. He'd
been in the army and they'd taught him how to shoot
laying down. He was an expert with a rifle. He fell
on his stomach and started shooting, as he'd been
trained, and wasn't missing a lick. He only stopped
because he ran out of shells.

And after that everyone was scared. We were
scared to stay home and scared to leave.[4]

Freestone County newspapers reported a different, cautiously crafted tale. The story in the June 9 edition of the *Fairfield Recorder*, after conceding that many conflicting reports of the incident had been received, stated that Leroy Gibson had been arrested "on suspicion" in Kirven, but had escaped after receiving "a slight wound." The next afternoon, it was "alleged" that six men, John T. King, Otis King, Bob King, Drew King, Bill Norman, and Walter Yerby, went to Simsboro to "investigate the trouble," and it was further alleged "that when they were about 200 yards from the house shots were fired at them from the house, and at the same time Leroy Gibson attacked Walter Yerby. Leroy was killed and shots were fired toward the house. Allie Gibson was found dead in the yard."

The report in the June 9 edition of the *Teague Chronicle* was shorter, and slightly more artful, stating that "when about 200 yards from the house, firing began and both Leroy and Allie Gibson were killed, and the third negro in the house, Floyd Gibson, escaped. No white men were hurt."[5]

In fact, at least two white men were killed, and others may have been wounded. One was killed on the Gibsons' property and a second died on the way to the hospital. Dr. Whiteside tended to them and telephoned Bertha Williams to give her a full report.[6] The Gibsons saw the men fall. Even a newspaper in faraway Chicago received a report that one white man was killed, but added that "his body is said to have been carried to the city and secretly hidden to avoid inciting others to riot."[7]

The news of white men being killed was hushed, and the reason for the cover-up, or mendacity, was a peculiar local notion of civic-mindedness.

When word spread, on June 3, that blacks were killing whites, hundreds of armed white men turned out, ready for open warfare. The state of crisis that had existed in the county for a month had reached a breaking point. All the rumors and fears about blacks "rising up" from their downtrodden condition seemed, finally, to be coming true. The county was perched on the ragged edge of a genuine race war, and nothing would prod it over that edge faster than confirmation that black men were outgunning and killing white men.

An editorial in the *Fairfield Recorder* danced around the subject, saying, "reports coming to Fairfield last Friday that a number of white men had been killed in an uprising of the negroes at Kirven caused considerable excitement and uneasiness. Many seized arms and left immediately for Kirven, while others prepared for local emergencies."[8]

Armed rebellion by blacks was the Southerners' terror. Official verification of the deaths would have been invitation for, or admission of, a race war. Other local newspaper articles would vehemently deny that any whites were killed. It was thought best to suppress the truth in the hope of preventing further bloodshed.

Besides, this time, the whites' fears were not unfounded—black men *were* arming themselves. Whites were not the only ones preparing for local emergencies.

After the murder of Leroy and Allie, but before the mob of armed whites arrived, families of blacks from the surrounding area converged on Simsboro.[9] Foster Foreman, who would become Lutisia Gibson's husband, saw the showdown developing.

Foster was a boy working in a cotton field near Simsboro when Leroy and Allie Gibson were killed. He heard the shots and assumed somebody was bird-hunting. When he returned home, he learned the facts, and the next morning, he saw black families coming to Simsboro by the wagon load. He also witnessed the very beginning of what would ultimately be a standoff:

> Bob Riley was a banker. His building was on this corner down from the red light [on the Fairfield–Mexia Road]. Riley was an old man, an older man. He had a lot of livestock down in here and he started out to see about his stock, and when he come, there was a bunch of black people down in here, they owned all the property down in here—they don't own it now—and they stopped him and told him it was best for him to not go down no further. They wouldn't let him go no further. He went back and told the rest of the white people.
>
> They told him that if he thought anything of himself, he'd best stay out of here. The black community had armed themselves and were ready. . . . So no white people attempted to come down here, whether they were Ku Klux Klan or who. It didn't matter who they was. If they was white, the people down here was gonna shoot them.
>
> They were barricaded in the bushes. They weren't out in the road. There would be a group here and you'd go another half a mile and there'd be another group. If you got by this, that other'n was gonna get you.[10]

Federal agents arrived, as did Sheriff Mayo and his deputies. Anyone who wanted to go into Simsboro would have to contend with opposition from law-enforcement officers as well as blacks.

Carter Sessions, recently acquitted of murder but still immensely respected, assumed the role of mediator. The black and white communities would listen to him, and he felt confident enough to go into Simsboro alone. When he returned from doing so, he asked the members of the white mob to go home. The angry whites milled around for a while and began to drift away, leaving only a hard core of about fifty rabble-rousers to stalk about in Kirven. Surprisingly, mercifully, there was no more violence.

The *Chicago Defender,* an African American newspaper, carried an account on June 10 headlined "Revolt on Lynchings Stirs South," and beginning, "When gun met gun at this place last Friday an armistice was soon signed by the two races. It wasn't a case of guns, bullets and knives versus prayers, but weapon against weapon." The article reported that armed white men "paraded" the streets of Kirven, "but dared not venture into Simsboro, where members of the Race were barricaded in barns awaiting the attack." Sheriff Mayo was quoted as saying that "the men at Simsboro had 30-30 rifles and were honeycombed in the swamps to fire on the whites from all angles." Carter Sessions was also quoted as saying, after venturing into Simsboro, that "men came from all parts of the woods armed with rifles and pockets loaded with bullets." [11]

Lutisia Gibson remembered Carter Sessions coming into Simsboro, and also remembered federal officers whom she believed were FBI agents arriving in what she called a helicopter—although it was probably Texas Rangers or National Guardsmen in Lieutenant Taylor's biplane—and staying for two days to protect her family.

The shootout in Simsboro was the final straw for many people. The county was receiving attention from all over the state—indeed, from all over the nation—and "Freestone County" was becoming synonymous with "lynching" and "race war." Leading white citizens took action.

The following Monday, District Judge Blackmon called a mass meeting of citizens at the county courthouse in Fairfield. Hundreds attended. Judge Blackmon gaveled the meeting to order, a chairman, secretary, and assistant secretary were elected, and speeches were made by ten prominent citizens, including Sheriff Mayo, Judge Blackmon, and three ministers. A resolutions committee was appointed which crafted a lengthy epistle to the world, and which was printed in the local newspapers, declaring, in part:

Whereas, we realize that the time has come when
those citizens who believe in the supremacy of the law
and who are jealous of the reputation and fair name of
Freestone County, should band together to show the
world that we are not only capable of, but that we are
determined to bring to an end the reign of demoraliza-
tion that has spread over the County, therefore be it

Resolved, by the citizens of Freestone County in
mass meeting assembled, that we call upon every citizen of the County to resume the normal and peaceful
pursuits of every day life; to see that all who are obey-
ing the laws of the land be accorded every right and
protection of the law; that the colored people whom
circumstances have placed within our midst, and who
have done no wrong, be given assurances of protection as long as they attend to their own business and
obey the law of the land; that no negro be harmed or
molested without a full, fair investigation; that the officers charged with the enforcement of the laws be
assured of our full and hearty cooperation, as long as
such officers diligently discharge their duties.[12]

The resolution went on and on, the people pledging to go to the
grand jury with information bearing on the peace and liberty of any
man, woman, or child, regardless of race, and denouncing the newspapers that reported wild rioting, because "even the most cursory investigation showed that no body of negroes had congregated anywhere
to resist or attack the whites, and that not a white man was injured." It
concluded with a final resolution that "the killing and terrorizing of
Negroes in the county must now cease."

The same day that the resolution appeared in the newspapers, the
Fairfield Recorder contained a separate editorial about the rally that
may have stretched the truth a little in order to smother more threats of
race war:

Resolutions adopted at a mass meeting in Fairfield
and printed in this issue explain the falsity of the wild
reports circulated over the State which were to the
effect that the negroes in this section had risen against
the whites, and that a race riot was raging. Nothing
was farther from the truth, and this only served to

intensify the feeling already existing. It is a mystery
how such absolutely groundless reports can obtain
such wide circulation. The women and children of the
county have been so badly stirred since the tragedy
at Kirven, that many of them are afraid to be on the
crowded streets, and it is high time that all of our
people resume their normal and ordinary pursuits,
and refrain from exciting discussions.[13]

However well-meaning the *Recorder* editor may have been, and certainly there was need for some well-intended reassurances of peace, he also seemed determined to demonstrate that he would not be totally reformed, and that the *real* problem in the county continued to be that of blacks assaulting whites. The same June 9 issue of the paper contained an article on the refusal of the *Dallas News* to publish a letter from State Senator W. E. Doyle of Teague denouncing the *News* for trying "to reform" people from engaging in mob law. Doyle claimed the *News* was ignoring the apparent epidemic of blacks assaulting whites, and the *Recorder* editor, agreeing with Doyle, added commentary on the same topic:

> In its editorial columns, the Dallas News grows rather
> hysterical over the "growing tendency of mob law,"
> but nowhere do we find any condemnation of the
> "growing tendency" to commit heinous crimes
> against the womanhood of the South, nor do we read
> any articles on the general breakdown of justice in
> our courts. . . . Too much prominence is given in the
> newspapers to the commission of crimes, and not
> enough to the punishment of the law breaker.[14]

Finally, the June 9 newspaper carried a short piece entitled "Old Negro's Prayer 'Kivers' the Case." On first glance, the little article seems to be an innocent attempt at 1920s-style humor through imitation of black dialect. Its conclusion, however, was either an extreme case of bad timing and poor taste or was intended to convey a darker, more ominous overtone:

> Those who are depressed and feel the heavy hand
> of hard times closing its grip about their epiglottis
> should read and take heart from this simple faith of
> this old colored man.

"O Laud, give thy servant this maunin' the eyes of the eagle and the wisdom of the owl, connect his soul with the sun of heaven, pizen his gospel telephone in the central skies, 'luminate his brow with light and his mind with the love of his fellow man, turpentine his imagination, grease his lips with possum oil, loosen his tongue with the sledge hammer of thy power, 'lectrify his brain with the lightening [*sic*] of the world, luberacate his joints with saving grease and saturate his muscles with tireless ointment, put perpetual motion into his limbs, fill him plumb full of the dynamite of thy glory, 'noint him all over with kerosene oil of thy salvation and set him on fire. Amen."[15]

Public opinion was very mixed, and people were still excited. They could not know whether more violence would occur, but the leaders of the community, and a majority of the county's citizens, desperately wanted the craziness to end.

Floyd Gibson's action in Simsboro tolled the reign of terror linked directly to Eula's murder. Like a playground hero who finally stood up to the school bully, he showed the Kings, or whoever was committing the crimes, that there was a limit to how far blacks would be pushed. He had done everyone a favor.

As Bertha Williams opined wistfully at the end of her interview in Kirven sixty-five years later, "They were coming after them, but none of these people here, they were so cowardly . . . all over the land. If they'd been like Floyd, it wouldn't have lasted half as long."[16]

The next week's papers, on June 16, contained no reports of murders, lynchings, or shootings. There were oil-field activity reports, local news items, and the following article, which can only be regarded today as sadly comical.

Ministers in Teague—the Preachers Association of the City of Teague—had gotten together and arrived at a momentous decision. Having had only flyswatter effectiveness on the elephant-sized evil stampeding about them, they had united and resolved to fire a cannon at gnat-sized sin:

PASTORS CONDEMN SUNDAY BASE BALL

The following resolution, passed by the Teague Pastors Association at their regular meeting Monday morning, have [*sic*] been received with request for publication:

Whereas, for the past three Lord's day afternoons our city has been cursed with base ball games, and

Whereas, it is universally known that gambling is engaged in at such times and places, and

Whereas, men and women who profess to be Christians and members of the church give and support to the games by attending them on God's day and paying the gate fees, and

Whereas we are commanded in God's word to "shun the very appearance of evil," and to "be ye separate from them," and to "keep yourselves unspotted from the world" and to "remember the Sabbath day to keep it holy," therefore be it

Resolved, that we, the Preachers Association of the City of Teague, place our disapproval on Sunday base ball games as in strict violation of the law of God and insist on our people staying away from them.

— E. HOMER TIREY, PRES.
L. F. BAIN, CLERK, PRO TEM.[17]

Perhaps the ministers were merely trying to assure everyone that life was getting back to normal in Freestone County.

 *Greater Irony*

By the end of 1922, Kirven had nearly ceased to exist. What had been a boom town was nearly a ghost town. Kirven had burned, and was still burning, for its sins.

Blacks were the first to go. Many were already gone before the echoes of gunshots died in Simsboro. The rest, all but a dozen or so, moved on during the next few months.

The reason for their mass departure is obvious. People do not tend to linger in areas where they are in danger of being castrated, burned, hanged, or shot. As Bertha Williams recalled, people were "running for their lives. On Saturdays, you'd hear that train go north, you'd think they were meeting a corpse" [i.e., there was a large, solemn crowd]. She went on, "I know some of them went to Oklahoma and California, but the majority of them went up around Waxahachie, Palmer, and Garrison [Texas]."[1]

Bertha stayed, along with her sister, Mamie, Mamie's family, and their brother, Littleo. Jenkins Carter, his family, a man named Monkey Bucher, and a small handful of others stayed also. They were the protected ones.

The Kings, Dr. Whiteside, the Sessions, or other respected white men put the word out on the street: "Leave these people alone or answer to us." Those closest to the power were the safest: another Southern code was honored.

No other blacks were secure. By August, almost the entire black population around Kirven—probably the 103 men who petitioned for peace and their families plus 200 to 300 living within five miles of town—had gone. Only the handful named above remained within the city limits, while one family, the Sullivans, remained on a farm about three miles from Kirven.[2]

The situation, if not permanent, would be long-lasting. "Used to be," Bertha Williams recalled in 1987, "from Kirven to Highway 75 [about eight miles], from Palamino's Cove, from here to Lanely, nobody was afraid to walk 'cause there'd always be a [black person's] house, all the way to 75. Now there's about two."

In subsequent years, other blacks could not be coaxed to move in from other areas for the same reason the natives left. The Gibsons, in Simsboro, recalled that they avoided going near Kirven for decades. They were afraid of what kind of people must live in a town where whites burned blacks and displayed a charred plow in the town square to prove it.[3]

Harry Hughes and his family moved to Kirven in 1930 and brought a black family from Navarro County to help work their land, but the family did not stay. The Hughes acquired the former home of Jerry Winchester, the man accused of incest who was shot by Horace Mayo. There were still bullet holes in the walls. They tried to board their hired help there, but when the black family heard what had happened in Kirven eight years earlier, and then learned that a shooting had occurred in the cabin, they disappeared.[4]

And as soon as the black exodus was over, white flight began.

The departures were not as dramatic, but were very apparent to those watching. Bertha Williams said the town was dead in six months. Another Kirven resident who stayed said that Kirven "just dried up" after the burnings. Sheriff Mayo's youngest daughter, Ruth Mayo Ditto, said it "went downhill immediately."

Grace Mayo, Mayo's middle daughter, was one of those who moved away, leaving in June 1922, with her new husband, Bill Norman. She was not sure how long the town took to die, and could only say that Kirven "went down to nothing" and "it didn't take too long."

Lura Bess Mayo Sprague, the oldest daughter, who stayed and continued teaching school and giving music lessons after the troubles, became particularly emotional about the town's decline:

> It [the burning of the three black men] just ruined the town. That was the nicest little town. It had a music store! It had a piano and music store! It had everything good in that little town, a tailor shop, a women's dress store, a confectionery, a movie theater. I just couldn't believe we moved into all that stuff over there. The people thought it was the boom town of Freestone County. Everyone wants to go where it's new and invigorating and everything is new and everyone is exciting, and that's the feeling we had, and then to just think that it died, and overnight almost.[5]

The people left for more than one reason, but the burnings were the root cause. Some white residents moved because they were tired of being afraid, weary of rumors of marching mobs and vengeance-seeking people of both races. Life was too short to live in fear, so they moved on, or back to wherever they came from.

Many moved because of the reputation Kirven and Freestone County had acquired in other parts of the state and the nation. As one resident of Kirven who stayed recalled, "You could go anywhere in the state and tell them where you were from and they would know it was the place where they burned the three Negroes."[6]

People who once boasted of being from Kirven became sick of being identified with lynching, burning, and lawlessness. If they were not genuinely ashamed, they were genuinely fed up. For others, perhaps most, however, the reason for moving was simple economics.

Blacks comprised the area's labor force, the backbone of its economy, and they went away right at the time when their help was most critical. June to August was when cotton needed the most attention, and with no available force of affordable white workers to fall back on, white landowners could clearly see what would happen. Selling out and moving somewhere with abundant, cheap labor made more sense than staying and either losing their crops or doing the work of several men.

Still, the white flight would not have happened so quickly, and would not have affected Kirven so dramatically, had human nature and fate not intervened. Some of the first to leave experienced the tragedy of their house or business burning down, either as they departed or shortly before they left. A stable and blacksmith shop near downtown Kirven was among the first to go. The oldest of the two adolescent brothers who witnessed the burnings recalled hearing the screams of the dying horses. The building was lost completely, but luckily it was insured. The insurance company paid on the policy and the owner moved away.[7]

The house of another resident also burned, but it was also covered by insurance. The owner had had a lucky break. Then a store caught fire. This time the insurance company investigated and ruled there had been arson, a fire set for the specific purpose of collecting insurance. The policy holders were, however, already absent from the county.[8] As J. C. Whatley said,

> Some of them just left, and some of them burned
> when they left, and had a good excuse to lay on it.
> Carl Norman moved to Venus, up by Fort Worth. He

had a big fine home, right across the street here, just
a block up there. It burned. And the banker's building
up here, it burned, and they just burned all over town,
see. I don't know if it was insurance, but enough
burned that none of us left could get any insurance.
My daddy went without insurance until he finally got
it back and on the gin.[9]

The house and business burnings were not immediate, nor even
confined to the year 1922. Apparently they continued throughout the
twenties. Sarah Goolsby, who would later marry Batchelor Nettle,
moved into town from Caney Creek around 1925, in time to go to the
eighth grade in Kirven. She remembered walking to school and said it
"seemed like every week there'd be another pretty house that had
burned down. We had beautiful houses and stores, and they burned
for insurance." She recalled that the Baptist church, the house "catty-
cornered" from the church, the banker's house, and Pott's store, a mil-
linery, feed, and dry goods store, "all burned."[10]

Documentary evidence of the departure of whites exists in newspapers, but would not be obvious to a casual reader. An advertisement
in the June 30, 1922, issue of the *Fairfield Recorder* offered six acres
of cotton, farming implements, household goods, and livestock near
Kirven for sale by G. C. Mayo. The property was described as "a bar-
gain." On September 22 of that year, C. H. Richardson offered for sale,
in the same paper, "175½ acre farm on Kirven and Fairfield road. Will
sell cheap, part cash and good time on balance. Might take small place
as part pay."[11] A year later, Richardson was still trying to unload the
175 acres, and had added 100 acres in cultivation "priced cheap."[12]

That autumn, the largest department store in Kirven, Bonner's,
closed, and late one night there was another fire, this time in a wooden
shop downtown near the store. Bonner's, which was brick, was safe,
but the flames spread to other wooden frame buildings. A large portion
of the business section of downtown was lost.[13] The buildings were not
ebuilt. Their owners moved instead. The brick buildings stood until
the building boom following World War II, when they were torn down
for their bricks.

At least one of the intentional fires was not set for insurance purposes. Shiloh, a Negro church located a few miles outside of Kirven
burned to the ground on December 29, 1922.[14] Two young white
men bragged about doing it, and were arrested, along with two friends,
the next day. As punishment, the families of the young men were re-

quired to rebuild the church, even though there were hardly any worshipers left to attend services. The perpetrators then "took a hitch" in the army.[15]

In November 1922, the Kirven State Bank closed its doors and combined its assets with those of the First State Bank of Teague. The *Fairfield Recorder* reported, with lame optimism, that the liquidation and consolidation would enable R. M. Thompson, president of both banks, "to get the business of the two institutions together where he can give them better attention and insure a fuller and more detailed service to the depositors of both."[16]

The oldest of the two brothers who witnessed the burnings remembered his apprehension at hearing about the bank's closing. Although he was only twelve at the time, he still had money to keep there, and he worried about what the closing of such an important institution of the town could mean.[17]

It meant people were getting "the hell out of Kirven," as Ruby Kate Whatley Richardson put it, "just as fast as they could."

Sheriff Mayo's family was touched early by the emigration. On Sunday, June 18, daughter Grace, Mayo's middle daughter, married William H. Norman of Kirven. Norman was editor of the *Kirven Commercial Record.* He may also have been the same Bill Norman who was named by the *Fairfield Recorder* as accompanying the King brothers to Simsboro to "arrest" Leroy Gibson, although Grace denied the possibility.

Getting married was just one of the new, big changes in Norman's life, however. He had decided to sell his newspaper and move to the town of Blooming Grove, in order to publish the *Blooming Grove Times.*[18]

Lura Bess recalled that her father was very sad at the wedding. Much of his despondency must have stemmed from the loss of a daughter, the first of the three to wed. Another reason for his sadness was surely tied to recent events.

In one of its last issues under Norman's editorship, the *Kirven Commercial Record* reported the appointment of J. W. Gurley to fill the unexpired term of office left vacant by the resignation of J. T. King.[19] The office was not identified, but was probably that of deputy sheriff, even though it did not typically have a specified term. Evidently the events of May and June had satiated John T.'s law-enforcement aspirations.

Other factors conspired to ensure that Kirven would continue to decline. The oil boom never materialized in Kirven as it had in the Mexia fields, and as it would near Wortham in 1924 and 1925, so the boom-town atmosphere faded and people moved. Later still, cotton ceased to be a profitable cash crop. During the thirties, the federal government started paying farmers not to plant. Tenants and share-croppers were supposed to receive a portion of the subsidy, but land-owners often found ways around this rule. Any sharecroppers who still remained would surely have moved on then. When the Great Depression is added in, the reasons to stay become fewer and fewer.

Census records, because they do not reflect the influx of people who came with the oil boom between 1920 and 1922, do not reveal a dramatic loss of people. The 1930 census shows the town contained only about fifty people less than the 400 counted in 1920, while the 1940 population had declined by only seven more people. It is not until 1950 that the population dropped significantly, to 152. The 1990 census reported 107.

Additionally, many of those who moved away were farmers and sharecroppers who did not live within the corporate boundaries of the town, although they were as much a part of the community as anyone who lived in town. Their disappearance added to the sense of abandonment and desolation felt by those left behind.

Perhaps a better reflection of the plummeting size of the community and the plummeting morale of those who remained is provided by a notice published on February 23, 1923, in the *Fairfield Recorder*. It announced that an election would be held in Kirven on the question of abolishing the corporate existence of the town. Pursuant to Texas law, thirty-six property owners in Kirven had signed a petition asking that the town be disincorporated, and the ballot was to be voted upon on March 24, 1923.

Disincorporation elections occur rarely in Texas. State law authorizes the formation, or incorporation, of a town principally for the purpose of providing services to the citizens. Incorporated villages are authorized to finance and provide police, fire, water, sewer, gas, and electric services and other amenities that are not readily available in the unincorporated countryside.

Once the services are available, reasons seldom exist to abolish the town. Even if a town's citizens move away, most municipalities simply cease to operate rather than formally disincorporate. By statute, in order for a disincorporation election to be called, a requisite number of citizens must decide, and state in writing, that there is insufficient reason for the town to exist to justify its continuing authority to collect property taxes, and they must present the petition to the town's governing body, which orders the election.

Such was the state of mind of a number of Kirven's citizens. Perhaps they were taking affirmative steps to erase the town from the map in order to put an official end to the agony and gloom that had been created.

No record of the results of the election exist, but the proposition apparently failed. Kirven is still carried in the files of the Texas Municipal League as an incorporated town.[20] A few stores remained in Kirven, but there were only two by 1952,[21] and today there is only one on its outskirts, a convenience store on Highway 27, which runs between Fairfield and Wortham.

The end of 1922 closed the door on Kirven, Texas, but the town did not die easily, and neither did the year. The remainder of 1922, even after the resolutions and civic demands for peace in June, saw one unpleasantry after another in Freestone County, beginning with an outbreak of new Ku Klux Klan activity in the county immediately after the Simsboro shootout.

Despite what one might assume, and what must have been the case, there is no hard evidence implicating the Freestone County Ku Klux Klan in any of the burnings and lynchings following Eula's murder. Newspapers document the existence of at least two chapters of the Klan in the county, in Teague and Wortham, and most witnesses interviewed remembered seeing Klansmen at some time in the county, but no one could associate them with the lynchings of 1922. Nevertheless, beginning in June, Freestone County Klan membership exploded.

The Ku Klux Klan was experiencing a major comeback during the period from 1919 to 1922, not just in Texas, but across the South. The secret organization became a major political force in local, state, and even national political races. Support for or opposition to the Klan was not merely a racial question, although the recent lynchings in Freestone County were bound to have been a major reason for the local outburst of activity.

The June 9 edition of the *Fairfield Recorder,* which also reported the deaths of Allie and Leroy Gibson, carried an article reporting a Klan initiation in a field north of the Cotton Gin cemetery in which 100 new members were initiated, a cross was burned, and speeches were made to a crowd numbering from 3,000 to 10,000. Whether by coincidence or design, the site of the ceremony was only a few hundred yards from the graves of Allie and Leroy Gibson.

In August, another initiation ceremony in the same field was reported, with another 100 initiates and another crowd numbering in the thousands.²² At about the same time, more Klan activity was reported north of the county. The Dallas Ku Klux Klan marched in a huge, post-election parade in that city, and in Corsicana, twenty-five miles from Kirven, six robed Klansmen entered a Baptist church to deliver a letter declaring the purposes of the Klan to preachers who were there.²³

A list of the purported members of the local Klan was delivered to the *Recorder* in August, but the newspaper declined to print it, merely acknowledging its receipt and saying many of the citizens listed were known not to be members of the Klan.²⁴

A week later, the *Teague Chronicle* put a larger spin on the latest initiation ceremony at Cotton Gin, describing it as having "175 initiates, a very interesting talk, able speaker, and a crowd estimated at five to ten thousand."²⁵

In September the *Recorder* reported that "several robed and hooded klansmen visited Kirven and left a letter to Mrs. Sallie McCown to assist her with $40 deposited in the Kirven State Bank." A letter from her thanking them was also printed, but there is no explanation of the basis of her need. One wonders if Mrs. McCown suffered a loss in June during the Simsboro shootout, and whether her husband was one of the men killed by Floyd Gibson.²⁶

The next round of painful events occurred that fall, and was preceded by a flurry of local politics.

After the Simsboro shootout, Mayo renewed his campaign against moonshiners, arresting two white men and a woman in possession of 1,600 bottles of beer near Wortham on June 27.²⁷ Then, on July 22, the Democratic primary election was held. There were three candidates for sheriff, Mayo, David Terry, and Jim McDonald. Mayo received the most votes—1,565 of the 3,322 cast—but not a majority. The other two candidates received 1,065 and 692 votes, respectively, which meant Mayo and Terry would be in a runoff election.²⁸

The runoff was called for August 26. Although today Texas has uniform election dates four times a year to avoid the cost and inconvenience of opening the polls numerous times, in 1922, there was also a primary election on August 16, for lieutenant governor, state treasurer, and district judge. The sheriff's primary race runoff, ten days later, was scheduled for the same date as runoffs for the offices of U.S. Senator, county treasurer, and county tax collector.

Mayo's opponent, David Terry, won the runoff, by 1,744 votes to 1,566.²⁹ The turnout for the runoff was almost exactly the same as that for the primary. Only twelve fewer people voted in the runoff, but Mayo picked up only one of the votes previously cast for McDonald, while Terry acquired 679. In Mayo's hometown of Kirven, 172 votes were cast, 91 of which were for him.

Mayo was devastated, but he did not give up. On October 6, he sent a statement to the local newspapers announcing his candidacy for the office at the November general election as an independent. The letter revealed that there had been political treachery afoot, or at least that Mayo believed there had been, and that he was still smarting from his experiences during martial law. The letter also contained some statements about the Ku Klux Klan that, by today's standards, would be considered courageous.[30]

He knew that bolting the Democratic party was tantamount to treason in many people's eyes, but he sincerely believed there were evil forces at work, and that many of the citizens of the county still believed in him. He had come in first in the primary, after all, and perhaps the time had come for a good man, as he considered himself to be, to stand up to the tyranny of the Klan. He had nothing to lose, he must have decided, and stated his feelings on the Klan very clearly, for all to read:

> In the State today we see the regular Democratic candidate opposed by an independent in the race for United States Senate, brought about by the surrender of the party to the way of the Ku Klux Klan. And in this connection, it might be well to say this organization was chiefly responsible for my defeat.
>
> Wherever it was popular to support the Klan, it was given out that I was opposed to the order; and where the Klan was unpopular I was held up as a member. So I was fought by Klan and anti-Klan. Now, as a matter of fact, I have decided views upon the question. I will be perfectly plain here and now, and leave no room for doubt. I am unable to see how any officer of the law can subscribe to anything so lawless as the Klan. Instead of being for law and order, it is the very opposite. Instead of an orderly enforcement of the law, they would inaugurate mob law. A law that requires men going about with hidden faces and robed in disguise is hardly worth enforcing. Law enforcement first of all should be open, above-board, fair and impartial. The Klan is the very antithesis of the spirit

of law enforcement. Do I make myself clear? As your
Sheriff I do not need the assistance of white-robed
masked men to force [sic] the laws of our State, nor
will I need them in the future. To be sure you understand me absolutely, I am unequivocally opposed to
the Klan and all its methods.[31]

Mayo's brave gamble failed miserably. At the general election in November, he received only 480 votes, against Terry's 1,787—less than
one-third of the number he had received in August. The headlines of
the *Teague Chronicle* for November 10 trumpeted the outcome of the
general election: "Democrats Overwhelm Independents Locally."

The flavor of the political times is evident in the statewide race for
the U.S. Senate. A Klan candidate, Earle Mayfield, ran against an anti-
Klan independent named George Peddy, and Mayfield received 198,710
votes to Peddy's 85,898. In Freestone County, Mayfield received 1,638
votes to Peddy's 491. Painfully for Mayo, his name was printed on the
ballot while the anti-Klan independent Peddy's name was not, but Peddy
still received eleven more votes than Mayo, all of them write-ins.[32]

The message to Mayo was loud and clear: The Klan was a powerful
political force to reckon with. His political and law-enforcement careers
were over.

Autumn was upon the county, the traditional closing-off and gath-
ering-in time, the putting-away and covering-up time. The election was
over and racial events reported in the papers seemed to be bumping
back to what people of the day considered normal. Tom Cornish,
Johnny's uncle,[33] was arrested for shooting and killing another black
man, Lee Read, for "fooling around with his wife." He was released
on bond.

On September 1, a white man, Herman Daniel, 22, of Lanley, shot
and instantly killed a black man, Jam Willis, 21 or 22. Daniel and his
brother were "keeping batch" on the Wilson farm three or four miles
southeast of Turlington. Willis had been warned to stay away from the
still, but he did not and was reported to have a pistol in his hand when
Daniel killed him with a single-barreled shotgun. Daniel was placed
under $500 bond.[34]

Mayo was still in office, and would be until January. He had suffered
a lot, but there was more to come.

On November 30, his wife, Bess Mayo, gave money to J. L. Johnson,
a black trusty in the Fairfield jail, to go to the store and buy groceries.
Johnson was 25, and had been convicted of killing another black near

Dew the previous December. He had been sentenced to fifteen years at his trial, but the case was on appeal and he was considered to be dependable. As the papers said, he "had a bad reputation among the negroes, but his conduct under arrest had won the confidence of officials."[35]

What Bess Mayo may not have known was that Johnson had received word the previous day of the outcome of his appeal. His conviction was affirmed, and he would soon be going to the state prison in Huntsville.

When Johnson returned, about 6:30 P.M., Mrs. Mayo was in her bedroom, straightening up. She shouted to him to put the groceries in the kitchen, but she did not come out, and did not think anything more about him until she heard a footstep at the bedroom door. Bess looked up. The black man was staring at her. He held one hand behind his back.

"What do you have behind your back?" she asked.

He brought his hand out slowly. He was clutching a cloth sack. Mrs. Mayo understood what was intended just as he dived for her.[36]

J. L. Johnson must have been one foolhardy, audacious individual. To attack the sheriff's wife in her bedroom in the county jail, after what had been done recently to blacks for lesser crimes, borders on the fantastic, if not the fanatical.

Johnson seized Bess Mayo, and tried to force the sack over her head. Mrs. Mayo screamed and fought desperately. Bess was not the type to wilt in the face of danger. They struggled and she broke free. Her daughter said she dove for the bed, where there was a pistol beneath her pillow. The newspaper said the weapon was on a dresser. Wherever it was, she seized a .32 caliber automatic pistol, today in the possession of a grandson, and took aim. Johnson called off the attack and made tracks.

He fled out the bedroom door, through the kitchen, and into the great outdoors, heading northeast. Bess Mayo chased him to the door and squeezed several quick shots into the dark that had enveloped him.

People came running and Bess told them what had happened. A posse formed immediately. Once again, the word spread through the county, and once again, hundreds of armed men took to the woods to search for a black man.

Sheriff Mayo was furious. For the last year he had known nothing but insult, disparagement, personal attack, embarrassment, and injury. Now fresh and more personal affronts were occurring in his own bedroom.

This time he led the armed mobs instead of opposing them, and the next night they surrounded the house of Johnson's uncle, Perry Grayson. They had tracked Johnson toward the house, and believed the fugitive was inside.

About midnight, they closed in. Mayo called out, telling Johnson to surrender, not to resist, that the house was surrounded.

There was a noise inside. Mayo and another posse member swore later that they heard the sound of a shell being pumped into a Winchester rifle. The door opened and someone came out. Mayo thought he saw the rifle. He fired. The man in the doorframe fell.

The man was not Johnson, but Grayson. The newspapers said he had a rifle in his hands, and added helpfully that several years earlier he had been convicted of killing a black man in Winkler County, for which he had served time in the penitentiary. He was 67 years old, and dead.[37]

The search, while not turning up Johnson, was not completely fruitless, however. Deputy Sheriff Ed Foreman stumbled onto a seventy-five-gallon copper moonshine pot in the woods a few miles northeast of Fairfield. The still was near the road and the deputy happened to stop his car nearby, perhaps to answer a call of nature. "A large quantity of mash was on hand," the *Fairfield Recorder* reported, "ready for cooking."[38]

Apparently, some sort of insane full moon, floating in a high stratosphere of violence, was bobbing over Freestone County again, because a week later, another white woman was assaulted by a black man, or so she claimed. What followed was an evil, grotesque comedy.

On Monday, December 11, Miss Florine Grayson—no relation to the dead Perry—reported the attack. She was a 20-year-old school teacher living in Streetman. A well-known lady, she was the sister-in-law of R. M. Thompson, president of the Teague bank, and the former Kirven bank, and also the sister-in-law of Associate Justice Dexter Hamilton of the Dallas Court of Appeals.

The accounts of the attack, as well as the levels of Miss Grayson's distress and humiliation, vary considerably. One newspaper said that Florine was seized in the "garden" of her home at about 6:30 or 6:45 in the morning. Another paper said the attack was in the back yard. One of the Mayo sisters delicately described the place of attack as being "her service room." Another newspaper breached propriety and said, without mincing words, that she was in the outhouse.

Some of the newspapers said the black man stuffed rags into her mouth. Another said it was cotton. Some reports said he put a sack over her head. Most said he tried to assault her. One said he was simply surprised in the outhouse and ran away as fast as he could on being discovered there.

Some accounts said that Miss Grayson struggled desperately and escaped. One said she staggered to "the gallery" and fainted. One lady who knew Florine scoffed at the whole idea of her being assaulted.

"She wasn't like me," the witness stated. "I was particular about who I dated. Florine was not."

A male contemporary of Florine harrumphed. "She wasn't attacked. She just got caught."

Still another stated the same opinion, but put it more delicately. "Florine was the kind of girl everyone wanted to go out with, and most everyone did." [39]

Whatever the degree of Miss Grayson's innocence or complicity, the good white people of Freestone County and its environs knew exactly what to do. They had had plenty of practice recently, and this time they acted just as crudely and barbarically as one would expect their actions to be if described in a Northern, African American, socialist, or other anti-Southern, anti-lynching newspaper.

There was no silent determination, no unified planning, no grim conviction. Most of the mob started drinking and casting about for a victim. George Gay, a 25-year-old black man from Fairfield, ambled into their gunsites.

There is a remote chance that Gay was guilty of whatever Florine claimed had happened to her, or of using her outhouse without permission. A piece of cloth found near her home was supposedly identified by Gay's landlady as part of a handkerchief she had given to the young man the day before. Florine, however, "failed to identify Gay when confronted by him," and the Grayson family pleaded that Gay not be mistreated, and be carried to the jail instead. [40]

The mob was reported to number 1,500, made up of people from Freestone, Limestone, and Navarro Counties. Some people, including several women, arrived by buggy.

Mayo and County Attorney J. E. Woods drove up together and tried to talk to the drunken mob. They pleaded. Woods's speech was said to be eloquent. The words, however, fell on deaf ears.

Luther A. Johnson, Congressman-elect from Corsicana, mounted a soapbox and "made an impassioned plea that the negro not be lynched until positive identification was made." He closed his address with the statement, "Will you join me in adopting David Crockett's motto, 'Be sure you are right. Then go ahead.'?" [41]

The drunken mob was somewhat impressed, somewhat confused. Like the bears old Davy used to tangle with, they were critical of anyone who would attempt to reform them. Several voices answered "yes" to Johnson, but several more shouted something to the effect of "You'd better not try to move the nigger."

While this was going on, Mayo and Woods somehow managed to sneak Gay into a car, just as Mayo had spirited Curry from the Wortham bank months earlier. They started driving away. A roar went up from the crowd, and they gave chase. Once again the harried sheriff found himself making a run from a lynch mob with a black prisoner. Once again, the mob telephoned ahead.

Two miles out of Streetman, on the road to Teague, the sheriff's car was stopped by a barricade of automobiles across the highway. Dozens more pulled in behind.

Gay was taken from the car to a nearby tree. A chain was wrapped around his neck. A mule was obtained from a nearby pasture and Gay was placed on its back. One of Mayo's deputies, whose allegiance to Mayo had apparently evaporated sometime around election day, climbed up the tree and began wrapping the other end of the chain around a limb.

The mob was out of control. Shouts and brays of laughter broke out like jets of a flood through patches on a flimsy dam. Cutting racial epithets and country witticisms filled the air. Somebody slapped the mule.

With the deputy still up the tree, the animal trotted out from under the hapless Gay, and set him to dangling. The members of the crowd whooped, jumped back, drew their pistols, and began peppering the swinging body.

The deputy, afraid he would miss out on the fun, lowered himself from the limb, and began kicking the dying man in the head.

More than 300 bullets were pumped into Gay's body. A couple went wild and injured members of the mob. A memorable time was had by all.

Their fever up, the members of the mob began looking for more opportunities to serve justice. A black man named Roger Payne was seized. Someone said Gay had implicated him. Freestone County lynch victims apparently had a penchant for doing that.

A member of the mob stepped forward and spoke in Payne's defense, however. He was "a good nigger," the white man testified. The code was honored. Payne was released.[42]

A message was delivered to Sheriff Mayo. J. L. Johnson, the attacker of Bess Mayo, had been captured and was being held in Palestine, just across the Trinity River. Surely relieved, Mayo took a constable, Harry Robinson, and drove away. The man in Palestine turned out not to be Johnson at all, but somebody else.

The restless crowd, meanwhile, surged back to Streetman. There, the mob burned an empty hotel in the town owned by a black man named R. Castile. The *Fairfield Recorder* observed sagely that the unoccupied hotel "had long been considered a den of vice and a sore spot in the town."[43]

Soon the nation was reading about Freestone County again. On December 16, the *New York News* ran an article about Streetman entitled "Texas Mob Holds Lynching Bee." The story began, "This town is noted for lynching, or, rather, for burning men at the stake, as three colored men have met their fate in that manner during the last three months."[44]

New York readers did not care if the article was confused about the exact town or time or number of the previous lynchings. It was the same county, same year. Close enough.

Mercifully, 1922 finally drew to a close, and with it, the outrages and violence in Freestone County that had captured so much attention. The local newspaper stories of 1923 were refreshingly free of gut-slamming news, until late summer, at any rate.

On August 13, 1923, a barn belonging to another Kirven man named Mayo burned mysteriously at two in the morning, destroying a cow, a mule, and a large quantity of feed.[45]

On September 4, 1923, Teague Klan No. 68 held a cross-burning ceremony at the Reunion Grounds in Fairfield. Ceremonies were opened by "the planting of the torch, the raising of the cross, and the burning of the signal and beacon lights." The Reverend Slaughter, of Killeen, addressed the crowd on "The Principles of the Ku Klux Klan and its Place in National Affairs Today." After the speech, a number of new members were initiated.[46]

13 *A Place in Blackest History*

The effect of the lynchings of 1922 on Freestone County was quite dramatic, but the events affected other people in ways the participants could never have imagined, in places they never visited. Some of the effects were immediate, while others played out over years. Some were dramatic, others subtle. Ultimately, the outburst of violence in that quiet little corner of Texas touched people in distant parts of the world, and helped work a change in the course of American history.

The violence that occurred around Kirven in May and June of 1922 was not merely a local reaction to the murder of a favorite citizen's favorite granddaughter. The events fit into, and affected, the national pattern of lynching, and neither Freestone County citizens as a whole nor the King brothers in particular were solely culpable. There is enough guilt to cut up and apportion among Americans like a birthday cake.

Lynching of blacks, even burning, was as common in the United States in 1922 as changes in the weather. Other countries and other peoples devised their own quirky methods of doing away with their citizens, but in America, the atrocity of choice was lynching, and its heyday was from the end of the Civil War to 1923.

The practice was born at the same time as the nation, shortly before the Revolutionary War. Some historians attribute its start to a Captain William Lynch, of Pittsylvania, Virginia, but a more credible namesake appears to be Charles Lynch, who was, appropriately, from Lynchburg, Virginia.[1]

Initially, lynching was not synonymous with hanging, nor even with killing; it was simply the practice of punishing wrongdoers in a manner not sanctioned by the law. It began because official courts were not available, and after such courts became available, it remained as a customary means of dealing with an accused criminal by extra-legal means. Hanging was one method of punishment, but others were whipping, beating, tarring and feathering, burning, and shooting, along with more creative forms of civic punishment. After the practice matured, lynching was typically inflicted by a mob.

Thousands of lynchings occurred in the United States prior to the 1880s, but data and statistics for their exact number and locations are incomplete.² Relatively accurate recording of the number of annual lynchings started in 1882, when the *Chicago Tribune* began listing mob murders with its annual summary of the year's crimes, disasters, and other phenomena. In 1905, Professor James Elbert Cutler of Yale University and Wellesley College published *Lynch-Law,* which contained summaries of lynchings that occurred from 1882 through 1903. Some lynchings, however, were unreported and unrecorded.

The Tuskegee Institute, of Alabama, founded in 1881, under the direction of Booker T. Washington, also maintained records, and the National Association for the Advancement of Colored People (NAACP), founded in New York City in 1909 and chartered in 1911, not only kept count, but broke the atrocities down by race, region, state, method, and reason. Statistics were even tallied by the association on how often lynchings were prevented.³

Approximately 5,000 lynchings, north and south, were reported between 1882 and 1925. In most years, the average number of reported lynchings was one or two per week. The major American newspapers published during the 1910s and 1920s contain dozens of accounts of lynchings.⁴ People became calloused to the horrors. As Walter White, a prominent opponent of lynching during the twenties, wrote:

> From the days when one John Malcolm was "genteely Tarr'd and Feather'd" at Pownalborough, Massachusetts, in 1773, mobbism has inevitably degenerated to the point where an uncomfortably large percentage of American citizens can read in their newspapers of the slow roasting alive of a human being in Mississippi and turn, promptly and with little thought, to the comic strip or sporting page.⁵

The twenty years prior to 1903 witnessed over fifty percent more lynchings than did the next twenty years. However, the latter two decades were marked by three trends: More of the lynchings occurred in the South; the proportion of black victims to white was much higher; and the lynchings were marked by much greater cruelty and barbarism. A new outburst of lynching began shortly after World War I, and some scholars consider the homecoming of the 369th United States Colored Infantry to have been the catalyst.

At noon on February 17, 1919, the division passed in review down Manhattan's Fifth Avenue, marching to Harlem. They were home from Europe, home from the War to End All Wars, home from proving they were men.

Two years earlier they had been known as the 15th Colored Infantry National Guard, or, more popularly, as the Harlem Hell Fighters.[6] They were not the only division of all-black American troops, but they were one of the most famous. In Europe they had been segregated from other American troops and trained and commanded by French officers. When going into battle, they went with French rather than American units. Now, back in America, each company marched through New York in a close-order phalanx formation distinctive of French troops.

In eight ranks, sixteen men across, officers and noncoms in the lead, the troops of the 369th swung down Fifth Avenue in squares measuring thirty-five feet wide by thirty-five feet long, stretching from sidewalk to sidewalk in perfect alignment. Company after company swung by as Jim Europe's Army Band blared out a raucous, jazzy marching tune and thousands of enthusiastic citizens lined the streets, cheering and waving.[7]

The men of the 369th did not cheer or wave back. They were combat veterans, having served their country in dozens of battles along the Rhine, and 171 members of the division had been decorated by the French for gallantry in action. This was their last parade, but their first chance to show the folks at home what a well-trained division of black soldiers looked like. They were proud, and the pride was obvious to anyone watching them. One of their number may have been Floyd Gibson, from Freestone County.[8]

The black spectators were wild with enthusiasm. Most of the white spectators were not. They had heard tales about the performance of men of black units in France, both on and off the battlefield. These black men had been trained to kill white men, and had done so with enthusiasm and efficiency. They were also said to be considered unique by the French people, and were popular with French women. The white spectators had heard of black soldiers having sexual relations with white French women . . . and now they were home.

Shortly after the 369th's demonstration of racial pride, a new, vicious round of lynchings and mob violence broke out. Bloody race riots erupted in Chicago, in Omaha, in Washington, D.C., in Longview,

Texas, and in Elaine, Arkansas. Blacks, particularly those in uniform, were dragged from streetcars, sidewalks, and their homes, and were threatened, beaten, and often killed.[9]

When Private William Little returned home to Blakely, Georgia, in late February 1919, a mob of white men was waiting for him on the depot platform. He was ordered to take off his uniform and walk home in his underwear. He refused to do so, and another group of whites came to his rescue, prevailing upon the mob to let him go home unmolested. For several weeks thereafter, he continued to wear his uniform, for he had no other clothing. Anonymous notes were delivered and threats were made, but Little ignored them. On April 3, he was found lying at the edge of town. He had been beaten to death. He was still wearing his uniform.[10]

Nine other returning black veterans were lynched in four Southern states in 1919; two of them were burned alive; others were hanged and mutilated in their uniforms. Dozens were beaten. Hundreds were hounded or threatened. The principal offense of each was being a black veteran.[11]

Lynching was politically controversial before the end of World War I, but the new epidemic of violence that began in 1919 played into the hands of anti-lynching activists, and gained greater support for the movement than ever before. The fresh, senseless killings and brutality toward American veterans, coming on the heels of the great democratic victory in Europe, focused and gave much-needed momentum to their cause. Other lynchings carried the same old Southern trappings and excuses, but the murder of brave American soldiers by Americans, merely because of their skin color, rallied supporters as nothing else had done.

The NAACP sponsored more than 2,000 public meetings on mob violence in 1919, spent several thousand dollars investigating particular lynchings, and vowed never to be intimidated by white supremacists again. In Texas in 1919, the organization's membership shot from 872 to more than 5,000.[12] One of its new recruits was probably Dan Kezer Kelly.

The drive continued through 1920 and 1921. For every person who longed to return to the good old days and put blacks back in "their place," there was at least one, or more, who did not want to slide backward into hatred and boorishness. To the latter, the practice of lynching "was so antithetical to the professed aims of the society" that they called on their fellow Americans to "act to bring an end to such barbarism."[13]

Outside the country, other nations were noticing and speaking out. Newspapers in Europe, South America, Canada, China, Japan, and Africa frequently carried articles about lynchings, burnings, and race riots in the United States.[14] The issue of the *Asian Review* dated May–June 1921 and published in Tokyo, Japan, for example, contained an article decrying lynching which stated: "Americans vociferously claim to be the champions of justice and humanity, yet they do not hesitate to trample upon those very principles and perpetuate the foulest deed ever conceived."

On April 12, 1921, President Harding delivered a message to Congress declaring the need for a wide-ranging series of actions to resolve problems at home. One of his points concerned lynching. He condemned the practice, declaring that "Congress ought to wipe the stain of barbaric lynching from the banners of a free and orderly, representative democracy."[15]

Shortly thereafter, four bills were introduced in Congress, two in each house, to make lynching illegal and to punish not only members of mobs, but law-enforcement officers who permitted lynchings to occur. Another bill was filed in the House of Representatives in July. Anti-lynching bills had been introduced before, but had never previously had any chance of passage by Congress.

One of the House bills, H.R. 13, was sponsored by Representative L. C. Dyer of St. Louis, Missouri. Dyer had filed an anti-lynching bill in each session of Congress since 1911, but all had been ignored. The same fate, however, did not await the one he introduced in 1921.[16]

The NAACP rallied behind the Dyer Bill. Other groups galloped to the fray, some new and some a stronger, more vocal version of earlier anti-lynching organizations.[17]

By December 1921, the Dyer Bill was still in the House, but newspapers were alluding to it each time another lynching occurred. The headline for a story recounting only details of a mob lynching in Watkinsville, Georgia, that month, for example, was "Bill Against Lynching is Given Boost," even though the article did not even mention the proposed law or, indeed, any question of politics.[18]

In January 1922, the Dyer Bill went before a committee of the whole House. Dyer pleaded with his fellow representatives, arguing that law, precedent, duty, and obligation supported his proposal. He praised brave black veterans and cited examples of lynchings in which "little children were taken from their mothers' arms and thrown into the fire." [19]

Southern congressmen, led by Hatton W. Sumners of Texas, responded that the white people of the South should have the right to lynch blacks as a matter of law, but on January 26, 1922, the Dyer Bill passed the House by a vote of 230 to 119. [20]

At first the anti-lynching crusade supporters were elated. Never before had a house of Congress come so far. Perhaps they would finally taste victory.

When the bill went to the Senate, however, it was assigned to the Judiciary Committee, where it was utterly stalemated. The committee was evenly divided, split down the middle on the issue of lynching. For five months the bill languished. By May, when proponents saw they did not have a majority of the committee that would vote to pass it out for debate on the floor of the Senate, they began searching for ways to apply pressure.

On May 3, the Senate of the Commonwealth of Massachusetts concurred in a resolution urging the Senate to pass the Dyer Bill, saying that "national repute among the nations of the world requires that an end be put to this practice of mob murder and lynching in the United States." It was presented to the United States Senate on May 10. [21]

On May 6, another petition was presented to the U.S. Senate which began, "The killing and burning alive of human beings by mobs in the United States is a reproach upon our country throughout the civilized world and threatens organized government in the Nation." It was signed by 300 prominent citizens, including 24 state governors; 38 mayors of principal cities (including San Antonio, Texas, and Charleston, South Carolina); three archbishops; 85 bishops and church leaders of all denominations; 47 lawyers, including two former attorneys general of the United States; 19 judges and appellate court justices; 29 college presidents; and dozens of newspaper editors, presidents of civic organizations, and other eminents. Many were Southerners. [22]

Then, just at that critical moment, as the national debate seemed to be reaching a climax, out of the smoke of a violent Saturday morning in Texas and into the national spotlight came the stories of the burning alive of three black men in Kirven, Texas.

The timing could not have been more crucial. Without dreaming that their acts would have national impact, the King brothers and their neighbors in Freestone County had committed what newspapers claimed was the first triple burning in American history, and had performed the deed for a national audience that was fervently watching for just such a development.

Furthermore, the Kirven burnings were the first, and most dramatic, of a rapid-fire volley of other hangings and burnings in the South that same month. Shadrick Green was killed on May 8. His death was followed by the lynchings of Tom Early, in Plantersville, Texas, on May 17; Hulen Owens, in Texarkana, Arkansas, on May 17; Charles Atkins, in Davisboro, Georgia, on May 18; Joe Winters, in Conroe, Texas, on May 20; Mose Bozier, in Alleytown, Texas, on May 20; Jim Denson, in Irvinton, Georgia, on May 23; and Jesse Thomas, in Waco, Texas, on May 26.[23]

So many lynchings in so short a period could not be ignored. The NAACP made certain that key senators saw the list. Their response was predictable.

"I am shocked and amazed at the list of lynchings," wrote Senator Frank B. Willis, of Ohio. "It is unfortunate that in this country dedicated to law and order, there should be eleven lynchings within the space of twenty-two days. This is an average of one every two days. Such a condition is most threatening and dangerous, and should be condemned by all good citizens."[24]

Senator Charles Curtis of Kansas agreed. "I do hope something can be done to stop the outrages," he told the NAACP. "I have talked to members of the Committee in regard to the Anti-Lynching Bill but the Committee does not seem to have reached a conclusion about it. I will talk again with members of the Committee."[25]

On June 24, the *Chicago Defender* predicted that the recent lynchings in Texas would prove to be the undoing of Michigan congressman Pat Kelly because he had voted against the Dyer Bill. To many of the paper's readers, "recent lynchings in Texas" was synonymous with Freestone County.

Shortly thereafter, the *St. Louis Argus* reported the receipt by the NAACP of several recently published French, Belgian, and Czechoslovakian newspapers. All contained the same story, reading in part: "the recent murder of three Negroes by an excited mob in Texas was the single event which had called public attention to the matter in a very decided manner."[26] There can be no doubt that the incident on European minds was the one that occurred in Kirven.

Public pressure continued to mount through June, and on July 5, 1922, the Senate Judiciary Committee passed the Dyer Bill out favorably by a slim, one-vote margin, and sent it to the floor of the full Senate with a recommendation for passage.

The final-straw catalyst for this anti-lynching victory, however, was not Kirven, but Herrin, Illinois. The Kirven event was shocking, but it occurred in the South and involved the deaths of black men. Southern senators could not break ideological ranks over such an incident. Herrin was different.

There, on June 22, 1922, 5,000 striking coal miners at a strip mine attacked workers who had been imported by the Lester Coal Company to break the strike. At least forty people died, many of them foreigners, some army veterans, all white. Most were shot. Some were weighted down with rocks and thrown in a pond.[27]

The incident was massive and appalling, and it both contained the right ingredients and occurred at the perfect time to break the stalemate in the Senate committee. The killings did not involve blacks and they occurred in Illinois. Thus, fence-straddling senators could condemn lynching and mob violence without betraying racist sentiment back home. Southerners could rail against barbarism that occurred in a Northern state.

Interestingly and bizarrely, the Herrin incident was even reported with rage and criticism, or hypocrisy, in Freestone County, the *Fairfield Recorder* editor waxing eloquent with the following diatribe: "The Herin [sic] massacre must remain a black spot on the escutcheon of the United States, a free country whose constitution guarantees the highest and lowest life, liberty and the pursuit of happiness. Surely we have cut loose from the old moorings."[28]

Passage of the Dyer Bill out of committee unleashed a flurry of excitement among leaders of the anti-lynching movement. At long last, they believed, the United States Congress would take action and put an end to lynching.

Not so. The Dyer Bill's opponents kept it off the Senate floor until November, when Senator Samuel M. Shortridge of California moved to make it the unfinished business of the year, or, in other words, to bring it to full debate and vote before the session ended.

Southern senators, led by one of their number from Mississippi, began a filibuster that lasted until the Thanksgiving break.[29] When the senators returned from their holiday, Senator Oscar W. Underwood of Alabama took the floor to say that he and his fellow Southerners were determined to block all legislation, even confirmation of presidential appointments, until the Republicans agreed to abandon the Dyer Bill. Republicans delayed a few more days, then relented.

The death of the Dyer Bill by filibuster was decried by its supporters as a "disgrace to modern civilization." A Northern Democratic senator was quoted as saying, "It is a sorry plight. Where will it end?" "None can say," an African American newspaper replied.[30]

But it had ended. Although no one could know it then, the Southerners' victory was only a battle won; they would lose the war. The dark days of lynching died with the Dyer Bill. Americans were fed up with the practice and the controversy. Even Southerners were catching on. The year 1922 turned out to be lynching's last big year.

The national annual lynching victim count had fluctuated from a high of 235 in 1892—more than 4 per week—to a low of 54 in 1917, and, not counting the deaths in Herrin, was 61 for 1922. In 1923, however, the count fell to 28, the lowest annual total since record-keeping began in 1882. In 1924, the count dropped to 16, edged up slightly in 1925 to 18, and edged up again in 1926 to 34, but that was the highest count for the rest of the century.[31] In 1928 the count was 11, and in 1929 it was 10. In 1932 there were only 8 lynchings nationwide.[32]

The total lynching body count since 1882 was shocking, and might be considered America's holocaust, but the nation, even the South, did not tolerate the barbaric practice after 1922. The violence had been too great, too savage, and had occurred too often. The practice did not end immediately—the number of lynchings continued to decline in baby steps toward extinction until the 1960s—but for all practical purposes, the "good job" in Kirven on May 6, 1922 caused one of the biggest steps of all.

In 1922, Freestone County was a crossroads where the nation's stinking racial past collided with its aching racial future. The acts committed there were mirror reflections of dramas being acted out across the country, particularly in the South. The atrocities committed were done with clarity of mind and with a bellow of multi-generational rage. Mercifully, ironically, the Freestone County outburst turned out to be one of the last, greatest bellows of the whole shameful phenomenon.

 *Burning Questions*

Assuming the accuracy of the Kelly report, the Northern newspaper accounts, and Foreman Carter's recollections, what are the consequences? How does this information fit into and affect the other details of the tale? What "burning questions" are left unanswered?

What was Snap Curry's role? Was he guilty, and if so, of what crimes? Did he confess, and if not, why did he run? Why did Curry implicate Mose Jones and Johnny Cornish, or did he? Even if he said no more than, "They are just as guilty as I," why did he do so? Why did he not implicate the Prowells? . . . Or, in fact, did he?

What of the Kings? Why, if Grandfather King believed the Prowells were guilty, did he assent to the burning of the three blacks? And why, if the Prowells were guilty, did the King brothers go on a killing rampage against other blacks? . . . Or, indeed, did they?

Finally, what was Horace Mayo's role? Was he a hero who tried to defend the three men, or a weak man who was more concerned about being reelected than about doing what was morally correct?

Can such questions be answered rationally, or has too much time and fact been lost? Can a single fabric be pieced together that bundles up all the loose ends, or must we merely speculate and discuss possibilities?

Facts can be uncovered, opinions can be formed, but the truth can never be known. No single fabric of truth can be knitted from an accumulation of eye-witness accounts and newspaper articles. Even if the accounts and articles were entirely consistent, which they are not, reconstruction and speculation cannot generate genuineness. All that can be done is to collect different perspectives from different sources.[1] All the facts were not known in 1922, and the passage of seventy-plus years, in addition to the frailty, arbitrariness, subjectivity, and selectivity of human memory, may have buried as much truth as has been uncovered.

Still, speculation and conjecture flow irresistibly from the Kirven story, and even without all the facts, enough information is available to supply a fairly convincing account of what really happened. What follows is, however, only one opinion, one attempt to weave one fabric, one bundling together of the loose ends.

Snap Curry was probably guilty of a minor role in the crime, to which he probably confessed, and much of the confession, as reported in the newspapers, was probably accurate. However, he was probably duped by the Prowells into participating, he probably did not help kill Eula, and certain details of his confession were probably changed and exaggerated.

The fact that newspapers across the state printed Curry's confession as early as May 6, the very day of the burnings, makes it unlikely that it was a total fabrication. Its publication was simply too soon and still in the midst of too much excitement and confusion. Nobody had time to manufacture a detailed account to feed to the press. Men like Sheriff Mayo and T. L. Childs, the post-lynching editorialist, probably heard Curry speak most of the words printed.

To believe otherwise is to argue that those men or others conspired quickly, with considerable foresight, and invented Curry's lengthy statement in time for publication almost as soon as Curry was dead.

Certainly, conspiracies and false testimony were common in the South when white men murdered black men, and newspaper editors were often the leaders of efforts to cover up acts of local racial rage. This particular case was not one of premeditated racism, however. Its outcome was not planned. Facts were still developing on May 6. At least one Prowell brother was apparently still at large and Grandfather King's suspicions were still viable. There was too much still happening for anyone to have time to invent and substitute a canned confession for the known facts that early.

On the other hand, by altering only a few details of Curry's confession, it was possible to report that the action of the mob was justified, and that only guilty men had been executed. Substitution of the names of Mose Jones and Johnny Cornish for those of Claude and Audey Prowell was the simplest modification.

Curry's crime was probably that he accepted fifteen dollars from the Prowells to stop Eula at the bridge. Foreman Carter said that he did so. Carter speculated that Eula would have run if she had seen the Prowells, her family's sworn enemies, but she would not have been frightened at the sight of her uncle's hired hand. Snap was probably thrilled to receive the windfall, and had no advance knowledge of what the Prowells intended to do to the girl.

Snap may have fallen against the fence while the Prowell brothers

were pulling Eula from the saddle. The frightened horse he was holding may have knocked or driven him into a post or the barbed wire,
cutting his chest. Such a wound would account not only for the broken
fence, but for Snap's story to his wife, recounted by Bertha Williams,
that his horse reared and drove the saddle horn into his chest. Such an
accident would be unusual, not the kind a man would dream up without supporting evidence, like a wound. Snap may have told Agnes
Curry only half a lie. A horse may have injured Snap and caused him
to get blood on his clothes.

Alternatively, or in addition, Eula may have struggled so violently
that the Prowells ordered Snap to help them, and once they were in
the woods, they persuaded him to help hold Eula down, so that his
clothes and shoes became bloody. They may have made Snap do this
on purpose, so that he would be implicated in the crime.

According to Snap's confession, he watched the others assault, stab,
mutilate, and stomp Eula. This makes sense if the other men were the
Prowells. If the two men were Jones and Cornish, and the trio had
planned to assault Eula for months, Snap surely would have participated. The fact that Curry confessed to only limited involvement in the
crime also supports its legitimacy. A phony confession designed by a
white Southerner would surely have exaggerated the guilt of all the
black men, rather than partially vindicate one of them.

Snap probably began running for the exact reason the mob suspected—he heard that bloodhounds were en route, and knew they
might follow his trail from the murder scene to his home. Thereafter,
once he was captured and in jail, he probably told the truth to Mayo
and the committee from the mob. In doing so, he probably implicated
the Prowells.

Foreman Carter addressed the issue of Snap's confession. When
asked how people first got the idea that Snap Curry was the murderer,
he replied by recalling what his poppa, Jenkins Carter, had been told
by the mysterious white man who delivered the news of the Prowell
confession:

A: What happened, the way the [white] man told it, they
              got Snap to stop the girl by telling her there was a
              cocklebur under her saddle blanket . . . to get off or
              get down and he'd take it out, or her horse might
              throw her. She got down and then these guys pulled
              her in.
Q: The two brothers?

A: The two guys, yeah. See, Snap didn't tell, he didn't
              go and tell the truth about it. Maybe if he'd told the
              truth, Sheriff Sessions [*sic*, actually Horace Mayo]
              might have saved him.
Q: Snap didn't tell the truth?
A: He didn't tell the truth until after he was caught. You
              see, when they had the posse, black and white was all
              looking together in this posse, and because we hadn't
              had no trouble around here at all, black and white got
              along very good up until that point, he was trying . . .
              and when he heard they were calling in the dogs, well
              he . . .
Q: He took off running?
A: Uh-huh . . . and Richard Spence saw him crawling
              along the road, crawling along the cotton rows, and he
              picked him up and said he was going back home, but
              he brought him in. . . . Richard Spence brought him
              back and he told the sheriff what happened, but it was
              too late then. You know how a mob is. They didn't
              listen. He should have told it to start with, but he
              didn't have enough intelligence to do that. 'Course he
              was scared. In that time, any white man could tell you
              what to do, and if your boss wasn't there to protect
              you, you had to do it, see.

Carter seemed to be saying that Curry might have saved himself if he
had immediately turned himself in to the sheriff—who was Jim Sessions for many years after the troubles—and if he had told the truth
about the Prowells. He was scared, however, and thought that because
blacks and whites got along, he could join the posse and help those in
authority, hoping that the Prowells would be caught without his having
to come forward. When he did tell the truth, after being caught, it was
too late—"You know how a mob is."

Even the committee members, whoever they were, may have believed Curry. Sheriff Mayo wrote on May 13 that "all three negroes were
landed in jail," after which the committee "decided to wait until two
more negroes suspected of being implicated in the matter were caught
and examined, before any further action against the three prisoners was
taken." Those two men were probably not Negroes. They were probably the remaining Prowell brother and his father, Tom Prowell. The
committee, after hearing Curry's confession and Mayo's recounting of

Grandfather King's theory, may have told the mob to wait until the other Prowell men were brought in before anyone took action.

If so, the mob either rejected the committee's recommendation or everyone deliberated and decided that, regardless of whether the Prowells were guilty or Jones and Cornish were not guilty, Curry was definitely involved, and he deserved to die. The mob had been at fever pitch all day, absolutely convinced of the guilt of Curry because of the bloody clothes and the fact that he had run from them. No one particularly cared if Jones and Cornish were innocent. They were black men who might have broken a Southern code. They needed to be taught a swift lesson.

If there was also a Prowell brother in jail, the same prejudice probably saved him from being taken to Kirven also. He was white, and thus deserved a trial. The authorities could decide his fate later.

But why, then, if Curry implicated the Prowells instead of Jones and Cornish, did Curry declare on his funeral pyre that they were as guilty as he, and deserved to die? Most of the newspaper accounts repeated this claim, and even Dan Kelly acknowledged the point in his report to the NAACP. His version of Curry's words was: "The others are as guilty as I, and if I burn, they deserve the same treatment."

We will never know, but what may have happened is that Curry felt totally alone, totally friendless, and totally betrayed by everyone, including Jones and Cornish.

Jones and Cornish were almost certainly arrested after Curry began running but before he was captured. The evidence at the murder scene indicated that there had been two or three killers. Curry was running, so he counted as one. The other two, someone decided, must be friends of Curry's. Jones and Cornish worked with him, and, according to some newspaper reports, they had been seen fishing with him earlier in the day, so they were arrested "on suspicion." Had Jones and Cornish been arrested after Curry, the mob would have stood between them and the jailhouse, and they probably would have been seized and lynched.

Once Snap was in jail with them, no matter what their relationship had been before, Jones and Cornish would have distanced themselves from him as much as possible, denying acts, knowledge, and friendship. To Curry, this may have been the last straw. He had been duped by the Prowells. His wife had helped turn him in. He had been double-crossed by Richard Spence. He had told the truth about the Prowells to the sheriff and the mob, to no avail. He had not helped murder the girl. He knew he was innocent and not deserving of such a horrible death, and yet nobody was sympathetic, not even the only two men left who seemingly should have been—his two black cellmates.

So, after being castrated and tied to the plow, seeing people piling wood, pouring gasoline, and preparing to strike matches, he was just not in a mood to do them any favors. The little that is known about Curry's personality, coming mostly from Foreman Carter—that he liked to pick fights, was "lower class," and was not very intelligent—do not describe a benevolent martyr. He was innocent. They were innocent. He was about to be burned. Why should they not burn with him?

Also, members of the mob needed a sign during the lull after burning Curry and before burning Jones. They wanted permission to burn Cornish and Jones, and nothing served their purpose better than words from Curry. His words may have been mumbled, garbled, taken out of context, or heard by only a few persons, but those who heard them seized upon them and championed them like a banner.

As for the Kings and their motives, the grandfather and the uncles probably suspected only the Prowells at first, and told the sheriff, who was in the process of arresting the guilty parties and solving the crime when Snap began running. After that, it did not matter what the Kings or anyone believed. No one, the Kings or Mayo, had control over the situation.

Thereafter, hearing that Curry had been implicated by his wife, that bloody clothes had been found, and that he was running was probably proof enough to convince even the Kings to join, or lead, the mob. Their pain over the loss of Eula was too great and too fresh; they were too firmly entrenched in the second stage of the grieving process, anger, to give anyone the benefit of the doubt. All the ugly heads of the mob pivoted from the Prowells and elsewhere to stare after the fleeing Snap, and the chase was on.

From then until the funeral pyre ceased smoking the next morning, emotion ruled. Everyone was seized by mob hysteria. Even Grandfather King, who believed most firmly in the Prowells' guilt, and who had begged the mob to go slow and not to lynch any innocent Negroes, was affected. His conviction was shaken by the "evidence." As he told Dan Kelly and Kelly repeated in his report, "I believe still, *although those rascals, some of them, may have been implicated,* they could not have thought of such a deed. I still believe that those Prowl boys are the ones who did it."

The question of what role the King brothers played in the reign of terror that followed the burnings is a knottier problem. There are essentially four pieces of information about their involvement available for consideration, but they yield conflicting conclusions.

First, and foremost, is the locally accepted story, or legend, in the area, handed down through generations and explained by such men as J. C. Whatley, that the Kings were the ringleaders, instigators, and principal participants in the reign of terror. Second, and supporting this, are the June 9 newspaper reports of the shootout in Simsboro which credit John T., Otis, Drew, and Bob King with leading the posse in pursuit of Leroy Gibson.

Contradicting the legend is, first, the published statement of Sheriff Mayo and the King brothers days after the burnings, asking people not to bring firearms into Kirven and saying that the family believed the guilty parties had been punished. Second, and more significant, is the testimony of three witnesses about who was responsible for the subsequent lynchings and terror. Foreman Carter declared that lots of different people committed the murders. Lura Bess Mayo Sprague described the killers as "sort of like professionals . . . [who] came from up at Streetman, and over at Corsicana and Mexia, and from all around; why, it just thrilled them to death to get out there and get those niggers, to have an excuse." Bertha Williams identified the killers as "just men, men here from seven or eight different towns," and declared adamantly that the Kings never did anything cruel to black people. None of these witnesses, two of whom were black, had any vested reason to protect the Kings seventy years after the event.

The most likely explanation of the reign of terror is that it was solely the product of racial hatred—something that cannot be explained rationally—and that many other Texans besides the King brothers seized upon the incident as an excuse to come to Freestone County and kill blacks. Eula's murder and the implication of Snap was a switch that turned loose the pathologically hateful, innately cruel, traditionally violent emotions that simmered in certain men's hearts. The King brothers may have participated, fueled by grief, frustration, and the belief that there were still conspirators in their niece's murder to be punished.

Perhaps the brothers went to Simsboro believing that Eula's blood on Leroy Gibson's clothes was evidence too damning to ignore, and perhaps their publicized presence at the shootout, the last outrage stemming directly from Eula's murder, caused people to remember the Kings as being involved in and responsible for all of the violence. Many different people probably committed outrageous, racially motivated acts during those four weeks, but as the years went by, the blame conveniently focused more and more squarely, and solely, on the King brothers.

The bottom-line explanation of the extent and reasons for the involvement of the Kings in the racial terror, if, in fact, their beloved Eula had been killed by their sworn enemies, the Prowells, remains a question that continues to burn, and that is still unanswered. The one surviving member of the family located who was present in 1922, and who might have cleared up the mystery of his grandfather's, father's, and uncles' involvement, declined to be interviewed, saying the recollections were simply too painful to think about.

The final, and most intriguing, of the burning questions, however, involves the nature and extent of Sheriff Mayo's role in the events that occurred after Snap Curry began to run.

Horace Mayo was essentially a good, intelligent man who was devoted to his family, attended church regularly, and loved to sing. He was also a sensitive but fun-loving man who needed and enjoyed people, who cherished his friends, who loved to pull pranks and tell stories, and who never should have become involved in the law-enforcement business, particularly during Prohibition days.

He tried to crack down on moonshining, only to have the governor pull the rug out from under him. The stand he took against the Klan is admirable. The KKK was wielding such phenomenal power in Texas in 1922 that it was said to control two-thirds of the state's county conventions.[2] Mayo had to have guts to step up to the microphone and say, "The Klan is the very antithesis of the spirit of law enforcement. Do I make myself clear?"

He apparently investigated Eula's murder carefully, tracked down the killers, and then tried to protect Curry, Jones, and Cornish from the mob, first by attempting to drive Curry out of the county, then by refusing to turn the three men over at the jail. After the prisoners were taken, he probably followed the mob to Kirven—his daughters said he did—still hoping, perhaps, to save a life. Later in the year, when George Gay was being held by another mob, by which time Mayo was a lame-duck sheriff with nothing to gain and with a recent outrage against his wife by a black man simmering in his mind, he still made a desperate, heroic attempt to save the man's life, at a risk to his own.

Nevertheless, when the moment of truth was upon him, he caved in, and became a spokesman in defense of the actions of the mob. He sold out, and that act ultimately destroyed him.

The moment of truth came on May 6 or shortly thereafter, after the burnings, when Mayo was forced to decide whether to continue to hold the Prowells for trial and seek to prove their guilt, or to capitulate to external pressure and let them go.

Horace Mayo certainly had human frailties. Indeed, his character may have been fatally flawed. His killing of Jerry Winchester has never been satisfactorily explained. He was an alcoholic. He was not successful at any job he pursued. He wanted to do right, but at the pivotal instant in his life when all that had gone before intersected with all that would be thereafter, when his future stood in the balance, he made the wrong choice. He capitulated, and then some.

Although he must have known about the guilt of the Prowells and the innocence of Jones and Cornish, he chose, in his letter to the newspapers dated May 13, to trumpet the white party line, or lie, regarding the lynchings. He did so not merely with silent acquiescence, but with affirmative invention.

First, Mayo's stated reason for writing the letter is untrue. There was no story in the Houston newspaper to criticize. He probably selected that newspaper because few, if any, Freestone County voters read it. The most popular out-of-county newspaper was the *Dallas Times Herald*. Dallas was closer than Houston and the paper was delivered daily by southbound train.

Second, his declaration in the letter that burning the men was a fitting punishment—"it would be a poor man who could have viewed the body or heard these negroes describe the manner in which they committed the crime, and then say burning was out of place"—could not have been his heartfelt conviction. He said it because he was involved in a cover-up, after which he told Dan Kelly that he believed Mose Jones was innocent.

The third, and most glaring, untruth in his letter is that "these negroes all confessed to taking part in the murder of Miss Ausley." Nobody else ever claimed that all three men, including Cornish and Jones, confessed. Even the very biased, pro-community local newspapers reported that they denied their guilt to the end, but Mayo wrote the opposite.

Finally, his statement in the letter about the committee coming out of Curry's cell and saying they were going to wait until *"two more negroes"* were caught before taking further action may have been Mayo seizing an opportunity to change a lot of perception by altering a little bit of fact. Saying that Curry identified two other black men, instead of two white men, allowed Mayo to caulk up a glaring crack in the official party line, and diverted attention from his decision to release the Prowells.

Perhaps Mayo did not act alone. There may have been secret meetings of key, influential players in Kirven and Freestone County between May 6 and May 13, which could have included anyone from prominent families to members of the Masonic Lodge. They may have analyzed what had occurred and what the best course of action would be for the future. They may have decided unanimously what course to follow. Pressure may have been put on Mayo to make certain declarations. He may have resisted and debated, or he may have agreed obediently.

Or perhaps Mayo made the decision to write the May 13 letter on his own. In it, he declared, "I am willing to take whatever criticism is directed at me, because my conscience is clear." This may have been the biggest lie of all. What he had done haunted Mayo until the day he died. What he had done probably killed him. Mayo would endure eight more years of failure and agony. Then he would commit suicide.

Dozens of other questions arise: Why did Dan Kelly talk to Grandfather King, but not to any of the King brothers before he made his report? Or did he do so, but was the information the King brothers supplied not supportive of his theories? Was the note in the bottle that was sent to the Dallas police from one of the Prowells? If so, what did the Prowell who wrote it mean by saying that the motive for Eula's murder was jealousy?

Perhaps there are answers somewhere. Perhaps the publication of this tale will cause a few more facts, instead of more questions, to float to the surface, if for no other reason than to correct mistakes in the foregoing interpretations.

There is, however, one other matter for speculation, one other type of burning question, but it does not involve motives, consequences, or analysis of insufficient evidence. It involves the arrangement of graves in the Shanks cemetery.

Grandfather John King and his wife, Permelia, lie together on the north side of the burial ground. Beside them is the grave and monument to Eula, and beside Eula is her mother, Eunice. Her uncle Bob and his wife, Maggie, lie on the same row, further south, while her uncle Otis and the grave of an infant son who died before Eula lie a few rows west of the other Kings.

Immediately east and slightly south of Eula's resting place, less than twenty feet away, is a plot containing four graves, two old, two more recent. Their monuments proclaim the family name of the three men and one woman who are buried in the plot: Prowell, Prowell, Prowell, and Prowell.

The occupants of two of the graves predeceased Eula. One was a 14-year-old boy who died in 1914. The other, A. T. Prowell, was 44 when he died in 1905. The full name of the father of Claude and Audey Prowell was Andrew Thomas Prowell. Was A. T. Prowell his father, the grandfather of Claude and Audey?

Texas death records and archives have not yielded an answer to this burning question, but a more interesting matter for contemplation is the effect, if any, that the sight of those graves had on the mourners who attended Eula's funeral on May 7, 1922. If Grandfather King believed the Prowells killed his beloved granddaughter, the sight of the name on the nearby headstones must have driven another cold wedge of sorrow into his laboring heart.

Similarly, when the other two Prowells died and were buried in the Shanks cemetery, in 1946 and 1958, did any Prowell family mourner stand within a few feet of the graves of Eula, her mother, and her grandparents, and contemplate the past? Both Claude and Audey would have been alive in 1946, and Claude was still living in 1958. He might have driven over from nearby Anderson County for the funeral of the wife of A. T. Prowell, who may have been his grandmother.

This is an irony-laden tale: Eula was "saved" on the same site where her "murderers" were burned alive; Mose Jones named his children after the town and man central to his own death; Johnny Cornish died because he had a "filthy" mouth; and the town of Kirven burned and died because of the burning and death of the three black men. The proximity of the Prowell graves to those of the Kings—not only Eula, but Grandfather and Otis too—adds just one more cosmic twist, an eternal twist, to the tale.

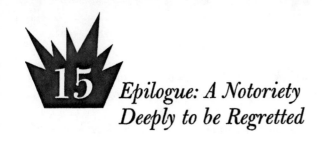

15 Epilogue: A Notoriety Deeply to be Regretted

The Kirven lynchings, and ironies, continued to claim victims, in different ways and in different places, as time went by.

The young bride of Johnny Cornish lasted only a few months. She did not recover from the shock of how her bridegroom was killed. She died "of a broken heart" a few months after Johnny. Additional details, including her name, are lost to history.[1]

Florine Grayson, the young school teacher whose assault resulted in the lynching of George Gay, apparently burned to death in Kirven. She was teaching there, a relative reported, and one winter day during the 1930s, she backed into an open-flame space heater. Her clothes caught fire. She did not recover.[2]

Horace Mayo committed suicide in September 1930.

After losing the election of 1922, he tried to return to his former life as a farmer, but lack of black labor and a despondent attitude held him down. He began drinking heavily, and soon deteriorated to the point where one of his only sources of income, and liquor, was shooting contests.

He would go to the cotton fields, not needing to feign intoxication anymore, and would inevitably be challenged to a contest by some of the white men working there. No matter how drunk he was, or became, he could still "skin" his challengers.

His family watched his descent helplessly. Sometimes he tried to act like the old Horace, showing affection, telling jokes, and laughing with friends, but he was different.

"He'd never been associated with the underworld," said his daughter Grace. "He was easily hurt and he was sensitive to everything. That will make a good person if you have the stamina to take it, but it's unfortunate my father even lived there, because of the type of person he was. I think being sheriff broke his spirit."

Of his drinking, his daughter Lura Bess said, "That was the only thing that gave him any relief. He did that just to drown himself so he wouldn't get so depressed thinking about how things were."

When Jim Sessions announced his candidacy for sheriff in 1929,

Mayo went to him and said, "Now Jim, I would love to help in any way I can." Sessions' reply was quick and straightforward: "No. I don't want your help."

J.R.'s rebuff may have finally brought home to him how low in life he had sunk.

He lamented to his family, recalling how well he had treated Jim Sessions when he and Jim's father were in jail for murder for nineteen days in 1921. Mayo never locked them in a cell. Instead, he moved his youngest daughter, Ruth, out of her room so they could stay there. The Sessions took all their meals with the Mayo family, and were treated like the friends they were. Now, in 1929, all Horace wanted to do was help, and this was how he was treated.

A few months after Jim Sessions took office, Mayo and a drinking buddy, Richard Hogan, took a long trip together. Mayo carried with him, like a comet's tail, the doubts, guilt, and frustration of the last nine years.

Lura Bess said the two men went to Alabama, where Mayo had relatives, to look for work. Ruth and Grace remembered the trip differently. "My daddy did something terrible," Ruth stated. "He sold all his cotton, but instead of putting that money on what he should have put it on, he spent it, and went on a trip with one of the Hogan boys."

Lura Bess said Hogan went along to drive, because her father was drinking so much in those days that he could not. A Kirven resident hooted at this, saying, "I don't think you get one alcoholic to drive another."

When they returned from the trip on September 13, 1930, with no work found and the money spent, they stopped at the Mayo farmhouse on the edge of town. Mrs. Mayo and Ruth were living in town. Grace and Lura Bess were married and living, respectively, in Arlington and College Station.

Mayo told Hogan to drive into town to get something, but not to stay away long, to return in half an hour. Hogan did as he was told. When he returned, he found Mayo lying in a pool of his own blood.

The ex-sheriff had shot himself in the head with the revolver he had carried during his law-enforcement career.

He was still alive, and Hogan rushed Mrs. Mayo and a doctor to his side. They moved him into the house in town, and called Lura Bess and Grace.

Grace had just given birth to a baby, and could not leave her bed, but Lura Bess rushed to her father's side. She was able to speak to him

before he died. He was conscious, but incoherent. Surrounded by hi~
wife, two daughters, and a collection of friends, he passed away shor~
after she arrived.

"Bless his heart," Lura Bess said. "We all grieved for him and we ~
grieved with him. We all knew, in our hearts, it was a relief. He was a
Christian, and you can commit suicide if your mind has been deranged
and you are not responsible."

He was buried in the Woodland Cemetery, near Kirven. Later, representatives of the bank came to the Mayo home to collect the money
Horace owed, but there was no money to be found.[3]

J. R. Sessions also committed suicide, although there is no reason to
link his death with what happened in 1922.

He served as sheriff of Freestone County from 1931 until 1949. He
was beloved, respected, and generally credited with wiping out moonshining and lawlessness in Freestone County. B. J. Ausley remembered
him as a crack shot and "a kind, loving man, but hard as heck."[4]

On January 21, 1949, Sessions drove home from his office in Fairfield
and parked his car in the driveway of his ranch house outside of
Kirven. His wife was gone, and when she returned she found him lying
dead in the front seat of the car, his revolver in his hand, a bullet in his
head. The death was ruled a suicide, but questions still remain in many
minds. The Texas House of Representatives passed a resolution in his
memory, describing him as "alert, fearless, calm, and with a poise and
dignity that commanded respect." He was also buried in Woodland
Cemetery.[5]

Otis King, credited by many as the leader of the reign of terror of
May–June 1922, lived a long but troubled life. He stayed in Kirven for
twelve years, but cotton farming and cattle ranching ceased to be profitable. The Great Depression set in and he moved his family to Houston, where he was hired as a motorcycle patrolman by the city on
March 16, 1934. His employment records have been destroyed, and
consist today of only one 3-inch by 5-inch personnel card, but the little
document speaks loudly.

He began his employment making 90 dollars a month and received
a raise to 95 dollars in September 1934. The next year, in October, he
received another raise to 105 dollars. In 1936, he received two raises,
to 110 dollars in February and to a whopping 140 dollars six months
later. Then the salary increases dried up. Nearly three years later he
received one more, to 150 dollars. Three and a half years afterwards,
he resigned from his job.

B. J. Ansley remembered hearing that his great-uncle received several disciplinary reprimands related to cruelty to blacks while on duty. The paucity of salary increases after 1936, together with his resignation, suggests something of the sort.

The personnel card also shows that he, Rena, and their two children moved five times in eight years. Finally, the line on the card to indicate marital status, originally marked "Mar." for married, was changed to an "S," for single.

Life in the big city, and his temperament, apparently took his job, his marriage, and perhaps even his ability to keep a house or apartment. He may have moved back to Freestone County. He is buried there, next to the grave of a baby boy who died before Eula. A small stone marked "Mother" is next to his, but there is no marker for Rena. Otis is in the same cemetery as his parents, his sister, his brother Bob, and his beloved niece, but is several dozen yards removed from them, having died on September 16, 1976.

Alva King, the youngest of the five brothers, did not participate in the lynchings, and was the first to leave the area. He was said to have been embarrassed by his family's involvement in the reign of terror, so he moved to Arkansas and did not come back until 1972, when he returned to attend a family reunion. Word of his visit leaked out, however, and an anonymous phone call was received at the house of the relative where he was staying. The caller said that if Alva remained in the county, he would be killed. He quickly returned to Arkansas.[6]

Other key players in the drama lived normal, happy lives, seemingly unfazed by their proximity to the violence of 1922.

Floyd Gibson, who single-handedly brought an end to much of the racial violence with his murdered nephew's rifle, left Freestone County immediately after the Simsboro shootout. He moved to Seattle, Washington, and stayed there the rest of his long life, returning to Freestone County only once, to visit his favorite sister, Sophie. It was only after Floyd returned to Washington that Sophie told the rest of the family he had been there. He died in Seattle, never having married.[7]

Mrs. Mayo and the three Mayo daughters lived long, contented lives. Bess Mayo stayed in Kirven and made a living renting rooms, primarily to school teachers, and cooking their meals. She died in 1977 and was buried next to her beloved Horace.

Lura Bess married Carl T. Sprague and spent most of her adult life in College Station, where her husband taught at Texas A&M University. Among other pursuits, Lura Bess taught music to the youth of College Station. She did so with the same passion she had displayed in Kirven.

Grace, who married Bill Norman, had two daughters and lived in Dallas. After her husband died and she became nearly blind, she moved to College Station, to be near her older sister.

Ruth, the youngest daughter, married Mike Ditto, and was a school teacher for many years, specializing in remedial reading. After she retired, an elementary school was named for her in Arlington, Texas. Her son, Dr. Michael Ditto, is the owner of the pistol his grandmother used to drive J. L. Johnson into the Freestone County night on November 30, 1922. All three of the Mayo daughters are widowed.

J. L. Johnson, the black man who assaulted Bess Mayo and ran away into the night, was never caught. Years later Lura Bess heard he escaped to Calvert, Texas, and lived there for the rest of his life.[8]

J. C. Whatley moved to Teague and worked for a grocery business. He also admitted to being forced to sell moonshine in order to eat, but swore he never made it. In 1942 he moved to Dallas and lived there for thirty-five years, working as a store manager for E. P. Compton, running a venetian-blind business, and serving as a night watchman and dispatcher for the Valley Steel Products Company. After working in Dallas for many years, he returned to Kirven and lived in a trailer house near the site of his father's cotton gin.[9] He died there in 1989.

Grandfather King's wife, Permelia, or Eubeza, died on April 5, 1930. He lived another fourteen years, until February 7, 1944, two months short of 90, and was frisky to the end.

B. J. Ausley, his grand-nephew, remembered how spry the old man was. In the late thirties, when John King was in his eighties, B.J. and his brothers decided to go skinny-dipping in a pond near the King house. Granddad joined in. There was a rope hanging from a tree and Grandfather King, as naked as the youngsters, swung merrily and repeatedly from it to drop into the water below.

Skinny-dipping was not the only proof of his virility. At about the same time he hired a 15-year-old girl to clean his house. Soon her parents were complaining that their daughter was spending more time at the King house than at home. It did not look right. People were beginning to talk. Old man King solved the problem by marrying the girl.[10] Perhaps he finally filled, at the very end, the aching longing for young ladies in his life.

The spot where Eula was murdered became a popular site for teen-agers and children to visit in the twenties, thirties, and forties. Every-one knew the story of her murder and the aftermath, and a large tree near where her body was found became a magnet for graffiti. Her name and date of death, along with the initials and names of dozens of visi-tors, were carved on its trunk over the years. The tree died and fell, probably in the sixties, and rotted away.[11]

The road along which she rode and was murdered was abandoned and the site was eventually bulldozed. Remains of the bridge where she was pulled from her horse may still be seen in the bed of Grindstone Creek, although the area is covered with trees and thick brush.

Through the twenties, thirties, and forties, several black baby girls born in Freestone County were named Eula, perhaps in an attempt to show support and to make peace by black families who still worried about the intentions of their white neighbors.

The plow around which Snap Curry, John Cornish, and Mose Jones were burned remained in the vacant lot in Kirven for twenty years. The implement was a symbol, some of the remaining whites of Kirven be-lieved, to remind blacks to stay in their place.

During a scrap drive early in World War II, a teenage Harry Hughes and his father saw the plow, but did not know its significance. They loaded it in a pickup, hauled it to Corsicana, and delivered it to a scrap-iron dealer.

When they returned they were informed of the significance of their act. Several natives were very upset, but nothing could be done. This was the first Harry had heard of the burnings, but he learned all he could about the incident thereafter. He worked most of his adult life for the Dow Chemical Company and returned to Kirven after retiring. He lives there today.

The site of the burnings was never built on, and was partially cov-ered with scrub trees and weeds for many years. On the part not over-grown, a volleyball net was erected. The teenagers and children who play there are happily oblivious to the dark history lurking nearby.

In 1996, Happy King, the son of John T. King, purchased the lot where the burnings occurred and donated it to the Kirven Baptist Church in remembrance of his grandparents. In February 1996, the lot was cleared of underbrush.

Of the black victims, only the grave of Allie Gibson is marked. He and Leroy are buried in the black cemetery behind the Cotton Gin,

Texas Cemetery, probably side by side. Allie's headstone reads: "A. G. Gibson, 1898–1922, At Rest."

The town of Kirven declined further with the years. It lost its school to Wortham in 1949, even though the Shanks school was consolidated with Kirven's in 1941. The school and the brick buildings downtown were torn down and their bricks sold to construction contractors. Very few of the town's original buildings, or those which were there in 1922, still remain. The Methodist church, from which the two brothers witnessed the burnings, is one exception. The little shack occupied by Jenkins Carter is another.

Shanks vanished completely. Today there is only the cemetery and a historical marker.

Freestone County remained isolated, provincial, and suspicious of outsiders until the mid-1970s, when the national energy crisis delivered an economic boom. The Dow Chemical Company, Texas Utilities, Tenneco, Shell, Houston Lighting and Power, and others rushed in to buy and lease up rights to mine lignite. Several natives became fabulously wealthy. Hundreds of outsiders moved in. By the time the boom was over, in the late eighties, the complexion of the county was changed forever.

Fairfield, the county seat, missed by the railroad in 1906, was not missed by Interstate Highway 45. The big road has added considerably to the town's commerce. Teague, not missed by the railroad, was, however, bypassed by I-45. The town that once threatened to take the courthouse away from Fairfield declined as railroading yielded more and more to automobiles. Fairfield is currently the largest town in the county.

The events of 1922 are nearly forgotten in the county today, and it is too late to learn how extensively they haunted earlier generations, the people who lived them. We cannot know how many white people who moved away knew the extent of their own, or their neighbors', guilt, or how many learned the truth and trembled at the realization. We can only speculate about how many members of the mob lay awake at night, turning the details of their involvement over in their minds, rationalizing their actions, assuring themselves of the rightness of their deeds, or praying feverishly to God for forgiveness. There may have been none.

Only bits and snatches of the people's trauma surfaced during the research for this book. The youngest of the two brothers who witnessed the burnings explained that his family never talked about the incident "because it was too horrible, because it caught in your throat, and you couldn't speak of it." Lutisia Gibson and other black witnesses commented that it was not a subject they discussed, even among themselves. Doing so was simply too dangerous. Willie Mae Beaver commented in 1986 that "there are families in the county now who deny ever living in Kirven. They'll say they used to live across the county line, or in Wortham or Mexia, but they didn't. They lived in Kirven and moved out after the burnings."

The county history book, published in 1978, contains a year-by-year summary of major events, reprinted from the county's centennial celebration in 1951. The entry for 1922 begins succinctly with, "Freestone County has gained a notoriety deeply to be regretted," then says nothing more about the troubles of that year.[12]

As one native put it, "Freestone County will get over its past one of these days, but it will take a lot of dying."

This story is now complete, but its messages can never be. The insanity of racial hatred, or hatred of any kind, the necessity of equal protection and due process of law, the danger of mob mentality, and the unforeseen consequences of deception and cover-up all hang from this tale like fruit ripe for the picking.

Perhaps most enlightening, most chilling, is the message this story conveys about the difference one man can make, and how horror may follow one man's decision to abandon his convictions. We can never know what would have happened if Horace Mayo had refused to participate in the cover-up, and had insisted on retaining and prosecuting the Prowells and revealing the truth. We can imagine that he still would not have been re-elected sheriff, but we cannot know. Perhaps Kirven would not have died. Perhaps this story would not have lurked like a tumor beneath the skin of the county for seventy-five years; surely Horace Mayo would not have lived and died so miserably.

Black and white, the people of Freestone County are like Americans everywhere, resilient, proud, unwilling to quit. They had hard times and they moved beyond them. They produced offspring who prospered, who learned to communicate, and who adapted. Many have forgiven, more have forgotten. Fairfield, the county seat, elected a black mayor in 1990. The county is a pleasant place to live, a pleasant place to raise children, a warm, caring world.

Still, the events of 1922 are an underlying, defining moment in the county's, and the nation's, history. The elastic flame that lurked beneath the surface of Kirven and all of America that year is no longer there, but doubt, and pain, still seep from the scars caused by the flame. Surely, after so many years, there has been enough denial, anger, and sorrow. The time for completion of the grieving process has surely come. If feelings other than healing and recovery regarding our nation's racial past can still be found in some places — if the world of care is still cold for some citizens — it should be cold no longer.

16 Epilogue to the Revised Edition

Consisting of information acquired by or furnished to the author during the decade following the book's publication

I. Prologue to the Epilogue

It was March 6, 1999, a Saturday. *Flames after Midnight* had been published for less than a month, and I was attending the first—and as it turned out, only—book signing held in Freestone County, Texas.

The preceding three weeks had been eventful. The book was released in February, which was both Black History Month and the month the first defendant in the murder of James Byrd of Jasper, Texas, went on trial. That man's name, John King, and the possibility that he was related to the King family of Kirven caused me to hire both a professional genealogist and a publicist. It turned out that there was no genealogical connection between the two King families, but the irony remained fresh, and several exciting events were scheduled. A friend in Oregon had secured a review of the book by *USA Today* newspaper, and the publicist, Phenix and Phenix of Austin, had scheduled three television and two radio interviews, as well as a Barnes & Noble book signing, for the two weeks following the event on March 6.

The book signing in Teague, Freestone County, was not the result of efforts by the publicist but of the daughters of Lutisia Gibson Foreman and Foster Foreman,[1] who had witnessed the shootout and threatened race war that occurred in Simsboro, Texas, in June 1922. The Foreman daughters were relatives of two of the Kirven lynching victims, and I had agreed to donate all profits from the book signing to their parents' church in Simsboro.

The event was accompanied by newspaper coverage in Teague, Fairfield, and Mexia, television coverage from Waco, and a small amount of resistance. A man named Quinton Morrow, of Teague, had written a long letter to the editor of the Teague newspaper declaring that "Mr. Akers released his book in an effort to cause problems for us in Freestone County, and the Jasper case was the ideal time to release it. . . . The Kirvin incident happened seventy-seven years ago and there is no reason to open up old wounds of this county . . . We sure don't need an agitator to cause problems. . . . I can find no praise, only contempt for what he has tried to do to this county."[2] His wife, Betty, would later weigh in, declaring that "[t]he residents of this county DO NOT APPRECIATE this writer's 'opening a can of stinky worms' for his personal recognition and gain."[3]

However, the closing of Mr. Morrow's letter was so ironically perfect that in hindsight I'm surprised I was not accused of writing it myself. After suggesting I was denigrating the reputation of the county's citizens and denouncing my efforts to make money at their expense, he offered, for just one dollar per copy, to send interested persons "the truth of the matter," along with "one page of my remembrance of the Ku Klux Klan in the year 1926, before they became a radical group."[4]

In spite of, or perhaps because of, the controversy, the book signing was well attended. Most of the people who came were black citizens of the county, some of whom were relatives of the victims, particularly Johnny Cornish. It was held in the Teague Community Center, several hundred dollars were generated for the Simsboro church, and I was in the midst of signing a book when I looked up and found myself confronted by four very angry looking white people, two men and two women.

They were handsome, despite looks of outrage on their faces, and before I could say anything one of the ladies asked accusingly, "Did you write this book?"

"Yes," I replied.

"And where did you get your information?" she demanded.

"From witnesses and newspaper articles mostly," I replied.

"Did you talk to anyone in the King family?" she demanded.

"I was only able to locate one of them," I said, "and he declined to talk to me."

"Who was that?"

"Happy King."

"Oh, Happy wouldn't talk to you, but this man here," gesturing to the stout, gray-haired man at her side, "has something to say to you. This is Roland King, and he is the son of Otis King."

Mr. King immediately launched into what was probably a speech he'd been thinking about for hours.

"How would you like it if this sort of thing happened to your daughter, or sister, or niece, and then someone came along and wrote a book about it?" he demanded. "How would you like it if she was dragged out in the woods and raped and stabbed thirty times and had her throat slit and her tongue cut out and her head stomped into the ground and if they took an old stick and jabbed it up into her . . . into her . . . if they took a stick and jabbed it up into her . . ."

"Her vagina, Roland!" the woman told him. "You can say it. Her vagina!"

The large room was absolutely silent. The fifty or so people in attendance, most of them black, some related to people supposedly killed by relatives of these people, had gradually formed a large horseshoe around the new visitors. Racial, and several other kinds of tension, seemed to be simmering. Anything might happen.

Except all I could think of was how thrilled I was to finally be meeting some of the King family. I had read and wondered about these people for a dozen years. Except for the portrait of Eula and descriptions of the men as large and nice-looking, I had no idea of their appearances or anything else about them. Now they, or their descendants, were standing in front of me.

I stuck my hand out to Mr. King. "Sir, it is a real pleasure to meet you. I've wondered about you and your family for years. I am so pleased that you decided to come today."

That might not have been the response he had scripted for me. I think he also noticed that he was the center of attention of a rather large, possibly unsympathetic crowd. He hesitated, then shook my hand.

A few more words and explanations were exchanged, then the Gibson/Foreman daughters, who are all charming, college-educated community leaders, stepped forward and initiated a dialogue. I talked to Roland's wife, Clara, while Roland and one of the sisters, Ruth, who was confined to a wheelchair, moved to the side to talk.

Mrs. King proved to be a well-spoken, insightful woman. They had not had a chance to read the book, but had assumed it contained nothing complimentary about their family and considered it their duty to set the record straight.

As I was talking to her, a friend, David McCartney, observed the exchange between Mr. King and Ruth Sloan. We don't know what was said, but he reported that Mr. King stood over her at first, then leaned down, then sat in a chair next to her. Soon she reached out, making a point, and touched his hand with the back of hers. A moment later he reached out and touched her shoulder. A few moments later they hugged.

Mrs. King and the other family members were also talking to blacks in attendance, and by the time the Waco camera crew arrived, a remarkable mood had settled in. Mrs. King, standing next to two of the Gibson/Foreman sisters, told the camera that it was time to put the past behind, to make amends, and perhaps even to have an annual reunion of the descendants of the events of 1922. She proposed to mark the event by having the fence torn down that divides white and black graves at the Cotton Gin cemetery, where LeRoy and Allie Gibson are buried. I was actually witnessing the kind of healing and forgiveness described by Archbishop Desmond Tutu in the quote I had chosen as the epigraph of the book.

After the event, David McCartney and I decided to drive to the Shanks Cemetery to visit the graves of Eula and her relatives. We were pleasantly surprised when the four King family members arrived shortly after we did, and we had the chance to talk further. They told me things that made it obvious I had misinterpreted motivations of their father, uncles, and grandfather, as well as actions of Snap Curry. Mr. King pointed to the trees along Grindstone Creek where Eula was murdered, less than a mile away, and told me how his father had taken him there when he was a boy in the 1930s.

"There was a big rock almost buried over there," he said, "and he rolled it out and told me to look in the hole. 'That's where your Aunt Eula's head was stomped into the ground,' he told me. I looked into that hole, and then Daddy rolled the rock back in place."

The rock is bound to still be there.

That day was the first when truly significant new, or additional, information was provided to me about the events of 1922 in Kirven, Texas. More recently, in June 2008, perhaps the most shocking information of all came to light.

Some of that new information is difficult to read. In particular, the man who was the source of the latter information occupied such a pivotal role in the events of May 1922 that the details he provided exceed the degree of detail a historical researcher expects to uncover—and challenge civil discourse as well. The words of this last source, who was an active participant in the burnings, did not become public until after his death and after the University of Texas Press agreed to add this epilogue, and even then, the information reached me almost by accident.

What follows in Section II presents this new information in the chronological order of events in 1922, while Section III contains observations, explanations of how the information was obtained, corrections, fresh answers, and one final, personal irony.[5] Like all the information in the book, it is presented for its historical and human value—something that should be preserved and considered—but it is not offered necessarily as the truth. We are no closer to the truth about this tale, or even to defining exactly what is truth, than we were in 1999. Yet we have facts and purported facts—some of which contradict each other—from which we can each fashion our own version of the events of May 1922. Nor does the new information, I'm afraid, draw us any closer to extinction of racial prejudice or mob hysteria, both of which seem alive and well in this eleventh year of the twenty-first century. Still, as long as we can talk and write rationally about the problems, there is hope.[6]

II. New Information

The commonly accepted local explanation for the motives of the three black men who supposedly killed Eula Ausley—that they sought revenge for having been beaten and horribly mistreated by their white employers, the King brothers—was, understandably, never directly communicated to the King family. Accordingly, when confronted with that suggestion in 1999, Roland King, son of Otis King, replied immediately with the statement, "I never knew of my father or uncles to punish or mistreat their colored hired hands, but if they ever did, it would have been Snap Curry."

Mr. King's words were accurate in the sense that his father and uncles had been wrongly accused of cruel acts they did not commit, both before and after Eula's death, and in the sense that Snap Curry deserved some type of punishment.

Curry, Roland and his siblings were told, was a troublemaker, and worse. He was remembered as a hovering, malignant threat to the safety of the King family for reasons that were never abundantly clear. He was not a good worker, had a short temper, and seemed intent on wreaking revenge for something the Kings had done to him, either real or imagined. Even before Eula was killed, they were afraid that he intended to harm one of their womenfolk.[7] His reputation was no better in the black community, and Johnny Cornish's sister, Lovie, told younger relatives that Snap was "a mean man."[8]

In particular, the King family remembered an event that occurred less than a week before Eula was murdered. Rena King, wife of Otis, was washing clothes in a washtub in the yard when she became aware of a presence nearby. She turned and saw Snap Curry standing a few yards away, glaring menacingly at her. Otis was not home, a fact the King family later theorized was known by Curry.[9] Startled and terrified, Rena fled to the house, grabbed a gun, and ran back outside, but Curry was gone.[10]

Curry's reputation for trouble was illuminated further by the recollections of the relative of a white family who lived near the Curry cabin. Agnes Curry, Snap's wife, was the daughter of Stamp and Molly Lewis, who were longtime tenant farmers of a local landowner named David Nettle. Agnes was born on the Nettle farm, and the family lived on a section of Nettle land known as the Aycock Place. For many years Molly came to the Nettle home and did the family's washing, which, due to there being twelve Nettle children, was nearly a full-time job. Later, Agnes took over the washing job and either confided to the family or, by carrying the marks of his blows, informed them that Snap was physically abusive to her.[11]

There really was, then, reason for the "differences" between Snap and Agnes mentioned in various accounts as an explanation for Agnes's willingness to reveal her suspicions about her husband to white authorities after Eula's murder (p. 107). Although those revelations were described in various ways, including that they were in response to torture—and by J. C. Whatley as a gratuitous confession to his father—the most reliable account of how Agnes implicated Snap was provided by Otis King's wife, Rena King, who told her daughter-in-law, Clara King.

Agnes regularly helped Rena do the washing at Otis and Rena's house. She and Snap had a baby that Agnes brought with her to the King home, whom Otis and Rena's daughter, Oleta, looked forward to playing with each washing day. The day of Eula's murder, however, Agnes called the King home by telephone, probably not from her own house, asked for Otis's wife, and when she came on the phone told her with a mixture of relief and panic, "Miss Rena, get out of there [meaning the King house] 'cause Snap has gone and done something bad, real bad. He come home with blood all over him and he won't let me touch his clothes."[12]

It was Rena King's speculation that when Agnes saw the blood, she immediately feared that Snap had killed her, Rena, but when Rena answered the telephone, Agnes realized she was not the victim, and so told her to flee. Rena did, calling her brother-in-law, John T., to come get her.[13]

The phone call to Rena King was not the only outcry Agnes made. She also told her parents, Mollie and Stamp Lewis, who urged her to report to white authorities about the blood on Snap's clothes.[14] According to one newspaper account, her reward for providing the information, once it became known that she had reported her suspicions, was that she was arrested and put in jail.[15] It is possible, of course, that she was taken somewhere for her own safety.

There was another, and more telling reason for the differences between Snap and Agnes, however.

In 2002, the brother of Foreman Carter, Hobart Carter, was located in a retirement home in Wortham, Texas. He was either 103 or 106 years old—he was sure it was one of the two—but he recalled the excitement of 1922 in detail.

He claimed to have been Johnny Cornish's best friend.[16] Both young men had white fathers, for one thing, and Johnny was an interesting person to run with, for another. Johnny was light-complexioned and sometimes "passed" for white. He was quite popular with women, even white women. Hobart said that Cornish went out with white women to "prove" he was "not just a negro," and sometimes flaunted these socially illicit relationships publicly.[17] According to Mr. Carter, this was one of the reasons the members of the white mob were happy to burn him alive.

But Mr. Carter was certain that Johnny was innocent, and he even provided the young man with an alibi, saying they were together the evening that Eula was murdered.[18] When asked why, then, Snap Curry had been so insistent that he and Mose Jones were as guilty as Snap, and should be burned, Carter did not hesitate to answer, "Because Snap thought that Johnny had been having an affair with his wife."

A question was immediately posed in response—"Well, was he?" Mr. Carter paused only a second, nodded his head and said "I believe he was."[19]

According to the recollections of Terry King, grandson of Drew King, the feud that existed between the King and Prowell families (see Chapter 9) began after cattle belonging to the Prowells broke through a fence into a cotton field owned by Drew King and trampled a portion of the crop. After it happened, probably more than once, Drew informed the Prowells that if the cattle got out again, he was going to lock them up until the Prowells paid for the damage. Relations deteriorated thereafter until 1920, when Drew King and at least two of the Prowells—probably Tom and his brother Rob—had a knife fight at either a café or a honky-tonk in Kirven.[20]

Despite Dan Kelly's report that Drew was cut with knives and "maimed for life," his grandson recalled seeing no scars or disfigurement. In fact, the version he heard was that his grandfather was the one who did the cutting, using a can opener—probably a "church key."[21]

A term paper written for a 1967 college course reported that Eula was supposedly scheduled to come home late the night she was murdered—around 6 P.M.—due to having attended practice for performance in the Kirven school play, "in which she was one of the leading participants."[22] She also had at least one more reason to be particularly happy that new spring day. She was engaged to be married to a fiancé named Layton Smith.[23] Nor was Mr. Smith the only man who had romanced her. Walter Yerby, one of the white men later named in the newspapers as being involved in the shootout at Simsboro on June 2, 1922, was also a suitor.[24]

The three men who were burned for her murder all worked for her grandfather, John King, and for two of his sons, Drew and Otis.[25] The story preserved by the King family of how the men stopped Eula as she rode home told how Snap stepped into her path holding a piece of paper, saying it was a note from her grandfather. When she reached for it, Curry seized her wrist, as well as the reins of her horse, and the other two men then helped him pull her from the saddle.[26] Such information, if accurate, could only have come from Snap Curry when he confessed, and was then recounted to one or more of the King men.

Another story recalled by the Kings was that a neighbor who lived near the scene of Eula's murder heard her screaming and thought it was "some kid getting a whipping." This information was reported in the *Austin Statesman* newspaper on May 6, 1922, but was remembered by the King family with additional poignancy, due to speculation that had the neighbor stepped out on his porch and fired a gun, it might have scared the murderers away.[27]

It was nearly dark when Eula's grandfather sent word to Otis to search for her. He and others did, and found her horse grazing unattended about two and a half miles south of Kirven at about 9 P.M.[28] Drew King, rather than Doctor Whiteside, found her body.[29] "Her throat had been cut, her head was crushed, and there were more than twenty-seven stab wounds in her face and on the upper portion of her body."[30] Her head was said to have been "battered into a pulp," although one newspaper reported that it was indented into the ground only four inches instead of completely, as virtually all other accounts declared.[31] Dr. Terry King, grandson of Drew King, was told that the murderers used a large rock to crush Eula's head and that the rock remained at the murder scene for years afterward.[32] Perhaps it was the same rock that Otis King showed his son, Roland.

Eula's body was taken to her grandparents' home, where it was laid on a bed and covered with a sheet. Before she was taken to the funeral home in Teague, the other members of her family saw her, including her cousin Alma, who had decided at the last moment not to stay after school and ride home horseback behind her aunt.[33] She recalled, and told her double first cousin by marriage, Clara King, that she went into the room where Eula was lying and Mrs. King pulled back the sheet to allow her to look, and that the sight was horrible.[34]

When the massive manhunt began the next day, calls for bloodhounds were sent to Fort Worth as well as Huntsville, and Fort Worth Chief of Police Harry Hamilton, accompanied by dogs and a detective named Salsberg, left by automobile for Kirven about 2:20 P.M., but got there too late.[35] The dogs from Huntsville had already arrived by airplane and were on Curry's trail, but their primary contribution turned out to be that news of their arrival caused Snap to run, thereby convincing everyone of his guilt.

After Curry was captured by Richard Spence and Homer Miller, he was turned over to Wortham Chief of Police J. V. Lee and night watchman George H. Laird. They first incarcerated him in the Wortham jail, but when a mob gathered, they snuck him down an alley to the Wortham Bank and placed him in the vault, where he remained for about three hours.[36] During that time he at first denied his guilt and declared that he had heard Mose Jones and Johnny Cornish discussing plans for the assault and saying that they must "do it at once" because soon she would no longer be going to school and they would no longer have a chance to seize her on her way home.[37] He explained the blood on his clothes by saying it was from a chest wound he had incurred while trying to stop a runaway team. When it was pointed out that the wound on his chest was festering and did not look fresh, he claimed the blood could be attributed to a beef that he had helped slaughter the preceding Tuesday. (It was then Friday.) He was not believed.[38]

Sheriff Horace Mayo was en route to Marlin, Texas, to pick up a prisoner while these events were transpiring, but when he was informed of the circumstances by McLennan County Sheriff M. Burton, who heard them from a Wortham deputy and who tracked Mayo down in a Waco hotel, the Freestone County sheriff left immediately for Kirven, arriving around 11 P.M.[39]

Before Mayo got there, Curry was reported to have made a full confession, and the mob had grown in size and impatience. They were threatening to storm the bank, so Mayo snuck his prisoner out a window and, accompanied by night watchman Laird, made a run in his Nash coupe for Mexia. The alarm was sounded almost immediately and several cars "loaded with armed men started in pursuit."[40]

Officer Laird had wrapped a chain around Curry's neck and the other end around his left arm. He was sitting in the front seat next to the passenger side door with the prisoner between him and the sheriff. Pursuers were close behind when Mayo drove around a sharp curve in the road "at break-neck speed."[41] The appellation was particularly well-chosen, because Laird's door flew open and he was thrown out and injured. He apparently managed to let go of the chain, or at least the newspaper failed to report any injury to Curry.[42]

Mayo stopped his car and, with Curry in tow, jumped out and disappeared into a cotton patch and the darkness. Those following must have either stopped and spread out or kept going, because Mayo managed to sneak back to his car after a few moments, start it up, and take off again, this time for Fairfield.[43]

The next day, by which time all three men had been burned, Mayo gave a statement to a reporter about how the mob took the prisoners from the jail, saying:

> I had arrived here with the Negro arrested at Wortham about forty minutes before the mob appeared. The men battered down the outer door of the jail, leading into my office. They then overpowered me, took my keys and went inside the jail proper and secured all three of the Negroes. There were several prisoners in the jail at the time but none of them were molested.[44]

His statement is at odds with the recollection of his oldest daughter, who said that when the mob took the prisoners she and her sisters and mother "did not hear a thing. . . . It was just as silent as could be, and we didn't, we were right there and we couldn't hear them coming down the stairs, even. They didn't make any noise or anything."[45]

Several hours before the men were taken from the jail, a core group of men had been selected, or had volunteered, to perform the real work—the heavy lifting—of burning the three black prisoners alive. There were nine of them: eight adult males and one fourteen-year-old boy. Two men led the group, one being, in all likelihood, Layton Smith, Eula's fiancé.[46] The other leader, described by one of the nine as a "born leader, somebody people listened to," and "like if John F. Kennedy was from country Texas," was reported to be none other than the oldest Prowell son, Claude.[47]

These nine individuals each had a particular role to play. The fourteen-year-old, whose name was John Ousterhous, and a twenty-year-old man, called "Mack" for the purposes of this epilogue,[48] worked together on a pig farm and possessed expertise at castrating. Mack, who lived to be 104, described himself as "keen with a knife." He was also anxious to prove his skill and show that he was man enough to perform his assigned task.[49] None of the nine were members of the King family.

Mack had been up since 4 A.M. that morning and was waiting in the vacant lot in Kirven for the mob to return with the prisoners. He was so tired that he dozed off several times while waiting.[50]

During the ride to Kirven, Curry provided more details to his confession, knowing he did not have long to live. He said that Cornish, Jones, and he had planned in advance and intended to murder another white girl whose name was not released. He said he met the other two men in a ravine and that Eula, knowing all three as men who worked for her uncle, stopped without hesitation. He claimed that he held the horse while Cornish and Jones dragged her from her saddle, saying that "the girl was so strong we had trouble in getting her off. Miss King screamed a number of times while she was being carried into the woods." He said the other two men "criminally assaulted her" while he watched, after which they stabbed her numerous times with a pocket knife, and finally beat her savagely with a large club.[51]

Through a failure of communication, half of the caravan of automobiles drove from Fairfield to the scene of the murder, believing the lynching would take place there. The other half went to Kirven. Word was sent to the others, and soon all were gathered in the vacant lot in the little town.[52]

One of the numerous families of newcomers to Kirven was the Cotton family. The father was an oil field worker who followed the march of new wells. He had a wife and three sons aged thirteen, eleven, and eight.[53]

The oldest, Reuben, and the youngest, Grady, were either awakened by the excitement or were already up when the crowd arrived, and they went to see what was happening.[54] Eighty years later, Grady could not recall what became of his older brother during the lynching and said that he did not know whether Reuben left or stayed. Another thing he did not know was that Reuben was a friend of John Osterhous, who was a year older and, like Reuben and Grady, was the son of an oil rig worker who had just recently moved to Kirven.

Accordingly, while Reuben probably did not perform any of the hands-on work of the core group of the mob, he joined Osterhous and witnessed what happened from up close. Considering that Osterhous, like Mack, was apparently assigned the job of waiting in the vacant lot in order to perform the castrations, it is quite possible that Reuben and Grady were present because Osterhous gave Reuben advance information about what was going to happen.

Grady reported that the three black men were lined up against a wall by the King brothers, who "went down the line and stabbed each one, saying 'how does that feel?' and 'how do you like it?' He did not witness this event, however, and arrived just as the cordwood was being stacked around Snap Curry, who was sitting on the seat of the plow.[55] What he was about to witness would stick with him for the rest of his life, remembered as the worst thing he ever saw, something which would permanently affect at least one of his perspectives of man's proper place and role in the world.

The "down the line" stabbing incident that Grady reported did not occur in the way he heard, and was not performed by any of the King men. What did happen was that Curry and Cornish were castrated by Mack and that young John Osterhous attempted to castrate Mose Jones, but succeeded only in cutting partially through the black man's penis before he gagged and had to stop. In addition, Snap Curry was cut across the chest, probably by Mack, so that his pectoral muscles were severed, and Johnny Cornish was cut "in his pretty face."[56] Mack compared the castrations to those he performed regularly on pigs, saying that kind of work "wasn't that much different from doing a nigger, especially a bad nigger."[57] What he did to Cornish and Curry was actually quite different than what he normally did to pigs, however, because he cut away all of the two men's genitalia.[58]

According to family memory, not only did the King brothers not help torture the three men, they were not even present; all five brothers stayed at home to protect their families. Rumors were running rampant that the "other King women were gonna get the same."[59] Eula's brother, Dowell Ausley, visited the scene in Kirven for a while, but left shortly after the three men "were secured" and before they were burned.[60] Newspaper and King family accounts both reported that Grandfather King was present, and Otis King was photographed kneeling in front of the funeral pyre after the men were burned but before it was doused again with gasoline in order to burn everything to ash, but none of the Kings performed the grisly deeds with which they would later be accused.

In fact, their absence was so noticeable that it was remarked on and resented somewhat by the nine men doing the work, who thought they should be helping, or "at least lending moral support."[61] These men believed they were acting on behalf of the King family, honoring them with their good efforts, and felt like they should be there to witness the retribution. That the King men were, for the most part, absent and yet were credited or blamed for the next seventy-five years as having been the primary perpetrators of the burnings adds one more injustice to this tale of great injustices.[62]

All three men were "screaming like little boys" as they were being mutilated.[63] The worst spectacle was provided by Mose Jones, who "cried like a baby," kept repeating "Why are you doing this?," and could barely endure the agony of having his member partially severed.[64] John Osterhous, embarrassed at having botched his assigned task, was given some whiskey to drink. He remained for the rest of the torture and murder, although neither he nor anyone else attempted any further mutilation of Jones.[65]

This young man, who was destined to die a soldier in 1943,[66] was memorable for another reason. Despite being blue-eyed and blond-haired and appearing younger than his fourteen years, with no hint of facial hair, he was described by Mack as bearing "an uncanny resemblance to a younger Johnny Cornish."[67]

Despite what had been done to him, Snap Curry remained defiant and malicious. Mack reported that he "had an evil glint" in his eye and that he began to brag about what he, Cornish, and Jones had done to "that little white bitch."[68] He provided grisly details about Eula's murder and the acts the three performed on her before they killed her, leaving no doubt in the mob members' minds of the guilt of all three. Mack said that Curry "never shut up until he was dead."[69]

Grady was only fifty feet from Curry once the man was seated on the plow seat. It appeared to Grady that Curry was not tied, or at least Grady could not see a rope. He said the crowd was large, but estimated it at only seventy-five to one hundred people. Of those, and consistent with Mack's account, Grady observed that only a few men were doing the real work, hauling and stacking wood, pouring kerosene, and asking questions. One, a forty-year-old, "was in charge of getting the fire going."[70] The rest of the crowd, like Grady, stood and watched quietly.[71]

An elderly man, possibly John King, Sr., possibly Tom Prowell, asked Curry if he realized he was going to be burned to death. Curry reportedly replied, "Go ahead and burn me. I am not afraid. Only burn those other two niggers. They are just as guilty as I am."[72] Curry may have felt grim satisfaction at the payback he was delivering to Cornish for cuckolding him. We can only wonder if Cornish realized the real reason he was about to die.

Even though none of them may have been present, the King family preserved and passed down the recollection that Curry was unrepentant to the end, saying that nothing the mob could do to him would hurt him as much as he and his companions had hurt Eula.[73] Grady, who said the wood was stacked on all sides of Curry to a level even with the seat, did not hear any such comments from Curry, whom he said did not scream or cry out, but only "sang a little song." Kerosene was poured and a match was applied.

The flames engulfed the doomed man, covering him entirely for a few seconds, then subsided enough to reveal that he still sat erect on the plow seat.[74] A member of the mob called out "Burn! That's the way you made her suffer!"[75]

Grady stated that he could see Curry clearly, and that as the flames did their damage he witnessed a horrible and macabre detail of the affair. Curry's scalp split, he said, and the skin of his head and face fell away and onto his shoulders, "like a woman's hair," revealing a white upright skull.[76]

It was more than Grady could stomach. He went home immediately, before either of the other two men were killed. Thereafter he was unable to eat anything for two or three days. Although the event was not spoken of later, it remained a vivid memory, and in later years he was unable to kill any sort of animal—even insects—due to the impact the scene had upon him. When asked eighty years later what the message of the event would be if he could convey it to the world, he said, "Don't even watch nothing like that. Don't. I wouldn't see another one like that if they paid me."

Cornish's and Jones's denials of guilt, of course, fell on deaf, unsympathetic ears, and the core group of the mob selected the next victim, Cornish.[77] In addition to being too pretty and light-complexioned for the comfort of local white men, Cornish made it easier to be hated by making a statement about the "private parts of white girls" that was "so disgusting I can't repeat it" according to Mack, who still would not do so eighty years later. He would say only that what Cornish said "just made us mad."[78] This is consistent with the account offered by Foreman Carter, who reported that Johnny's "nasty mouth" was one of the reasons he was put on the fire.[79]

Mack also claimed that it was not Curry, but Cornish, who sang a song, and that it was not "O Lord, I Am Coming," but "that Cohan ditty" popular during World War One, possibly "Over There."[80] Johnny Cornish was apparently a very cool, nervy victim.

A reporter for the *Corsicana Daily Sun* was either present or had access to witnesses who spoke to no other newspaper, as his article contained more gruesome detail than did other papers.[81] He wrote of Cornish that "[a]s a fish flops when it hits dry land, his body writhed and flopped from the fire. Again into the blazing pyre he was thrown and again he escaped."[82] Finally, the newspaper reported, one of the mob struck him in the head and threw him again atop the blazing mass where he died, still protesting his innocence.[83] This detail is described incorrectly in the first edition of *Flames* as the act of Otis King striking Mose Jones with a radius rod and knocking out one of his eyes (pp. 66–67). What actually occurred, Mack reported, was that Cornish was struck not by Otis King but by Claude Prowell, and not with a radius rod but with an ax handle. As for the effect of the blow, Mack observed that it left Cornish's eye "just dangling, like Jones's cock."[84]

The Corsicana paper supported the *Fort Worth Star-Telegram*'s account by reporting that Jones was the next, and last, to die. It also stated that he suffered the most.[85]

By now the crowd apparently wanted to drag the affair out in order to make certain its lessons were being seen and appreciated. Jones was first held over the fire, probably with ropes soaked in water, and then the crowd was asked to stand back so that the women and children present could see. A horseshoe-like opening was made, and several women and children gazed at the horrible scene. Jones was thrown on the fire, but, like Cornish, he rolled off and was thrown on again. This was repeated five times, during which "there were no murmurs of pity, only those of antipathy."[86]

Finally he was unable to crawl out of the fire: "[T]he flesh of his legs, his waist and hips a charred mass, [he was] still conscious and declaring he knew nothing of the affair for which he was dying. Losing control of the lower part of his body, the Negro used his hands to wipe the sweat from his blistered face and to tear away the collar of his shirt that had caught fire. In this condition he was asked if he was guilty, and in a voice choked with flame, denied the guilt."[87] Mack reported that both Cornish and Jones were naked when they were burned, and that the flesh melted from their bodies like wax from candles.[88]

Someone tired of the gruesome spectacle and threw gasoline on the fire. The flames leaped high and at 6:45 A.M., Jones emitted one last moan and "fell chest down in the pit of fire and released his life to avenge another."[89] This collapse may have been interpreted by some as the act of clasping the plow and inhaling flames in order to die quickly, an act attributed in the first edition of this book to Cornish.

As the flames died down, a photographer from Buie Photography Studio in Mexia arrived. He took at least eight photos and sold them as postcards, including two from opposite sides of the plow while it was nearly covered with charred wood, ashes, and bones, as well as an unburned hand or foot with a rope wrapped around the wrist or ankle; one of Otis King, Dog Sergeant Simmons, and the two Huntsville bloodhounds squatting in front of the pyre; one of a group of men holding something aloft said to be the heart or liver of one of the victims; and one taken after the fire had been renewed and burned down to ash, which serves as the cover photo for this book.

One of the original postcards, labeled with printing in the same hand as that on the cover photo, sold on eBay in 2002 for more than $500.00. It depicted the plow, covered with partially burned wood and ashes, including what appears to be a leg bone and a gallon can that probably carried gasoline. It was inscribed "The Mouldering [sic] Fire of Snap Curry, John Cornish, Mose Jones, Murders [sic] of High School Girl Kirven, Texas."[90]

These were not the only photographs taken. During the burnings a member of the crowd of watchers took pictures, probably with a Brownie dollar box camera, which was introduced in 1900 and was commonly accessible. However, either at the suggestion of other members of the crowd, from a personal feeling of guilt, or in response to a threat, the amateur cameraman threw the camera into the fire and let it burn to make certain that none of the photos would lead to prosecution of members of the mob.[91]

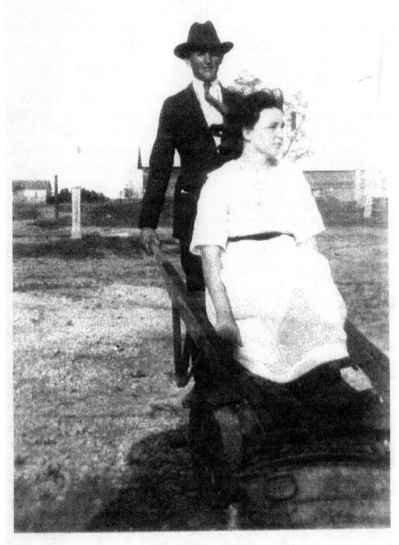

Eula Ausley- Layton Smith

*Eula Ausley and her fiancé, Layton Smith, a few weeks before
her murder. Pushing the bride in a wheelbarrow is an old
wedding custom. Smith probably served as one of the two
organizers of the eight men and one boy who carried out the
mutilation and burning of the three men accused of Eula's
murder on May 6, 1922.*

Front Row: Otis - John - John T. King   1922.
Back Row: Dow Ausley - Drew - Alva - Bobby King

*The King men in 1922. Seated, left to right, Otis King, John
King, John T. King; standing, left to right, Dowell Ausley,
Drew King, Alva King, and Robert King. Shortly after Eula's
murder, Mrs. King realized that the family did not have a
formal portrait of her and, fearing the loss of other loved ones,
convinced the men to pose for this photo.*

Otis King, right, Dog Sergeant S. O. Simmons, and the two bloodhounds flown in from Huntsville in front of the plow and pyre where Johnny Cornish, Mose Jones, and Snap Curry were burned alive a short time before this photo was taken. Despite his posing at the scene and community recollections of responsibility for the lynchings, Otis King was not present when the three men were killed. Note that they and other members of the crowd have donned their "Sunday best" for the event.

The plow and pyre where Curry, Cornish, and Jones were burned alive. A blackened arm or leg, with a rope wrapped around it, can be seen protruding from the right corner of the pile.

After Eula's murder, when the King family had a portrait made from the photo of Eula and Layton Smith, they took the opportunity to have a portrait of Eula's mother, Eunice, made from a snapshot the family owned.

Mrs. John (Permelia Alma or "Eubeza") King, with Otis, left, and Alva, in 1902.

After the crowd dispersed, young Grady Cotton decided to go look at the scene again. He found an elderly black man, nearly alone, raking coals and muttering to himself. The man said he had the heart of one of the three men and wanted to see it burn and to "kill it." Cotton speculated that the gentleman was upset that a member of his race had committed such a heinous crime, and rather than resent the treatment meted out to them, wanted to make certain the job was completed.[92]

This gentleman was the only black person Grady saw at the scene, but three others were reported to be in attendance during the burnings, including Johnny's uncle, Tom Cornish.[93] The *Fort Worth Star-Telegram* reported that when Johnny was thrown on the fire, Tom, overcome with emotion, began to cry and curse aloud and had to be restrained by his two friends from attempting to aid his relative.[94] This report sounds similar to the account provided by Foreman Carter of Johnny's actions just before he was killed, but whether Tom was alone in cursing the white men's actions or he was emulating his nephew, it may have had the same result. Tom was, according to Mack, lynched and killed the following Monday.[95] Mack also stated that Tom Cornish, with whom he had worked doing farm and "tree work," was normally better behaved than Johnny, and it was "a shame that he too got killed."[96]

Shadrick Green, who was lynched the day after the burnings, became a victim merely because he had skinned a rabbit. His son, Roy Green, was six when his father left that morning, and eighty-four years later he still recalled the incident, saying, "I will never forget. My father left that Saturday morning to go hunting and by Sunday we heard he was dead."[97] The rabbit had been fed to Shadrick's dogs, but when a group of white men came along and found the black man in the woods with blood on his pants and shoes, they needed no further proof of his involvement in the murder of Eula. They killed him where they found him, then took his body to the Kirven-Fairfield road and hanged it from a tree.[98]

How many other black men were killed during the subsequent reign of terror will never be known, but Walter Hayes, who was the sheriff of nearby Navarro County in 1922, was interviewed in 1966 and was not hesitant to confirm that there were many more than the three burning victims and Green.

> Hell yes! There was at least twenty—had to be that many—could've been more. No way of knowing how

many. Damn sure more than four. You see, a bunch
of niggers got together and signed an agreement not
to work for whites. After the burnings at Kirven this
memorandum was found and ever' last one of them
was hunted down and hung. Seems to me there was
fourteen or fifteen on that list. I know they was that
many besides the four. Racial hatred was so intense
after that girl's murder that that memorandum was
sufficient reason to kill a few niggers.[99]

Other witnesses claimed that forty or fifty men were murdered, and
Mrs. Anna Chambers, a black woman who lived in Kirven at the time,
said that many black people simply disappeared. People were afraid to
stay for fear of being hanged, but also were afraid that by leaving they
would appear to be guilty of something. She recalled that one man
she knew hid his wife and two children in a creek bottom for several
days, believing it was their only chance for survival.[100] In another case,
David O. Nettle, who was white, literally boarded up the house of his
friends and neighbors Stamp and Molly Lewis, the parents of Agnes
Curry, with the couple inside in order to keep their relationship with
Snap from leading to their injury or death. The Nettles were a well-
respected family. Their ancestors helped settle Freestone County in
the 1830s, and Mr. Nettle let it be known that no harm should come to
them. None did.[101]

Sheriff Hayes's story about the "memorandum" signed by black men
provides a new rationale for the reign of terror, but no other authority
mentions its existence. A memorandum that *is* documented was signed
by 103 local black men in May 1922. It declared that "the law-abiding
Negro citizens of Kirven . . . are in perfect harmony with the good
white people of this place," and "[w]e stand ready to assist our good
white people in any undertaking to bring about peace and harmony at
home."[102]

As matters began to settle, Eula's grandmother, Permelia "Eubeza"
King, found a new cause for concern. The family possessed no formal
portrait of the murdered girl, nothing they could gaze at to remember her. Furthermore, considering all the violence and killing that
was going on, it seemed likely that another loved one might be lost.
She decided, therefore, that the menfolk of the family should have a
formal portrait made, which was done before the year ended, quite
possibly at Buie's in Mexia. It depicts Grandfather King seated in the
center, flanked by Otis on his right and John T. on his left, with Dow-

ell Ausley, Drew, Alva, and Bob King lined up left to right standing behind them.[103]

Furthermore, the family possessed a snapshot of Eula sitting in a wheelbarrow being pushed by her fiancé, Layton Smith—an old wedding tradition. This they took to a photographer to have cropped, retouched, enlarged, and framed to become the "cheap enlargement of his granddaughter's picture at which he (Grandfather King) worshipped like a shrine" observed by Dan Kelly when he last visited the old man. While she was at it, Mrs. King decided it was time to have a portrait of Eula's mother, Eunice, to hang in the house. They had one unflattering photo, or a portion of one, made sometime before Eunice gave birth to Eula, and the photographer was directed to prepare a portrait in the same manner that he did for Eula's, of the same size and in a similar frame.[104]

Floyd Gibson, the brave World War One veteran who took a rifle and single-handedly brought an end to the reign of terror, fled to Seattle, Washington, after he shot and killed at least two members of the gang that killed his brother and nephew (pp. 126–127). That he and Claude Prowell should flee to the same state is ironic, but unlike Claude, who found a wife there and returned to Texas, Floyd remained for the rest of his life. A man related to Johnny Cornish, who asked not to be named, provided this information at the Teague book signing on March 6, 1999, and added a startling piece of information. The reason he was able to escape was because, the man said, he was aided by a white family—the Kings.

This may seem unlikely, but it is possible. Floyd's father, Ben, was a loyal hired hand of the King family, credited by some with finding Eula's horse the day of her murder. Grandfather King may have seen events play out the way he most feared, with innocent blacks being killed, and arranged to help smuggle Floyd away from the region out of friendship for Ben and because he understood that Floyd had bravely acted to defend himself and his family. Perhaps saving him was some small retribution for not saving Cornish or Jones.

Added to this little mystery is the ever-dubious testimony of J. C. Whatley, who claimed that his father was responsible for helping Floyd escape.[105] Given that Whatley also claimed that his father was the man who implicated Snap Curry; that he placed himself with Dr. Whiteside in finding Eula's body; and that he maintained he was safely in the drug store serving cold drinks while the burnings were taking place, his statement that his father was a hero by helping the heroic Floyd escape is unlikely to the point of insult.

Still, the story and its King/Whatley associations make it worthy of consideration for what it suggests as much as for its possible veracity. If members of the local black community believed that the Kings helped Floyd escape, it reveals that, in at least some areas, the family was remembered as helpful or heroic rather than murderous. By claiming credit for his family for Floyd's escape, J.C. also acknowledged that assisting Floyd Gibson's getaway was considered to be a heroic act. In 1922, many residents of Freestone County surely considered Floyd Gibson a killer who should be brought to justice, but over the years Whatley may have heard enough praise for whoever assisted his escape that he added the event to his collection of spurious claims.

Family members of Otis King who were old enough to remember the events of 1922 and who were still living in 1999, as well as those who came later, harbored no doubts about the guilt of the three black men who were burned.[106] The grandson of another King brother, Drew, who now practices medicine in Louisiana, took the initiative and contacted me in 2003. His grandfather had been a major participant in the events, and although he was not born until 1938, he had heard stories of the Kirven lynchings as he was growing up. He was appreciative to learn more details about the event and contributed the information he had heard.[107]

The King family may have been unfairly maligned over the decades if they did not actually participate in the burnings on May 6, 1922. Perhaps they did, as the newspapers reported, participate in subsequent killings, or at least in the shootout in Simsboro. In any event, Otis's reputation suffered unnecessarily in *Flames after Midnight*, in which I suggested that he fell on hard times after moving to Houston and becoming a police officer.[108] In fact, Otis became the Chief of Police of Pasadena, a large city that borders Houston.[109]

However, if King family members still considered the Prowells to be guiltless, the feeling was not shared throughout Freestone County. The same gentleman whose parents lived close to Snap and Agnes Curry in 1922, and who testified to Snap's mistreatment of his wife, recalled that as a boy growing up in the area he heard men sitting around the general store in Streetman speculating about whether the "Powell" family actually murdered Eula.[110]

Another former resident of the county, now living in Denver, was the grandson of Sheriff Mayo's deputy, Luke Marberry. He had been a law officer for ten years and an investigator for the Texas Alcoholic Beverage Commission. He wrote, after reading the book, to share his thoughts about who was guilty and who was not. After saying that he knew about putting criminal cases together, he wrote, "Well, to make a long story short, I come to the same conclusion of the book: there is a botched investigation, little if no evidence, several avenues of material issues revealing other suspects with motive to kill were not followed up. All of this in addition to mob control and overpowering the jail, and the killing-burning without even a trial. A TERRIBLE TIME IN HISTORY . . ."[111]

Indeed it was.

III. Corrections, Reactions, and Answers

Many readers of *Flames* praised it; a few condemned it; and a few offered corrections. One of the latter wrote to point out, correctly, that the members of the lynch mob would not have been armed with Springfield "303s" as is mentioned on page 50, but .30–30s, and that the 369th United States Infantry was not a division, as mentioned on page 151, but a regiment. A relative of the Cornish family pointed out that the "Uncle Charley" who first told Nettie Cornish of the death of Johnny was not merely a friend, as stated on page 71, but was actually an uncle named Charlie Cornish.[112] Occasionally some inaccurate information came in, such as a report that Howard "Buck" Kester, a social reformer of the period, also investigated the Kirven lynchings on behalf of the NAACP. Kester certainly performed that Dan Kelly-esque job on other lynchings, but when the Kirven incidents took place he was only seventeen years of age, attending Lynchburg College and serving as a student pastor in Grassy Meadows, West Virginia.[113]

Some readers simply expressed appreciation or compliments for the work and admired the "nerve" it took to produce the book. Many who did so had a connection with the story, and some asked if I knew anything about the involvement of a particular ancestor or relative. Two of my favorite responses came, respectively, from far away and from near Kirven.

The former was from a professional musician friend in Oregon who e-mailed after learning what occurred at the Teague book signing and the brief instance of reconciliation that occurred between the descendants of lynching victims and the King family. He said he had been sitting quietly, watching the sun rise and "re-reading the story over and over again." He conveyed emotional observations and concluded by saying:

But the real essence of the story, the real "grabber" is
how you gently point out that all this hate and violence, death and destruction of lives, is a part of all of
us. Born into us as a species. It's called human nature,
and it is happening all over the world, right now! It
happened in Germany during the war, it happened in
Vietnam and Cambodia, in South Africa and India.
It is happening in the Middle East, and in Ethiopia,
Rhodesia, Uganda, Central America, literally everywhere. Everywhere, except one small corner of Texas,
where for one very short afternoon a small group of
people rose above their hate and prejudice, and made
the conscious decision to defy human nature.[114]

The second was contained in a book review for the *Mexia Daily
News*, in which the reviewer began by saying,

"Damn" is the only thing I can say after reading
Flames after Midnight by Monte Akers, a study of the
May 4, 1922, burning of three black men by a mob for
the murder of a white girl. The little book will anger
some folks or at least embarrass them that such a hor-
rid happening could occur in nearby Kirven. Certainly no son or grandson should be judged by what
their father or grandfather did seventy-seven years
ago. Anyone who was directly involved is dead, but
Akers has been severely criticized for his efforts. Why
should he want to "dig around in something that happened so long ago?" It happened in Kirven many years
ago, but it happened in Jasper only a few months ago.
Maybe our collective souls need an occasional shaking
so such tragedies will never happen again.[115]

Some readers offered new information that, while possible, had the
ring of baseless rumor, such as a claim that Sheriff Mayo not only did
not resist the mob at the Fairfield jail, but that he gave its members a
peculiar, secret signal to let them know when it was safe to take the
prisoners. Another claim was that the three men were tied with ropes
behind three of the lynch mob's automobiles and were forced to run
the approximate twelve miles to Kirven before being burned.

Occasionally a person came forward claiming special, dubious
knowledge, such as a man who attended the Teague book signing,

identified himself as a cousin of Johnny Cornish, and asked, "Have you ever seen the fingers and tongues?" Receiving a baffled response, he explained that the lynch mob had cut off the fingers of the burning victims, so that they would not be able to untie the ropes with which they were bound, and had cut out their tongues, so that they could not scream. These appendages, he stated, were preserved in a jar of alcohol and were displayed in a store in Kirven for many years.

And what of the half-dozen questions posed in the chapter entitled "Burning Questions"? Have any answers come forth or become more likely? Yes.

The first question posed concerned the extent of Snap Curry's guilt and involvement, and essentially nothing has been discovered in nearly ten years to exonerate him. To the contrary, new evidence of his personality and actions depicts a man who was cruel to his wife and a threat to his employers well before May 4, 1922. The general conclusions of the chapter seem inescapable: that he played a role in the crime, particularly that he was hired by the Prowells to stop Eula's horse, and that he thereafter participated in her murder to a degree sufficient to spot his clothes and shoes with blood.

The particularly baffling question of why he implicated Mose Jones and Johnny Cornish was answered by Hobart Carter. He believed, probably correctly, that Cornish was having or had had sexual relations with Agnes Curry. Curry first blamed the crime on Cornish and Jones while being held in Wortham, before admitting to his own involvement. Thereafter, he stuck with the story of their guilt, and while being burned alive was certainly unplanned and unfortunate, being able to use the situation to get Johnny burned as well was, to him at least, priceless.

This does not, however, shed any light on why Mose Jones was implicated. Perhaps he had earned Curry's antipathy for reasons unknown, or perhaps Curry, believing he needed to account for and describe the acts of three murderers, chose Jones out of convenience. We may never know.

Yet, if Cornish and Jones were innocent and Curry helped the Prowells murder Eula, and if Claude Prowell was the leader of the men who castrated and burned Curry, why would Curry protect the Prowells to the very end? It defies logic, which is nothing new in regard to this tale. A possible explanation is that Curry was bound to the Prowells by a mutual hatred of the Kings, and that hurting them and simultaneously getting even with Johnny Cornish provided Curry with salvageable victories more important than implicating Claude, Audey, and possibly Tom Prowell.

If this Machiavellian set of motivations was present, one can only marvel at the audacity and cunning of Claude Prowell as it all transpired.

The question of why, if Grandfather King believed the Prowells were guilty and the black men innocent, his sons not only believed the black men were guilty but allegedly acted as leaders in the burnings and subsequent reign of terror has also been explained. After Roland and Clara King had the opportunity to return to their home in Grapeland, read the book, and discuss its contents, Mrs. King explained that Grandfather King had, indeed, decided the Prowells were guilty. He was the only one in the family who believed that, however, because the Prowells told the younger Kings something that resonated with their code of Southern honor in the time and place of its telling. When the Kings confronted the Prowells after Eula's murder, probably on the day of the burnings, the Prowells told them and Sheriff Mayo that their [the Prowells'] footprints were present near the scene of Eula's murder because they were operating a moonshine still nearby. More importantly, they told the King brothers that if they wanted to make war on them, they would have gone after the King men, never the King women.

To those who endorsed the chauvinistic, patronizing Southern honor code of 1922, this announcement may have sounded credible. Certainly the King brothers wanted to believe Snap Curry was guilty, and afterwards they had no desire to acknowledge that innocents had been burned alive. Their rage was still not spent, but they were not the kind of men who would suddenly declare, "Oops, the wrong guys were burned alive." They wanted to hear, and believe, that the Prowells were innocent and, like the Kings, honorable. To prove how much they believed in that honor, as well as the correctness of their actions, they apparently helped kill at least two more black men in Simsboro. If the guilt of the Prowells and the testimony of Mack are also to be believed, then Claude Prowell wrapped it all up in a neat package by becoming the self-appointed leader of the lynch mob.

The questions about Horace Mayo's role in the matter are more settled, and consistently so. He was, by all counts, a tragic hero and a tragic villain. Mack described him as "a lovable fool."[116] The new revelations concerning his attempt to save Snap Curry from the lynch mob by making an abortive run from Wortham toward Mexia elevate his character to a higher plane than the one he occupied earlier, even when it was known that he opposed the Ku Klux Klan, attempted to

save the three black men from the mob, and made a risky effort to rescue lynch victim George Gay (pp. 146–147). Yet it remains painfully
obvious that after telling the Prowells to leave the county and not come
back, he chose to join the cover-up, probably in the hope that doing so
would get him re-elected. His subsequent reaction—to defeat and to
the proddings of his own conscience—was not faith or resilience, but
alcoholism and a downward spiral to suicide.

And what of Thelma (see pages 94–97)?

Despite my confident boast that I would find her, I have not. The
most likely candidate continues to be Annie T. Gibson Prowell, wife
of Tom Prowell, mother of Claude and Audey Prowell. She was born
in 1876 or 1877, in or near Monroe, Walker County, Georgia, before
birth certificates were required by law, and she apparently never had
cause to file for a delayed certificate. Her parents were named John and
Sallie Gibson, and the family is shown as having a younger child, Mat-
tie, who was ten months old when Annie was three. By 1900 she was
twenty-three and living in Freestone County, married to Tom Prowell, and was the mother of children Claude, Annie R., and Joseph. I
was unable to locate her and Tom's marriage license in the Freestone
County records now on file at Sam Houston State University.

She was very consistent in completing various census reports, her
childrens' birth certificates, and other records with only her first name
and middle initial. This habit makes it seem unlikely that she would
have been so well known as "Thelma," instead of Annie, that Bertha
Williams would call her that seventy-four years later. She was probably
illiterate, however, and may have called herself Thelma but was in the
habit of reciting her first name for official purposes. It is worth noting
that a black woman in 1922 was unlikely to have been on a first-name
basis with an adult white woman and would have been more likely to
call her "Miss Thelma." It is even possible that Thelma was a servant
or employee of the Prowells.

In the end, however, the wife of Tom Prowell is the best candidate for the identity. Learning she was named Annie Thelma would
close one small loophole, but would prove only that Bertha Williams
believed the Prowells were the killers and that Tom, the father, was
involved. Learning that her middle name was something else would
simply muddy the murky waters a little more.

Reactions to the book among reviewers and scholars
surpassed my expectations, and reactions in Freestone County were
not as negative as I feared they might be.

Numerous newspapers and periodicals, mostly in Texas but from a few other areas as well, reviewed the book, and all contained favorable, supportive comments. Some were dramatic, such as the review printed in *Southern Art & Soul* magazine, based in Mississippi, which concluded with:

> If you sleep peacefully, you will not after *Flames after Midnight*. If you think your friends and neighbors are understanding people who will deal heroically with misfortune, this book will change your mind. If you want to know why some Americans distrust and shy from our justice system, then read this book. If you want to know what shadows of evil lurk in all of us, spend an afternoon visiting Kirven, Texas. If you watch the news of the Balkans and think that it can't happen here, find out how it almost did.[117]

The review did not compare the Kirven incident to either the murder of James Byrd, Jr., in Jasper, Texas, by white supremacists or the Rodney King beating in Los Angeles, and other than discussing Sheriff Mayo's failure to "rise to the occasion" and the fact that some Americans do not trust the justice system, it did not suggest that the government should take responsibility for what happened in Kirven. Nevertheless, in a letter dated April 11, 1999, a Mississippi resident responded to the *Southern Art & Soul* review by making such comparisons in a long, thoughtful letter. He laid much of the blame for lynching at the feet of federal, state, and local officials, indicated that government reparations were in order, and not only invited my thoughts on such matters, but hinted that I should join in an effort to secure compensation for the descendants of the victims of violent racism. I responded a few weeks after receiving the letter, thanking him and saying:

> [Y]our comparisons of the Jasper and Kirven incidents are very similar to mine—there are more dissimilarities than similarities. Jasper was the work of a few members of the lunatic fringe whereas Kirven was the effort of an entire community, including its most prominent families. The Jasper incident was so rare and horrible for its time that it shocked the nation, whereas Kirven's was just one more tolerated outrage in a dismal parade of tolerated outrages that spanned

half a century and were part of a political practice.
In Jasper the rule of law has apparently brought the
perpetrators to justice, or will do so, whereas in
Kirven there was only mob law, with its tragic results.
In Jasper there was immediate remorse, confrontation
with reality, and at least some healing. In Kirven there
has been seventy-seven years of denial. In many ways,
Jasper demonstrates that we have come a long way as a
civilized society in those years. . . .

. . . [M]y sincere hope for *Flames after Midnight* is
that it will do some small part to educate the public
about the senselessness of hate, the dangers of mob
justice, and the necessity of not repeating mistakes of
the past. More importantly, I'd like to think it can, and
has, accomplished some healing. . . .[118]

With regard to reparations, however, I declined support on the basis
of well-established legal principles. The other reviews speak for themselves, and need not be quoted here.[119]

Most gratifying, however, was the book's reception in colleges and
universities. It became required reading in various college courses,
which resulted in an amusing request posted on the Internet by a student in such a course who asked if anyone "has the Cliff Notes version
of *Flames after Midnight?*"

In addition to the college courses, the book and story occupied a
significant portion of a master's thesis[120] and at least one undergradu-
ate term paper.[121] It became part of Gode Davis's documentary film on
lynching,[122] and I occasionally received unexpected inquiries from unexpected locations.

A gentleman e-mailed from England to say that as a student of the
University of Newcastle, he was conducting research on democracy,
had come across the book, and was e-mailing to ask me about the effects that lynching has had on the African American community and
what impact this has had on their integration into wider American
Democracy.

I responded the best I could, directing him toward other scholars
on lynching and writing:

During the period that American lynching was most
prevalent, 1882–1922, the practice was an effective
tool that told Blacks and other minorities they would

not be allowed to exist in American society unless they adhered to a very strict, narrow regimen of behavior. In other words, for decades lynching helped ensure that Blacks were not treated democratically in America.

Thereafter, in the long-run, lynching led to racial tolerance in the sense that it was so wrong that it led to "right." The practice was so horrible, so barbaric (particularly after the 1906 *U.S. v. Shipp* trial), and ultimately so unacceptable to the majority of Americans that it helped serve as a wake-up call that things must change. As discussed in the book, the frequency of lynchings fell off dramatically after 1922. With that decline in violence began the glacial process of conferring civil rights to those so long denied them.

One may argue, then, that by existing, lynching had to be ended, and the drive to end it gave rise to the understanding, ideas, and enlightenment necessary to accomplish the African-American integration into American democratic society that has, in fact, occurred. A premise might also be advanced that the successful non-violent civil rights movement led by Martin Luther King and others in the 1960s was a reaction, in part, to the violence of lynching. Similarly one might postulate that it is often necessary for people to witness or experience extreme acts of senseless injustice (Wounded Knee, the Holocaust, 9/11) before they are finally motivated to put an end to senseless brutality.

In any event, I believe the United States is just now becoming willing to examine its aching racial past, particularly the lynching period. . . . We still have a ways to go; we have made a lot of mistakes and we continue to make more. All the people have not accepted the notion that "all the people" does not still exclude certain people. Nevertheless, compared to nations in which ethnic-cleansing, genocide, and suicide bombings serve as almost daily expressions of societal philosophy, America stands as a model for tolerance and acceptance of the differences among the world's peoples.

On the local, Freestone County front, my interviewing and quoting of J. C. Whatley served as a significant reason for condemnation of the book by "one of the greatest opponents of the book . . . a former sheriff and friend of Akers . . . J. R. 'Sonny' Sessions."[123] Sessions was the grandson and son of sheriffs of Freestone County, his father having been closely involved with the events of 1922 before he took office in 1929.[124] When I lived in Freestone County, Sonny was not only sheriff but a fellow member of the Freestone County Historical Commission, and he shared some of his recollections, particularly those unfavorable to Horace Mayo, long before the book became a project. Yet after the book was published he "never spoke to [me] again and told reporters he refused to read the book."[125]

Sessions ultimately did read it, however, and complained that it failed to mention that his family had gone to "extreme measures to protect the blacks who were working for them" during the reign of terror, whereas "an irrelevant side story, about Sessions' father, was [included]."[126] As for J. C. Whatley and the other people interviewed, he declared that "[a]ll his sources wouldn't have been good sources fifty years before, and they certainly weren't then [now]. Most of them are senile," and "Nobody believes what J.C. says."[127] He summed up the local response to the book as "[h]e [Akers] thought it was going to go big and it was a flop here. Local people just passed it by completely."[128]

In reality I never expected the book to be well received in the county. I was just relieved that those who harbored feelings like Sonny's did not respond the way the citizens of 1922 did. I cannot help wonder how many in the county read the book but were careful never to let Sonny know.

Yet the book did receive some favorable reaction in the county. One resident wrote to say, "I wish to compliment you on the fine and professional job you did in recounting the historical event of Freestone County. . . . I thank you for this education because now I can better relate to the people and their personalities and struggles more so."[129] Joycie Burns, a black businesswoman in Teague and respected leader of the black community, offered the book for sale at her insurance business and office supply store, the only place it could be purchased in the county.

"I loved it," she said. When asked by a Baylor college student if she thought I was "an agitator, trying to stir up trouble, or a healer, trying to facilitate healing between the black and white communities," she responded thoughtfully that "Yes, he is (an agitator). Let's say you have a pot of beans here and you're trying to cook them, and you never stir them. What happens? They're going to burn, they're just going to sit there, but you have to be an agitator. . . . You've got to stir it up before it can become what it is supposed to be. . . . If he had never touched this, you have people in Freestone County that knew all about it, but if he had never touched it, it would still be dormant."[130]

The favorable feelings that Roland and Clara King experienced on March 6, 1999, toward the book and its potential impact on local race relations were short-lived. After they returned to their home, other relatives who were not present, such as Roland's eighty-four-year-old sister, Oleta, and eighty-eight-year-old cousin, Alma, both of whom lived through the troubles of 1922, did not want to be bothered with the story.[131] They believed, as all of the family except possibly Grandfather King did, that the three black men who were burned killed Eula.

Furthermore, after giving it some thought, Clara King decided that Dan Kelly's story about interviewing Grandfather King was highly suspect.

> There is one other thing that I think, and it is just an opinion because I did not know Grandpa King—but what I have heard about him is that he would not have confided in the gentleman that posed as a reporter; in fact he probably would not have even talked with him or anyone else outside the family or close friends. He did not like or trust strangers—any strangers. (Mr. King could not read or write.) The gentleman wrote what he thought that the NAACP wanted to hear. They would not have paid him to write that three black men raped, tortured, and mutilated a young, white, eighteen-year-old female.[132]

The fence between the black and white cemeteries in Cotton Gin did not come down. Despite a letter-writing campaign, one newspaper article,[133] local efforts by the daughters of Lutisia and Foster Foreman and David McCartney, the initial support of Clara King, the fact that a similar fence was torn down in Jasper as a symbol of racial healing,[134] and an appeal to the Cotton Gin Cemetery Association board of directors, it stands to this day. Its removal would have been a minor but tangible symbol of racial healing in the region that has not come to pass.[135] Discussions and tentative proposals regarding the possible erection of a monument to the victims of the Kirven incident also died barren.[136]

Despite the many years that have passed since the incidents of May 1922, startling new information continues to filter through the decades. The most interesting, or shocking, concerns "Mack."

I learned of Mack's existence in 1999, shortly after the book was published. Despite the supposition in the book review of *Flames* in the Mexia newspaper that all those involved were dead, this man was said to have not only been a member of the mob, but to have proudly claimed over the years to have personally castrated one or more of the victims. In fact, it was reported, he considered the Kirven burnings to have been a highlight of his life.

I was told of his existence but was cautioned not to approach him as his family members were regarded as potentially violent and were said to be very protective of the old man, then in his nineties, fearing a belated attempt to prosecute him. This latter piece of information proved to be false, or exaggerated, but at the time, having no idea what directions publication of the book might go, I merely catalogued the possibility that such a man existed with the other reports and revelations that came my way. It was not my goal to see him prosecuted, and I believed that the statute of limitations had passed for any crime he might have actually committed.[137]

Then, in 2002, a filmmaker named Gode Davis came to Texas from Rhode Island. He was working on a documentary film about lynching that he hoped to sell to HBO, PBS, or a similar outlet. He had read *Flames* and enlisted my aid as a historical advisor for the film. One of his purposes in coming to Texas was to track down information on the Kirven incident he could incorporate into the film. When he learned of Mack's existence he announced an intention to talk to him. He was warned, not merely by me, that he might receive a rude welcome, or worse, if he approached the old man. Gode plowed forward anyway.

He visited the man at home, which was that of his son, and reported afterward that the son acted very suspicious of him and made certain that Gode noticed the Winchester rifle leaning against the doorframe when he arrived. Nevertheless, he ushered Gode into the old man's bedroom.

The interview was essentially fruitless. Mack acknowledged being present at the burnings and repeated the accepted explanation of the motives of the three victims, but at the time he did not add any new or startling information. One aspect of the interview was significant and quite telling, however. Hanging on the wall of the old man's bedroom behind his bed, nicely framed and aesthetically arranged, were six photographs of the Kirven burning scene taken by the Buie photographer from Mexia early on the morning of May 6, 1922.[138]

Later in the month, Gode returned to Rhode Island, and I subsequently had no contact with him for a few years. I did not know that he received a surprise phone call from Mack. It turned out to be the first of several he would receive, and of which Gode wrote in 2008 as follows:

> After my rather frightening visit to the (man's) residence in 2002, I was very surprised when he began calling me late at night in September 2002. I received six calls from him, all made from his home I assume, during that month. One call was not substantive, as his son or one of his family members went to the bathroom and was awake so he had to hang up. The other five calls kept me up way into the wee hours and were often disturbing enough that I was worthless the following day.
>
> He said that he wanted to talk about the "nigger lynching" and that he was a very old man and his family didn't want to know anything about it. The photos were on his bedroom wall in back of his bed because "I always want to remember it," he said. In the first and second calls, I tried to ask journalism 101-type questions just to ascertain if he was telling the truth as he remembered it. His memory was very good, better than Hobart Carter's, in fact. He was born in 1902 and was a century old when we spoke.
>
> Initially, he seemed to show little remorse. He spoke of working on a "pig farm" in the area towards Waco and of learning to castrate pigs there. This meant he had a skill to impress the others who were leaders of the mob, about eight men and one boy of fourteen he said. The boy was also a farm worker, and like Mack, had the "skill" of knowing how to castrate a pig, which "wasn't that much different from doin' a nigger," he said, "especially a bad nigger." So Mack told me that all three victims were castrated, but he "only did two of them." The boy did the other, he told me.

Another lyncher, a man of about forty whom he still wouldn't identify after eighty years had passed—even though the forty-year-old had to have been deceased—was "in charge of getting the fire going." A knife was used to painfully cut Snap Curry in the pectoral muscles of the chest, as he screamed, and again, the style of the cuts had something to do with farm labor. Johnny Cornish was cut in his "pretty face" as he was particularly despised. He was considered by people in the area to be "a miscegenation threat." According to Mack, "Nobody was surprised that Johnny Cornish was involved." He says that he knew Tom Cornish better, worked with him doing farm and tree work, and that he was better behaved, and it was "a shame that he too got killed."

In the third call, I asked him what made him do the castrating. "I was showing off. Proving that I was good enough so that people would respect me," he admitted. "In those days, young fellows had to prove they were men."

I also asked him in that call, why he'd decided to speak to me, a complete stranger. . . . "Because you are a stranger," he said, "and it's never left me, what we did that night."

By the fourth and fifth calls (as I said, one call was abbreviated), he became sadder sounding, and more wistful, if not exactly remorseful. "I give all the nig-gers a lot of extra peaches," he said, "and none of them know that I was even there."[139]

The other details of the man's involvement—how eight men and a boy were assigned specific duties they carried out to burn the three men and what those duties consisted of—were provided in other messages from Gode and are described in Section II of this epilogue. Of the disturbing events and shocking testimony I've encountered in twenty-nine years of association with this bizarre, horrible tale, I consider this man's testimony to be the most chilling. He was the consummate American lyncher. He hated, he participated in an utterly fiendish way, and he took pride in what he had done.

The legacy of the Kirven burnings, to the extent it can be known,

has already been perused, prodded, and pondered. No more great conclusions need be drawn, and no more Parthian volleys need be fired.
Instead, I will conclude with short anecdotes provided by three black
women that reveal additional insights.

Two of the ladies were born after the troubles and the third lived
through them. One of the former recalled that as a little girl, her grandmother would tell her and her sisters that they must not be outside after dark because they might be taken and molested by "bad men who
would stick sticks in them." She said she never understood why her
grandmother would say such an unusual thing until she read *Flames*
and learned of Eula's torture.[140]

The second lady, a great-niece of Nettie Cornish, did not learn the
details of what her family endured until after *Flames* was published.
She was deeply moved and gave sincere, serious thought to what the
story meant and what needed to be done:

> Aunt Nettie's life was a living HELL! Oh my God!
> The Blacks lived every minute (back then) in fear.
> Never knowing what a White person may accuse them
> of and they were doomed. Being a Black person myself
> . . . death would have been welcomed! How did Aunt
> Nettie stay sane? When things got where she could
> leave Fairfield . . . what made her stay? The old gen-
> erations of Cornish's were born in Fairfield and died
> and will die in Fairfield. With all the tragedy, fear, and
> hardship . . . what made them stay? Were the roots so
> deep with family history, that held her there? Did she
> believe that the secret (of what happened to Johnny
> and other family members) would be someday be set
> free or made right?
>
> From a relative that can't sleep or eat due to all of
> the questions running though my mind. What can we
> do to make this a better world for all? The story needs
> to be told so it won't ever happen again! My life will
> never be the same again. I now have a better apprecia-
> tion for the ones that lived through those times. I will
> tell the story and pass it on to the next generations, the
> sacrifices that those relatives who have departed this
> earth made for us to have the freedom we (young gen-
> eration) take for granted. The freedom we have today

came at a high price to those who came before us. The freedom we enjoy, has been paid in blood, heartaches, humiliation, elimination, slaughter, butchered, and a lost of history.

We ALL have to work together to make this nation a better place for ALL! In God We Trust!!!![141]

The lady who lived through the troubles, Anna Chambers, was interviewed in 1966 by V. Wayne Oakes, and her perspective was markedly different. She reported that conditions had improved greatly since 1922—schools were integrated, the races lived together in harmony, and the whites were contrite for how they had once treated blacks.

Still, a long life in Freestone County immunized her from optimism, and she revealed what must have been a common attitude in the black community by recounting a small anecdote that occurred when Fairfield celebrated its centennial in 1951. Nettie Cornish, Johnny's mother, was selected to ride at the head of the centennial parade down Commerce Avenue, the main street of the county seat. The elderly lady was dressed in red, white, and blue and was proud to be so honored. She must have been considered by many whites who knew the Kirven story as a wonderful symbol of the healing that had occurred and an example of how broad-minded and accepting the new generation of Freestone citizens had become.

"But," Mrs. Chambers observed wryly, "of course she was the monkey."[142]

Notes

Prologue to Part One

1. Letter of recommendation to Robert E. Lee from Joseph Mayo, Jr., dated October 10, 1867, recommending Captain Walter R. Bowie for the position of housekeeper of the boarding house at Washington College. In the collection of the Leyburn Library, Washington & Lee University, Lexington, Virginia.

2. These same sentiments were recently articulated by Archbishop Desmond Tutu of South Africa, who declared in an interview: "It is not enough to say let bygones be bygones. Indeed, just saying that ensures it will not be so. Reconciliation does not come easy. Believing it does will ensure that it will never be. We have to work and look the beast firmly in the eyes. . . . Without memory, there is no healing. Without forgiveness, there is no future." Colin Green, "Without Memory, There Is No Healing. Without Forgiveness, There Is No Future," *Parade* (January 11, 1998), 4.

Chapter One: Eula

1. *Kirven Commercial Record,* May 7, 1922; interview of Bertha Williams, June 5, 1987; interview of Sarah Goolsby Nettle, June 1, 1996. Mrs. Nettle recalled that graduating girls wore white dresses and graduating boys wore suits at Kirven until the late 1920s, when they began wearing caps and gowns.

2. Rain in Freestone County was heavy and continuous from April 24 through May 3. *Fairfield Recorder,* April 28, 1922 and May 5, 1922.

3. *Teague Chronicle,* May 27, 1921.

4. Interview conducted April 5, 1995.

5. *Fairfield Recorder,* April 28, 1922, May 5, 1922, and May 12, 1922; interview conducted April 8, 1995.

6. Interview conducted January 8, 1995; photograph of Eula Ausley provided by her nephew, B. J. Ausley.

7. Interview of Lura Bess Mayo Sprague, December 3, 1994. Mrs. Sprague was a 22-year-old teacher in the Kirven School on May 4, 1922, and said this would have been typical clothing for a girl of Eula's age to wear. The fact that Eula wore a hat is mentioned in several newspaper articles.

8. Interview conducted April 8, 1995.

9. Ibid.

10. Interview of Lura Bess Mayo Sprague, December 3, 1994; interview of Bertha Williams, June 5, 1987.

11. "Report of Dan Kelly on Investigation of Lynchings at Kirven, Texas, May 6, 1922" (NAACP Papers, Documents Division, Library of Congress, Washington, D.C.); interview of J. C. Whatley, May 5, 1987; supported in substance by B. J. Ausley, interviewed on April 9, 1995.

12. Interview of Lutisia Gibson Foreman and Foster Foreman, January 7, 1995.

13. Interview of Bertha Williams, June 5, 1987.

14. *Kirven Commercial Record*, May 7, 1922.

15. Interview of Foreman Carter, April 10, 1995.

16. *Dallas Times Herald*, May 5, 1922; *Kirven Commercial Record*, May 7, 1922.

17. Interview of J. C. Whatley, May 5, 1987.

18. *Austin Statesman*, May 5, 1922; "Report of Dan Kelly."

19. *Dallas Times Herald*, May 5, 1922.

20. Interview of Harry Hughes, January 8, 1995.

21. *Austin Statesman*, May 6, 1922.

Chapter Two: Kirven, the County, the Country, and the Kings

1. N. Graebner, G. Fite, and P. White, *A History of the American People* (New York: McGraw-Hill, 1970), 674; *Teague Chronicle*, May 5, 1922; interview of Willie Mae Beaver, October 24, 1986.

2. *Fairfield Recorder*, October 14, 1921, December 2, 1921, and December 9, 1921.

3. Ibid., December 20, 1921–February 18, 1922.

4. *Fairfield Recorder*, October 21, 1921 and October 28, 1921.

5. *Kirven Commercial Record*, quoted in the *Fairfield Recorder*, November 11, 1921.

6. *Fairfield Recorder*, February 18, 1922; *Teague Chronicle*, April 21, 1922.

7. Interview of Lura Bess Mayo Sprague, December 3, 1994. Mrs. Sprague remembered sitting on a front porch in Kirven and watching the oil derricks in the direction of Wortham and Mexia.

8. *History of Freestone County*, vol. 1 (Fairfield, Texas: Freestone County Historical Commission, 1978), 147.

9. Ibid., 171. The Trinity and Brazos Valley Railroad would later become the Burlington-Rock Island Railroad. *Handbook of Texas*, vol. 1 (Austin: Texas State Historical Association, 1952), 967.

10. *History of Freestone County*, vol. 1, 170–172.

11. Ibid., 140–141.

12. Ibid.

13. Interview of Lura Bess Mayo Sprague, December 3, 1994.

14. Interview of Willie Mae Keeling Beaver, October 24, 1986.

15. *Handbook of Texas;* Fourteenth Census of the United States (1920), Freestone County, Precinct Six. According to local tradition and the recollection of some witnesses, Kirven had a large population in 1922 compared with other towns

in the county; only Teague had more inhabitants. This belief is not, however, supported in available documents. One explanation may be that a large number of people who were not residents of the town visited Kirven regularly to shop. The number and variety of stores in Kirven apparently attracted people from other parts of both Freestone and Limestone counties. Another explanation is that cotton farming and sharecropping resulted in a larger, more concentrated rural population than that existing in the cattle-ranching community surrounding Kirven today, so that the population of the town and its environs was considerably larger than it was in later years. In any event, any dramatic population growth that occurred in Kirven between 1920 and 1922 was attributable to the oil boom.

16. *Fairfield Recorder,* November 28, 1919 and March 4, 1921.

17. Interview of Bertha Williams, June 5, 1987.

18. Interviews of Harry Hughes, April 10, 1995 and April 4, 1996.

19. Interview of Bertha Williams, June 5, 1987; interview of Foreman Carter, April 10, 1995.

20. *History of Freestone County,* vol. 1, 8–9, 14–15.

21. Ibid., 15.

22. Fourteenth Census of the United States (1920), Limestone County.

23. *History of Freestone County,* vol. 1, 15.

24. Lawrence D. Rice, *The Negro in Texas, 1874–1900* (Baton Rouge: Louisiana State University Press, 1971), 140–145; interview of Foster Foreman, January 7, 1995.

25. Rice, *The Negro in Texas,* 141–145.

26. Ibid.

27. Ibid.

28. *History of Freestone County,* vol. 1, 15.

29. Ibid., 24

30. *Fairfield Recorder,* February 20, 1920.

31. Graebner et al., *A History of the American People,* 984.

32. *History of Freestone County,* vol. 1, 203; interview of Uel L. Davis, Jr., October 28, 1986.

33. *Annual Report of the Adjutant General of Texas for the Period from January 21, 1921 to December 31, 1921* (Austin: Texas State Archives), 94–111; *Fairfield Recorder,* February 10, 1922; *Teague Chronicle,* January 13, 1922, January 29, 1922, and February 10, 1922.

34. *Annual Report of the Adjutant General; History of Freestone County,* vol. 1, 54–56; *Teague Chronicle,* January 13, 1922 and February 10, 1922; *Fairfield Recorder,* February 10, 1922.

35. *History of Freestone County,* vol. 1, 141.

36. Ibid., 568.

37. *Fairfield Recorder,* December 16, 1921; *Teague Chronicle,* February 21, 1922.

38. Interview of Foreman Carter, April 10, 1995.

39. Ibid.

40. *Fairfield Recorder,* December 16, 1921.

41. Ibid.

42. Ibid.

43. *Fairfield Recorder,* February 21, 1922; *Teague Chronicle,* February 21, 1922.

44. *Fairfield Recorder,* February 21, 1922; *Teague Chronicle,* February 21, 1922.

45. Interview of Foreman Carter, April 10, 1995.

46. Interview of Lura Bess Mayo Sprague, December 3, 1994.

47. *Fairfield Recorder,* May 12, 1922.

48. *Kirven Commercial Record,* May 7, 1922.

49. Ibid.

50. *Fairfield Recorder,* January 16, 1920.

51. All five boys were in the county, and Alva was living with his parents in February 1920, when the census was taken. Some witnesses interviewed named Alva as being present in May 1922, but according to J. C. Whatley, he was married and living out of the county.

52. Interview of J. C. Whatley, May 5, 1987; interview of Lura Bess Mayo Sprague, December 3, 1994; interview of Harry Hughes, January 8, 1995.

53. Interview of Lura Bess Mayo Sprague, December 3, 1994.

54. Interview of J. C. Whatley, May 5, 1987.

55. Interview of Harry Hughes, April 4, 1995.

56. Gravestone of Eunice Ausley, Shanks Cemetery, near Kirven, Texas.

57. *Kirven Commercial Record,* May 7, 1922; interview of J. C. Whatley, May 5, 1922; interview of B. J. Ausley, April 9, 1995.

58. Thirteenth Census (1910), Freestone County, Precinct Six; Fourteenth Census (1920), Freestone County, Precinct Six.

59. Interview of B. J. Ausley, April 9, 1995.

60. Standard Certificate of Death No. 2373, L. C. Ausley, filed January 21, 1920. Austin: Texas Department of Health, Bureau of Vital Statistics.

61. Ibid.

62. *Fairfield Recorder,* May 12, 1922.

63. Interview conducted July 19, 1995. More than one witness described Eula as being the "sunshine" of the John King household.

64. *History of Freestone County,* vol. 1, 88–91, 93–94, 99, 142–143, 147–148, 149–150.

65. Interview of Lura Bess Mayo Sprague, December 3, 1994.

66. "Report of Dan Kelly."

67. *Fairfield Recorder,* March 3, 1922.

68. Ibid.; interview conducted July 19, 1995.

69. *Fairfield Recorder,* March 3, 1922; *Teague Chronicle,* March 3, 1922.

70. Interview of Bertha Williams, June 5, 1987. According to census records for Freestone County in 1920, Dowell was living with Otis and Rena King in 1920. B. J. Ausley, the only surviving son of Dowell Ausley, was not certain whether his father was still in Freestone County in May 1922. He entered the service after

World War I, but his military records, like those of many American servicemen, were either lost or destroyed in a fire at the military records center in St. Louis during the Vietnam War.

71. Interview of Lutisia Gibson Foreman and Foster Foreman, January 7, 1995.

72. Interview conducted July 19, 1995; interview conducted October 28, 1986.

73. Interview of Willie Mae Keeling Beaver, October 24, 1986.

74. Interview of B. J. Ausley, April 9, 1995; interview of Lura Bess Mayo Sprague, December 3, 1994; interview of J. C. Whatley, May 5, 1987; interview conducted October 28, 1986.

75. Interview of B. J. Ausley, April 9, 1995.

Chapter 3: The Instant when Music Shatters Glass

1. Telephone interview conducted June 3, 1995.

2. *Dallas Times Herald,* May 5, 1922; interview of J. C. Whatley, May 5, 1987.

3. "Report of Dan Kelly."

4. Ibid.; interview of Willie Mae Beaver, October 24, 1986.

5. "Report of Dan Kelly."

6. Ibid.

7. Ibid.

8. Interview of J. C. Whatley, May 5, 1987.

9. Interview of John D. Nettle, June 1, 1996.

10. Interview conducted April 8, 1995.

11. Interview of J. C. Whatley, May 5, 1987.

12. Interview conducted January 8, 1995.

13. *Houston Chronicle,* May 7, 1922; *Dallas Times Herald,* May 7, 1922.

14. Interview conducted July 19, 1995.

15. *New York Call,* May 7, 1922.

16. Interview of J. C. Whatley, May 5, 1987. A newspaper account stated that her murderers "mutilated the body with a stick in a most horrible manner." *Kirven Commercial Record,* May 7, 1922.

17. Interview conducted July 19, 1995.

18. Interview of J. C. Whatley, May 5, 1987.

Chapter Four: Sheriff Mayo

1. *History of Freestone County,* vol. 1, 53.

2. Freestone County was staunchly Democratic. Often, no Republican candidate bothered to file, so election outcomes were frequently determined in primary races. Between January and July 1920, Mayo had three Democratic opponents, David Terry, Jim McDonald, and Samson Lamb. The primary election was held July 24, 1920, and Terry received the most votes, with 822; Mayo received 818, McDonald 611, and Lamb 314. A runoff was held which Mayo won. Terry

put his house on the market and dropped out of sight, but was back in 1922 to challenge Mayo again. Mayo was sworn into office on December 1, 1920. *Fairfield Recorder,* February 20, 1920, March 5, 1920, August 6, 1920, November 12, 1920, and December 3, 1920.

3. Interview of Harry Hughes, January 10, 1995; interview of Lura Bess Mayo Sprague, December 3, 1994; interview of Ruth Mayo Ditto, September 11, 1993; interview of Uel L. Davis, Jr., October 28, 1986.

4. *Fairfield Recorder,* December 17, 1920.

5. *Fairfield Recorder,* December 31, 1920, February 4, 1921, March 18, 1921, August 19, 1921, and September 2, 1921.

6. *Fairfield Recorder,* January 21, 1921; interview of Grace Mayo Norman and Ruth Mayo Ditto, September 12, 1993; interview of Lura Bess Mayo Sprague, December 3, 1994. Lura Bess had received a teaching certificate and returned to teach in Kirven, but she lived with her parents in Fairfield.

7. *Fairfield Recorder,* July 15, 1921.

8. *Fairfield Recorder,* September 9, 1921.

9. Interview of Harry Hughes, January 8, 1995.

10. Interview of Sarah Goolsby Nettle, June 1, 1996.

11. *Fairfield Recorder,* September 29, 1921.

12. *Teague Chronicle,* April 22, 1921 and May 13, 1921.

13. Interview of Grace Mayo Norman, September 12, 1993.

14. Interview conducted October 28, 1986, corroborated in substance by Harry Hughes, interviewed April 10, 1995.

15. Interview of Lura Bess Mayo Sprague, December 3, 1994; interview of Grace Mayo Norman, September 12, 1993; interview of Ruth Mayo Ditto, September 11, 1993.

16. Interview of Grace Mayo Norman, September 12, 1993.

17. Interview of Lura Bess Mayo Sprague, December 3, 1994.

18. Ibid.

19. Ibid.

20. Ibid.; interview of Grace Mayo Norman, September 12, 1993.

21. Interview of Lura Bess Mayo Sprague, December 3, 1994.

22. Death Records, Genealogy Section, Texas State Archives, Austin.

23. *Teague Chronicle,* September 23, 1921.

24. *Teague Chronicle,* January 13, 1922.

25. *Fairfield Recorder,* October 6, 1922.

26. *Fairfield Recorder,* January 16, 1920 and May 21, 1920.

27. *Fairfield Recorder,* February 10, 1922; *Teague Chronicle,* February 10, 1922.

28. *Fairfield Recorder,* February 3, 1922.

29. *Teague Chronicle,* February 10, 1922; *Fairfield Recorder,* February 10, 1922.

30. *Teague Chronicle,* February 10, 1922.

31. Ibid.

32. *Annual Report of the Adjutant General of Texas,* 94-95.

33. Ibid., 102.
34. Ibid., 103–105.
35. *Teague Chronicle,* March 17, 1922
36. *Teague Chronicle,* March 24, 1922. Mayo's letter read as follows:

EDITOR, TEAGUE CHRONICLE
TEAGUE, TEXAS

Dear sir:

I am taking this means of communicating to the public generally the attitude of this office in reference to enforcement of laws concerning the making and sale of liquor. I realize that there has been criticism of this department from various sources, due to what some have been pleased to term lax enforcement of the law in this respect. Such criticism and faultfinding has been based upon conclusions which do not take into consideration the difficulties and obstacles encountered by me and my deputies in any attempt to enforce the drastic measures applicable to the situation. The display of military power, under the short term of martial law, but added to the faultfinding and I feel that undue censure has been passed on this office.

However, all that is past and gone, and I trust that anyone in the future, having any fault to find with this office will come to me or those under me and speak it plainly. Those who come into possession of facts which would lead to the discovery of stills or stores of whiskey will not only be doing a favor to this office, but the failure to do so is a reflection upon their good citizenship. I wish to say here, however, that I do not appreciate the effort of informers to keep in the dark; anonymous letters never make much impression on anyone, for if a person has anything to tell he ought to be willing to do it frankly and openly and not under cover of darkness. This office will, to the limits its occupants possess, seek to protect anyone who furnishes information leading to arrests and convictions for violation of law.

Regardless of what any person may think of the merits of the law, of the justness or righteousness of the eighteenth amendment, it is and shall continue to be the purpose of this office to enforce to the fullest extent without fear or favor, with malice to none, but in even-handed justice, the law as it now stands. It is to be hoped that any who have engaged in this unlawful enterprise has learned a lesson; that such practice shall cease, but if the law is violated, whoever the transgressor is, regardless of color, standing or position in society, he must suffer.

It may occur to some that a statement should not be necessary from an officer of the law, but in view of the misapprehensions which seem to have gotten abroad, I am making this statement to the public, and will thank you to give it publicity.

H. M. MAYO, SHERIFF
FREESTONE COUNTY

37. *Dallas Times Herald,* May 5, 1922; *Austin Statesman,* May 6, 1922.
38. *Austin Statesman,* May 5, 1922.
39. *Dallas Times Herald,* May 5, 1922.
40. Interview of B. J. Ausley, April 9, 1995.
41. *Dallas Times Herald,* May 5, 1922.
42. Interview conducted October 28, 1986.

Chapter Five: Manhunt

1. "Report of Dan Kelly."
2. *Austin Statesman,* May 5, 1922; *Houston Chronicle,* May 6, 1922.
3. *Dallas Times Herald,* May 5, 1922; *Houston Chronicle,* May 5, 1922; *Houston Chronicle,* May 7, 1922; interview conducted April 5, 1995; interview of J. C. Whatley, May 5, 1987.
4. Interview of J. C. Whatley, May 5, 1987.
5. "Report of Dan Kelly"; interview conducted January 8, 1995.
6. *Houston Chronicle,* May 6, 1922.
7. *Dallas Times Herald,* May 5, 1922.
8. Interview of Foreman Carter, April 9, 1995.
9. *Kirven Commercial Record,* May 7, 1922; *Dallas Times Herald,* May 7, 1922; "Report of Dan Kelly"; interview conducted April 8, 1995; interview of J. C. Whatley, May 5, 1987.
10. Fourteenth Census (1920), Freestone County, Precinct Six; interview of Foreman Carter, April 9, 1995.
11. Fourteenth Census (1920), Freestone County, Precinct Six.
12. Interview of Foreman Carter, April 9, 1995; interview of Bertha Williams, June 5, 1987.
13. Interview of Foreman Carter, July 19, 1995.
14. *Dallas Times Herald,* May 6, 1922; *Dallas Times Herald,* May 7, 1922; *Kirven Commercial Record,* May 7, 1922; interview conducted April 8, 1995; interview of J. C. Whatley, May 5, 1987.
15. "Report of Dan Kelly."
16. Interview of Bertha Williams, June 5, 1987.
17. *History of Freestone County,* vol. 1, 52–53, 567–568; interview of Ruth Mayo Ditto, September 11, 1993; interview of Bertha Williams, June 5, 1987.
18. "Report of Dan Kelly."
19. Interview of J. C. Whatley, May 5, 1987.
20. "Report of Dan Kelly"; *Houston Chronicle,* May 7, 1922.
21. *Houston Chronicle,* May 7, 1922.
22. *Kirven Commercial Record,* May 7, 1922.
23. *Houston Chronicle,* May 6, 1922; *Kirven Commercial Record,* May 7, 1922.
24. *Dallas Times Herald,* May 5, 1922; *Austin Statesman,* May 5, 1922; *Brooklyn Citizen,* May 6, 1922; *Houston Chronicle,* May 7, 1922.
25. *Houston Chronicle,* May 7, 1922.

26. *Dallas Times Herald,* May 5, 1922.

27. *Houston Chronicle,* May 7, 1922.

28. Interview of J. C. Whatley, May 5, 1987.

29. *Houston Chronicle,* May 7, 1922; interview of J. C. Whatley, May 5, 1987.

30. Interview of Bertha Williams, June 5, 1987.

Chapter Six: A "Good Job" in the Early Hours of the Morning

1. *Dallas Times Herald,* May 6, 1922; *Houston Chronicle,* May 7, 1922; *Kirven Commercial Record,* May 7, 1922.

2. *Dallas Times Herald,* May 6, 1922; *Fairfield Recorder,* May 19, 1922.

3. *Dallas Times Herald,* May 6, 1922; *Houston Chronicle,* May 7, 1922; *Kirven Commercial Record,* May 7, 1922.

4. *Teague Chronicle,* May 19, 1922.

5. This critical piece of information was not revealed in any Texas newspaper, nor in any non-Texas African American paper, but in the *New York Call,* a predominantly socialist paper, on Sunday, May 7, 1922. The source of the information was stated to be Sheriff Horace Mayo.

6. Interview of J. C. Whatley, May 5, 1987.

7. *Austin Statesman,* May 6, 1922; *Houston Chronicle,* May 6, 1922; *St. Louis Argus,* May 12, 1922.

8. Fourteenth Census (1920), Freestone County, Precinct Six; interview conducted April 8, 1995.

9. Interview conducted November 19, 1995.

10. Ibid.

11. Fourteenth Census (1920), Freestone County, Precinct Six.

12. Interview of Foreman Carter, April 9, 1995; interview conducted November 19, 1995.

13. Interview of Foreman Carter, July 19, 1995.

14. Interview conducted November 19, 1995.

15. Fourteenth Census (1920), Freestone County, Precinct Six.

16. *Kirven Commercial Record,* May 7, 1922; *Fairfield Recorder,* May 19, 1922.

17. *Kirven Commercial Record,* May 7, 1922.

18. Interview conducted July 19, 1995.

19. *Fairfield Recorder,* May 19, 1922.

20. Ibid.

21. Interview of J. C. Whatley, May 5, 1987.

22. Interview of Lura Bess Mayo Sprague, December 3, 1994.

23. *Kirven Commercial Record,* May 7, 1922.

24. *Houston Chronicle,* May 7, 1922.

25. Ibid.

26. Interview conducted July 19, 1995; interview conducted April 8, 1995; interview conducted April 5, 1995.

27. The *Houston Chronicle* of May 7, 1922 said the crowd in Fairfield numbered

800. Other papers, such as the *Kirven Commercial Record* of May 7, 1922, placed the number at 500. The *Chicago Defender* of May 13, 1922 said there were 1,000 men, women, and children.

28. *Kirven Commercial Record,* May 7, 1922.

29. Interview of Harry Hughes, January 9, 1995.

30. *New York Call,* May 7, 1922; interview conducted January 8, 1995; interview of J. C. Whatley, May 5, 1987.

31. *Houston Chronicle,* May 7, 1922.

32. Interview of J. C. Whatley, May 5, 1987.

33. Interview conducted November 3, 1986.

34. Although the *Brooklyn Citizen* for May 6, 1922 is quoted to this effect in Ralph Ginzburg's *100 Years of Lynching* (New York: Lancer Books, 1974: 162), that issue of the newspaper does not, in fact, contain the statement. The date may be incorrect, or Ginzburg may have applied literary license to a statement in the *Chicago Defender* of May 13, 1922 that "no independent organ of the body was left untouched," and attributed the statement to the wrong newspaper.

35. Photograph provided by B. J. Ausley; interview of Harry Hughes, January 9, 1995; interview conducted January 9, 1995; interview of J. C. Whatley, May 5, 1987.

36. *Houston Chronicle,* May 7, 1922.

37. Once again, Ginzburg cites the May 6, 1922 issue of the *Brooklyn Citizen* for this information, but that issue of the *Citizen* does not, in fact, mention the preachers. The *Chicago Defender* for May 13, however, does refer to the preachers conducting a ceremony, although that newspaper describes it in a mocking manner. A witness who knew the Methodist minister said that it would have been consistent with his personality and ministry to pray for the condemned men.

38. Interview of J. C. Whatley, May 5, 1987.

39. *Dallas Times Herald,* May 7, 1922; *Kirven Commercial Record,* May 7, 1922; *New York Call,* May 7, 1922; "Report of Dan Kelly"; *Brooklyn Citizen,* May 6, 1922, as quoted by Ginzburg in *100 Years of Lynching* (p. 162).

40. Interview of B. J. Ausley, April 9, 1995; interview conducted July 19, 1995.

41. *Kirven Commercial Record,* May 7, 1922.

42. Ibid.; *Brooklyn Citizen,* May 6, 1922; *Houston Chronicle,* May 7, 1922; *New York Call,* May 7, 1922; *Fairfield Recorder,* May 12, 1922; *Teague Chronicle,* May 12, 1922.

43. Interview of B. J. Ausley, April 9, 1995.

44. Interview of J. C. Whatley, May 5, 1987; interview of Willie Mae Keeling Beaver, October 24, 1986; interview conducted October 28, 1986.

45. Interview of Harry Hughes, January 9, 1995.

46. Interviews conducted January 9, 1995 and April 5, 1995.

47. Ibid.

48. Again, Ginzburg cites the *Brooklyn Citizen* of May 6, 1922 for this statement, although it is not, in fact, in that newspaper article, nor is it in the *Chicago Defender.*

49. Ibid.

50. *Houston Chronicle,* May 7, 1922.

51. *Brooklyn Citizen,* May 6, 1922, as quoted by Ginzburg in *100 Years of Lynching* (p. 163).

52. "Report of Dan Kelly."

53. *Kirven Commercial Record,* May 7, 1922.

54. Interview conducted October 28, 1986. The "Report of Dan Kelly" partially substantiates this version, at least with respect to one of the three victims.

55. Interview of J. C. Whatley, May 5, 1987.

56. Interview conducted January 9, 1995.

57. Interview conducted April 5, 1995.

58. Interview of Harry Hughes, January 9, 1995.

59. *Brooklyn Citizen,* May 6, 1922, as quoted by Ginzburg in *100 Years of Lynching* (p. 163).

60. Interview of Foreman Carter, April 9, 1995.

61. "Report of Dan Kelly"; interview conducted October 28, 1986.

62. *Dallas Times Herald,* May 7, 1922; *Houston Chronicle,* May 7, 1922; *New York Call,* May 7, 1922.

63. *Kirven Commercial Record,* May 7, 1922.

64. *Houston Chronicle,* May 7, 1922.

Chapter Seven: This Cold World of Care

1. *Brooklyn Citizen,* May 6, 1922, as quoted by Ginzburg in *100 Years of Lynching* (p. 162).

2. *Houston Chronicle,* May 6, 1922.

3. *New York Call,* May 7, 1922.

4. *Chicago Defender,* May 13, 1922.

5. *Dallas Times Herald,* May 6, 1922.

6. Interview conducted January 9, 1995.

7. Interview of J. C. Whatley, May 5, 1987.

8. Ibid.

9. Sylvia Norman, *The Flight of the Skylark: Development of Shelley's Reputation* (Norman: University of Oklahoma Press, 1954), 265-266.

10. Ibid.

11. Interview conducted January 9, 1995.

12. Interview of J. C. Whatley, May 5, 1987; interview conducted October 28, 1986.

13. Interview conducted November 3, 1986.

14. Interview of Bertha Williams, June 5, 1987.

15. Interview conducted November 19, 1995.

16. *History of Freestone County,* vol. 1, 580; interview conducted November 19, 1995.

17. Interview conducted November 19, 1995.

18. *Houston Chronicle,* May 7, 1922.

19. *Dallas Times Herald,* May 8, 1922.

20. *Houston Chronicle,* May 7, 1922.

21. The Reverend Starnes took his evangelist troop back to its hometown of Waco after conducting the revival in Kirven in March. He held more tent meetings in Waco, adding 451 new members to the Baptist congregation and setting the Texas record for the most new additions to a church for the second year in a row. He was scheduled to begin a two-week revival in Fairfield on April 16, but was delayed leaving a Waco revival meeting and did not get there on schedule, although his tent arrived. The meeting was re-scheduled, and started on Sunday, April 23, but heavy rains also began, and the tent was blown down on Monday. Because the pews in the Baptist church had been moved to the tent, the revival was held in the Methodist church. On May 5, he heard of the murder of Eula Ausley and was asked to preside at her funeral on May 7, the same day the revival ended. When the Fairfield meeting was finally over, Starnes had added 85 new members to various churches of Fairfield, but the closing ceremony was marred by the unexpected announcement by the Reverend Etherridge, of the Fairfield Baptist Church, that he was resigning as pastor. (*Fairfield Recorder,* April 21, 1922, April 28, 1922, May 5, 1922, and May 12, 1922.)

22. *Kirven Commercial Record,* May 7, 1922; interview conducted October 28, 1986.

23. Interview of Willie Mae Keeling Beaver, October 24, 1986; Interview of J. C. Whatley, May 5, 1987.

24. Interview conducted January 9, 1995.

25. Ibid.; interview conducted April 5, 1995.

26. Interview of John D. Nettle, June 1, 1996.

27. Interview of Willie Mae Keeling Beaver, October 24, 1986.

28. Interview conducted January 9, 1995.

29. *Kirven Commercial Record,* May 7, 1922; *Houston Chronicle,* May 8, 1922; *Austin Statesman,* May 8, 1922; interview of Bertha Williams, June 5, 1987.

30. Interview conducted November 19, 1995.

31. *Dallas Times Herald,* May 8, 1922.

32. *Teague Chronicle,* January 28, 1921.

33. *Houston Chronicle,* May 8, 1922.

34. The Texas legislature had cut the budget of the Rangers in its 1921 session, requiring the dismissal of several officers. (Correspondence files of the Texas Rangers, Texas State Archives, Austin.)

35. Ibid.; *Dallas Times Herald,* May 8, 1922; *Austin Statesman,* May 8, 1922.

36. *Houston Chronicle,* May 8, 1922.

37. Ibid.

38. *Houston Chronicle,* May 9, 1922.

Chapter Eight: Terror

1. Interview of Bertha Williams, June 5, 1987.
2. Interview conducted October 28, 1986.
3. Interview of John D. Nettle, June 1, 1996.
4. Ibid.; interview conducted October 28, 1986.
5. Several persons interviewed mentioned this story or one similar. All of the stories may have been about the same victim, who may have been Tom Barry. Barry was the only documented victim whose death was not reported in the newspapers and who was not remembered by any person interviewed. Considering the number of lynchings elsewhere in Texas in May and June and later in the year in Freestone County, the dozens of murders attributed to Freestone County may have been a conglomerate of fact, rumor, and killings in other counties. The documented killings of blacks by lynching or mobbing in the county in 1922 were those of Snap Curry, Mose Jones, Johnny Cornish, Shadrick Green, Tom Barry, Leroy Gibson, Allie Gibson, George Gay, and Perry Grayson.
6. Mr. Nettle was named for Dr. Claude Batchelor of Kirven. Interview of John D. Nettle, June 1, 1996, and correspondence, August 13, 1996.
7. *Chicago Defender,* June 10, 1922.
8. *Fairfield Recorder,* May 12, 1922. The complete editorial read as follows:

The awful crime of last week staggered and horrified the people of Freestone County. John King, whose granddaughter was so brutally slain, is one of the County's grand old men, possessing the esteem of a large circle of acquaintances. It is our painful duty to publish details of this horrible crime, and the punishment of the perpetrators, and we do so in just as few words as possible. Naturally, our people will be criticized for the mobbing of the guilty, yet so long as our women are attacked so long will the people of the nation mete swift and terrible punishment. Had the perpetrators of this crime been of another color, the punishment would have been the same. Had the innocent victim been of another race, her people would have clamored for swift punishment just the same. The relatives of the dead girl have declared themselves satisfied that all the guilty have been punished. Let's stop discussing the awful affair and return to a normal condition, for the good of all.

9. *Teague Chronicle,* May 12, 1922. The complete editorial read as follows:

THE KIRVEN TRAGEDY
BY T. L. CHILDS

The recent tragedy in Kirven in which Miss Eula (King) Ausley, grand daughter of John King, one of the highly respected citizens of Freestone County, lost her life, was one of the most deplorable in the long history of Freestone County. The crime was committed in such a brutal and diabolical manner and the young girl mutilated in such a way as to stamp the crime of such fiendish character that the strongest of men were nauseated. When brutes capable of such revolting acts are caught, human nature cannot be expected to stand up to the high tests of every day life, and the punishment of the negroes at Kirven did not even in a small way pay them their just desserts [*sic*]. We resent insinuations from the outside world that Freestone County citizens are savages, but they are just ordinary red-blooded American citizens who are always ready to defend their womanhood with their lives and when their loved ones have had the hand of the rape fiend on their throat, be that hand black or white, they are quick to avenge the crime with the life of the murderer. Such is the red blooded American whether he lives in Freestone County, in Missouri, in Indiana or in Illinois. No person who gazed upon the sad sight of that 17 year old school girl's mutilated body could ever criticize any punishment meted out to the brutes responsible for it. And the men who coolly, calmly and deliberately examined the evidence against the negroes executed; who listened to the calm confession of Snap Curry as each word fell slowly and with cool decision from his lips, narrating in the most minute detail every little act of himself and his accomplices in the commission of the offense will ever in this world be convinced that innocent men were executed or that they received more than their just deserts. The men who executed those negroes were not irresponsible boys, but were men whose matured years had brought them the respect and confidence of their fellow citizens for their cool and ripened judgment. The people of the outside world, even though they might not countenance the citizens of the county taking unto themselves the task of punishing those brutes, can rest assured that any Texas jury hearing the evidence in this case would not have hesitated a moment in rendering a verdict that would have carried against those negroes the extreme penalty of the law.

But now that the guilty ones have been punished and pretty Eula Ausley avenged, so far as human hands can accomplish that vengeance, if we are to retain the respect and not deserve the censure of the world, our citizens must return to their usual vocations and see that no innocent persons be harmed. I have such abiding confidence in the people of Freestone County that I believe they will follow the request of the relatives of the dead girl that no further acts of violence be tolerated. If these relatives are satisfied, surely no one else should complain. The example of swift and sure punishment cannot fail to have impressed any others of the fate which such fiendish crimes will ever bring, and this matter should now rest.

10. *Dallas Times Herald,* May 12, 1922. The complete article read as follows:

MEXIA MAN SAYS HE KILLED GIRL

"I guess the people are satisfied now. They have lynched four innocent men for a murder I myself committed. I am the man who killed Eula Ausley," is the partial contents of a letter received by police Thursday.

Police believe the writer is demented or wrote the letter as a practical joke.

The message was written on tissue paper, carefully rolled and placed in a small round bottle. The bottle was sealed and addressed to the Chief of Police, Dallas, Texas.

The package was mailed from Mexia and received in Dallas Thursday morning.

The letter stated that jealousy was the cause of the act.

"While the mob was burning three negroes at Kirven for the murder, the real murderer was making his escape," the letter said.

11. Interview conducted July 19, 1995.

12. Interview of B. J. Ausley, April 9, 1995.

13. *Fairfield Recorder,* May 19, 1922; *Teague Chronicle,* May 19, 1922. The introduction to the letter and the complete letter read as follows:

The *Houston Chronicle* made some statements in reference to the recent lynching in this county which Sheriff Mayo considered unwarranted by the facts, and he proposes that the paper right itself. His statement is self-explanatory, and follows:

FAIRFIELD, TEXAS MAY 13, 1922
EDITOR, *HOUSTON CHRONICLE*
HOUSTON, TEXAS

Dear Sirs: I read your article of the 7th inst. relative to the execution of the three negroes at Kirven, this county, and was surprised at the inaccuracy of the whole article, for the reason that you obtained the true facts from this office before its publication. The facts given you and the article published were very far apart.

My duty demands that I protect the negroes, and I did so by carrying them to the Fairfield jail, every other road of Wortham and Kirven being guarded by citizens determined to see that the negroes should not be carried out of the county. All three negroes were landed in the jail, and not two, as your article stated. Several hundred men gathered around the jail and asked that several men be permitted to question the prisoners, which request was granted. After examining Snap Curry, I gathered from the committee that they had decided to wait until two more negroes suspected of being implicated in the matter were caught and examined, before any further action against the three prisoners was taken. Later, I was again requested to parley with the crowd, and when I opened the door, was seized and held while men rushed the jail and took all three negroes. Resistance to the determined citizens would have been folly as well as suicide on the part of myself and three deputies. The men had formed and carried out their preparations too calmly and thoroughly to brook opposition and I feel certain they would have torn the jail down stone by stone if it had been necessary to take the negroes. Furthermore, these negroes all confessed to taking part in the murder of Miss Ausley, and no doubt is entertained in any quarter of their guilt. The horrible manner in which the girl was mutilated, on account of the revolting details, could not be published in the papers, and it would be a poor man who could have viewed the body or heard these negroes describe the manner in which they committed the crime, and then say that burning them was out of place. I am willing to take whatever criticism is directed at me, because my conscience is clear. But I do not think it just of a great paper to hark back to other incidents in order to condemn the people of a county or community. It is true that this county was placed under martial law, and a spectacular expedition headed by such advertising stunts as an airplane, etc. arrested scores of innocent people, in addition to a very few guilty ones. In justice to the county and its people, I think your paper should investigate and publish how many arrests were made by the rangers and State officers in those raids, how many men complaints were filed against by the State authorities, and how many convictions were obtained. All the cases having been filed in the Federal court . . . [words illegible in original] in a stockade while under martial law, but a peace officer under bond and desiring to harm no innocent man, will not lock them up indiscriminately without even filing charges against them. As for the "notorious road houses" referred to in your article, fairness on your correspondent's part should have caused him to state that they were barely over the line in this county and were occasioned by the oil fields at Mexia. "The backwoods people" mentioned in your article were probably the best citizenship in Navarro, Limestone and Freestone counties, and the color of the criminals' skins did not govern the punishment meted out to them. If it had been proven that white men committed this revolting outrage with its unheard details, I am sure that they would have been burned at the stake just the same.

We feel that the citizenship of Freestone county will compare favorably with that of any other county in Texas, or for that matter, in the country. We do not feel that a great daily newspaper published in a southern city should cast "slurs" that reflect upon a great people of its own State. Because your paper called my office and asked for the facts at the time of the offense, I feel that you should publish this communication. Further, the references made to the former period under which martial law was declared, while having nothing under the sun to do with the Kirven affair, will be taken as evidence by the uninformed that this county is composed entirely of outlaws and moonshiners. Because of the unfairness and unjustness of such references and insinuations, I believe that a sense of fair play will cause your paper to use its great resources in ascertaining just how many complaints were filed by the military against Freestone county citizens, how many were confined in the stockade without complaints being filed, and incidentally, the people of Texas might be interested in learning how much of the tax payers' money was expended in this "campaign," especially as sufficient funds could not be given our free schools on account of not having the money.

As an officer of the law, I am opposed to mob law and will endeavor to prevent its happening.

H. M. MAYO

14. *Dallas News,* May 26, 1922. The complete statement from the committee of Kirven Negroes read as follows:

The News has received the following communication relating to the recent lynchings at Kirven:

To Whom it May Concern:
   This is to certify that the law-abiding negro citizens of Kirven, Freestone County, Texas, desire that the world should know that they are in perfect peace and harmony with the good white people of this place. And we further desire that the world should know that when the interests of our good white friends are disturbed ours are disturbed. We also desire that the world should know that there has not been one word of dissatisfaction as to the punishment of the desperate murderers. We sincerely hope that all such characters have been cleaned up from among us not only in Kirven but in the entire race. The negro citizens of this place gave every assistance possible in helping to capture the murderers. If we only knew we had other such characters among us we would be perfectly willing to see them go in the same like manner, as we feel that death in its severest form would be too good for any individual of this character. We desire the good white people to know that it is the desire of the negroes of this place to live here for their interest as well as ours. We stand ready at any time to assist our good white people in any undertaking to bring about peace and harmony at home. We the committee, L. C. Carter, A. T. Thomas, Lee Carter, secretary, respectfully present to the world the following names of the negro citizens of Kirven. (Here follows, under the heading "Peace: We are for Peace," the signatures of 103 men.—Editor *Dallas News*)

Chapter Nine: A Visitor from Waco

1. Microfilm section, Registrar's Office, University of Texas, Austin.
2. See, for example, *St. Louis Argus,* June 30, 1922. This story, unlike the *New York World* report of January 2, 1923, reported Kelly's speech at the NAACP convention, and named the Prowell brothers as the murderers. The focus of the *World*'s report was on the number of lynchings that occurred in 1922, of which the "most ironic" was the Kirven event, particularly in light of Kelly's report.
3. The source of this question is not clear, but the answer matches the testimony of J. C. Whatley regarding the conclusion of Dr. Whiteside.

Chapter Ten: Confirmation

1. *Dallas Times Herald,* May 5, 1922; *Austin Statesman,* May 5, 1922; *Houston Chronicle,* May 7, 1922.
2. *Fairfield Recorder,* June 4, 1920.
3. *State vs. Tom Prowell,* Cause No. 4623, filed June 30, 1920, formerly ar-

chived on the third floor of the Freestone County Courthouse, Fairfield, Texas, now stored off-site.

4. Interview of B. J. Ausley, April 9, 1995.

5. Interview of Bertha Williams, June 5, 1987.

6. Fourteenth Census (1920), Thirteenth Census (1910), Twelfth Census (1900), Freestone County, Texas, Precinct Six.

7. *Fairfield Recorder*, April 14, 1920.

8. In addition to Bertha Williams and B. J. Ausley, discussed previously, a witness who preferred not to be identified said she remembered the Prowell family, but could not recall any details about them.

9. Standard Certificate of Birth No. 88766, Bureau of Vital Statistics, Texas Department of Health, filed December 2, 1925.

10. Standard Certificate of Birth No. 375, Bureau of Vital Statistics, Texas Department of Health, filed March 24, 1929. This certificate, as revised in 1986, shows Mrs. Prowell's place of birth to be Sentel, Washington, rather than Eltopia.

11. Standard Certificate of Birth No. 57520, Bureau of Vital Statistics, Texas Department of Health, filed August 25, 1934. The child's name is not given, and this time the mother's place of birth is listed as Eltoba, instead of either Eltopia or Sentel, Washington. Eltopia, Eltoba, and Sentel are not listed in a modern atlas of Washington state. No attempt was made to search census or other records for additional information on the family or background of Lavada May Burch.

12. Standard Certificate of Death No. 59308, Bureau of Vital Statistics, Texas Department of Health, filed November 18, 1959.

13. Standard Certificate of Death No. 30905, Bureau of Vital Statistics, Texas Department of Health, filed April 29, 1952.

14. Standard Certificate of Death No. 40275, Bureau of Vital Statistics, Texas Department of Health, filed June 10, 1969.

15. Interview of Foreman Carter, April 9, 1995.

16. A telephone call to the New Jersey attorney general's office failed to confirm or deny Mr. Carter's claim of employment. Computer records of prior employees extended back only a few years, and I was informed that a driver for the attorney general might have been employed by another state agency in the past.

17. Interview of Harry Hughes, January 8, 1995.

18. Interview of Foreman Carter, July 19, 1995.

Chapter Eleven: Doll Rags

1. Bertha Williams knew Leroy was in town to visit his girlfriend. The Gibson family information was provided by Lutisia Gibson Foreman and Foster Foreman. Interview of Bertha Williams, June 5, 1987; interview of Lutisia Gibson Foreman and Foster Foreman, January 7, 1995.

2. Interview of Lutisia Gibson Foreman, January 7, 1995.

3. Ibid.

4. Ibid.

5. The careful drafting and evasiveness practiced by local Southern newspapers when reporting racial incidents is well-illustrated by comparing the eyewitness account of Lutisia Gibson Foreman with two local reports, which follow. The following report appeared in the *Fairfield Recorder* on June 9, 1922:

TWO NEGROES KILLED NEAR SIMSBORO

Last Friday afternoon about 3:30 PM Leroy and Allie Gibson, negroes about 21 years old, were killed on Mose Gibson's place, east of Simsboro on an old road known as the Mexia-Fairfield Road.

There have been so many conflicting reports that we will only make a brief account of the trouble.

It is reported to us that on the day previous to the killings, Leroy Gibson was taken by some white men and escaped, receiving a slight wound from a shot.

It is alleged that on Friday afternoon, John T. King, deputy Sheriff, and Otis C. King, Marshall at Kirven, accompanied by Bob and Drew King, Walter Yerby and Bill Norman, went to Mose Gibson's house to investigate the trouble. It is alleged that when they were about 200 yards from the house shots were fired at them from the house, and at the same time Leroy Gibson attacked Walter Yerby. Leroy was killed and shots were fired toward the house. Allie Gibson was found dead in the yard.

From this trouble reports spread all over Texas that a race war was in progress in Freestone County, and considerable excitement naturally followed.

In a short time armed men began pouring into Simsboro from every section; and by sundown, it is estimated there were over 1000 armed men, and also a flying machine.

Sheriff Mayo took hold of the situation promptly and with a firm hand, and with the assistance of local officers at Teague and other places, guards were thrown out on the roads leading into the negro section, and the public was kept out.

In the *Teague Chronicle* on June 9, 1922, the following report appeared:

TWO NEGROES KILLED IN SIMSBORO COMMUNITY

Leroy Gibson and Allie Gibson, negroes, were killed at the home of their grandfather, Mose Gibson, last Friday by a posse headed by Jno. T. King, deputy sheriff, and Otis C. King, city marshall of Kirven. The officers stated that Leroy Gibson was under suspicion and had been arrested the night before and escaped, after being shot in the leg. Learning he had gone to his grandfather's home, they went to Mose Gibson's, obtained Leroy and started back to Kirven. When about 200 yards from the house, firing began and both Leroy and Allie Gibson were killed, and the third negro in the house, Floyd Gibson, escaped. No white men were hurt.

6. Interview of Bertha Williams, June 5, 1987.
7. *Chicago Defender,* June 10, 1922.
8. *Fairfield Recorder,* June 9, 1922. The remainder of the editorial stated the following:

No one obliges the citizenship there for circulation of this report, as the people of Kirven were just as much in the dark about what was transpiring as were other places, since the stage of the trouble was several miles south of Kirven and no accurate reports could be obtained for quite awhile.

9. Interview of Foster Foreman, January 7, 1995; *Chicago Defender,* June 10, 1922.
10. Interview of Foster Foreman, January 7, 1995.
11. *Chicago Defender,* June 10, 1922. The complete article read as follows:

REVOLT ON LYNCHINGS STIRS SOUTH
RACES CLASH WHEN ATTEMPT IS MADE TO BURN YOUNG TEXAS FARM BOY

Simsboro, Tex., June 9,—When gun met gun at this place last Friday an armistice was soon signed by the two races. It wasn't a case of guns, bullets and knives versus prayers, but weapon against weapon. Authorities feared the situation would terminate in wholesale massacre, and busied themselves seeing leaders of both races. The town is quiet today.

Fifty or more heavily armed white men paraded the streets of Kirven, a short distance from here, but dared not venture into Simsboro, where members of the Race were barricaded in barns awaiting the attack. According to Sheriff Horace Mayo, the men at Simsboro had 30-30 rifles and were honeycombed in the swamps to fire on the whites from all angles.

Carter Sessions (white) wealthy property owner, took that nerve to venture into "no man's land" district announcing himself a federal agent. According to Sessions, men came from all parts of the woods armed with rifles and pockets loaded with bullets. He declared the lynching of five men of our Race here recently had occasioned the heavy firing. Sessions brought word back to Kirven that nothing would happen if whites put away their guns.

The trouble occurred when two officers, acting apparently without authority, drove into Simsboro and attempted to arrest Leroy Gibson in connection with the death of Miss Ousley, a 17-year-old school girl. Five men have been burned and lynched as penalty for her death. All were innocent.

When the officers appeared at Gibson's house, they covered the family with revolvers and ordered him to enter an awaiting auto. Relatives feared another lynching and Gibson's brother, Alley, fired on the officers. Leroy attempted to escape, but was killed. A member of the auto party was also slain. His body, however, is said to have been carried to the city and secretly hidden to avoid exciting others to riot.

Manual T. Gonzualles (white), a federal prohibition agent, is given credit for avoiding a bloody conflict. When Gonzualles attempted to invade Simsboro, he saw a sentry hiding in a tall tree.

"What's your business?" a voice yelled at him. Gonzualles waved for the man to come down for a talk.

"I ain't got time to talk," came the answer from the lookout; "you white folks is trying to raise hell."

Gonzualles finally persuaded the sentry to come down. He carried a high-powered rifle and aimed it at Gonzualles' head during the conversation, to "play safe" as he stated.

Sheriff Horace Mayo, in reviewing the case, scored the officers for attempting to arrest Gibson when there was no charge pending against him. It was revealed that the officers planned to do a "favor" for John King, deputy sheriff, and Otis King, town marshall, uncles of the dead white girl, by placing Gibson in their hands.

12. *Teague Chronicle,* June 9, 1922; *Fairfield Recorder,* June 9, 1922.
13. *Fairfield Recorder,* June 9, 1922.
14. Ibid.
15. Ibid.
16. Interview of Bertha Williams, June 5, 1987.
17. *Teague Chronicle,* June 16, 1922.

Chapter Twelve: Greater Irony

1. Interview of Bertha Williams, June 5, 1987.
2. Ibid.
3. Interview of Lutisia Gibson Foreman and Foster Foreman, January 7, 1995.
4. Interview of Harry Hughes, January 8, 1995.
5. Interview of Lura Bess Mayo Sprague, December 3, 1994.
6. Interview conducted October 28, 1986.
7. Interview conducted April 5, 1995.
8. The county history book contains a record of Kirven, emphasizing its boom days but never mentioning the troubles except to say, "In the middle 20's, several wooden stores burned and Kirven started 'going down hill.'" (E. M. Prouty, "Kirven, As I Remember It," *History of Freestone County,* vol. 1, 141.)
9. Interview of J. C. Whatley, May 5, 1987.
10. Interview of Sarah Goolsby Nettle, June 1, 1996.
11. *Fairfield Recorder,* September 22, 1922.
12. *Fairfield Recorder,* August 3, 1923.

13. Interview conducted April 5, 1995; interview of J. C. Whatley, May 5, 1987.

14. *Fairfield Recorder,* January 5, 1923.

15. Interview of Harry Hughes and Foreman Carter, April 9, 1995.

16. *Fairfield Recorder,* November 17, 1922.

17. Interview conducted April 5, 1995.

18. *Teague Chronicle,* June 23, 1922.

19. King's resignation was reported in the *Fairfield Recorder* on June 30, 1922, and attributed to the *Kirven Commercial Record.* The only issue of the *Commercial Record* located during the research of this story was dated May 7, 1922.

20. *1995-1996 Directory of Texas City Officials* (Austin: Texas Municipal League, 1995), 49.

21. *Handbook of Texas,* vol. 1 (Austin: Texas State Historical Association, 1952), 967.

22. *Fairfield Recorder,* August 18, 1922.

23. *Fairfield Recorder,* July 28, 1922, in which the following report appeared:

DALLAS KLAN IN UNMASKED PARADE
DALLAS, JULY 23 — THE DALLAS KU KLUX KLAN
UNMASKED EARLY TODAY.

Following receipt of election returns clearly showing the entire klan ticket in Dallas County had swept into office by a big majority, 3500 Klansmen, unmasked and unrobed, followed leaders of the local organization through the streets while election crowds cheered. George Butcher, Z. E. Marvin and other well known Dallas business men were at the head of the procession which paraded the streets.

Standing on an automobile bearing the insign of the organization, Rev. A. C. Parker proclaimed himself cyclops of the local organization and George Butcher declared the parade was being staged in response to the insistent demands of certain local papers that the members come out from behind the masks.

One of the successful candidates for District Judge says: "The voice of the people is the voice of God," and he hoped certain Dallas Newspapers had heard it. Other than that the speeches were confined to the wishes that the bitterly fought campaign would be forgotten and that the opposition would get together with the klan for the betterment of all conditions.

There was an insistent report in political circles today that the anti-klan faction would not discuss the matter. They said "church is not over until the singing is done" and the last vote had not been counted in the election of Saturday.

Republicans were busy today, preparing to go after these anti-Klansmen who are dissatisfied with the results of the election. It was said today the Republicans would have out a complete county ticket and would make an especial appeal to the dissatisfied Democrats who participated in Saturday's election.

24. *Fairfield Recorder,* August 18, 1922.

25. *Teague Chronicle,* August 25, 1922.

26. *Fairfield Recorder,* September 22, 1922. Many witnesses who were inter-viewed remembered that the Klan was once active in the county, but only four related specific anecdotes. J. C. Whatley recalled the Klan tarring and feathering an alcoholic white man named Burleson who had been beating his wife or had been unfaithful.

The youngest of the two brothers who witnessed the burnings remembered the same story, and also recalled the Klan entering the Kirven Methodist church one Sunday during church services. There were about fifteen of them, in full robed regalia, and they paraded down the center aisle, took seats in the front pews, stayed until the service was nearly over, and paraded out. They may have been showing their strength, or they may have been trying to intimidate the min-ister, who had earlier declined an offer of money from them. J. C. Whatley was present at the same incident.

Harry Hughes had an uncle, a Mr. Allen, who was visited by the Klan later. It was during the Depression and Mr. Allen was successful in luring a black family to the Kirven area to help harvest his crops. One night he was awakened by a shout and found a semi-circle of hooded and mounted Klansmen in his front yard. They informed him it wasn't right, when there were so many white men out of work, for him to bring "niggers" in.

Mr. Allen looked at the riders and calmly retorted, "I recognize you men. I recognize your horses. I know who you are." He then proceeded to call his hooded neighbors by name and told them to go back home, concluding by saying, "Or you can stay and help me get in my crops, if you're so wise and anxious to work." They left and did not bother him anymore.

Only one witness, Ruth Mayo Ditto, suggested the Klan was more active. When the subject came up, she declared:

> "Oh, I remember. Now that I remember, the Ku Klux Klan.
> I remember that everywhere we went, here they were, just
> standing around."

Q: "Standing around? In their robes and hoods?"

A: "Yeah, in their robes and hoods."

As a ten- or eleven-year-old, Ruth may have seen the Klan a few times and been so impressed she remembered them being everywhere. None of the other witnesses supported her, and some denied the possibility. Nevertheless, it is dif-ficult to believe that the Klan was not actively involved.

27. *Fairfield Recorder,* June 30, 1922.

28. *Fairfield Recorder,* July 28, 1922.

29. *Fairfield Recorder,* September 8, 1922.

30. *Fairfield Recorder,* October 6, 1922.

31. Ibid. Mayo's letter was labeled a "political advertisement." On October 27,

1922, the *Recorder* carried the following letter from D. A. Haddick entitled "Reply to Mayo":

I believe it is time for someone to call Mr. Mayo's hand on the article published in the County papers October the 6th.

In making his announcement for sheriff on the independent ticket, he made some broad assertions. He claims he could not get any cooperation in the enforcement of the law. We happen to know that he did not ask for our cooperation here at New Hope, at one of the worst hell holes that was ever let run in a civilized nation. After we had signed a petition to the County Judge and County Attorney, asking for help and pledging our cooperation, we stood ready to assist in any way we could. Did we get help from our Sheriff or any of his men? If so you could not tell it. The Rangers had to come and put that gang out of business. There are a good many citizens condemning our Governor for declaring Martial Law in Freestone County. If the Chicken Garden of Wortham and the Winter Garden at New Hope had been controlled and never let run wide open in violation of our laws, Governor Neff would never have declared Martial Law. Therefore we have no one to blame but our own officers. And again, Mr. Mayo accuses the K.K.K. for his defeat. I can't say how they voted, but I can say that there is no K.K.K. in the New Hope community, and if Mr. Mayo will look up the record he will find others that did not belong to the K.K.K. voted for Mr. Terry, and I believe that the big majority that voted in the primaries think more of their word and honor than they do for any bolter that is seeking to be elected on an independent ticket in Freestone County or the State of Texas.

I am not K.K.K. myself, and I am not writing this article to defend them, but I want to say this, and you boys that love your God and want to live in a civilized country where you will be protected from hijackers, bootleggers and other law breakers: You will have to stand for men who will enforce the law or else we will have to line up with the K.K.K. History will repeat itself. We old men remember when the Republican party was in power in the South, and we say God forbid that it ever comes to our Southland again. But we have men yet in the South that would sell their birth right for a mess of pottage today, and will fuse with the worst enemy the South ever had in order to carry out their schemes.

I want to repeat it again. If the Republican party gets in power, we will need the K.K.K., and don't you forget it.

Boys, go to the polls on Nov. 7th and vote a condemnation of such tactics.

D. A. HADDICK

Haddick's letter was also labeled "A political advertisement."

32. *Teague Chronicle,* November 10, 1922.

33. Interview of Bertha Williams, June 5, 1987.

34. *Fairfield Recorder,* September 8, 1922.

35. *Fairfield Recorder,* December 8, 1922.

36. Interview of Lura Bess Mayo Sprague, December 3, 1994.

37. *Fairfield Recorder,* December 8, 1922; *Teague Chronicle,* December 8, 1922.

38. *Fairfield Recorder,* December 8, 1922.

39. *Fairfield Recorder,* December 15, 1922; *Teague Chronicle,* December 15, 1922; *New York World,* December 16, 1922; interview of Foreman Carter and Harry Hughes, April 9, 1995; interview of Harry Hughes, January 8, 1995; interview of Lura Bess Mayo Sprague, December 3, 1994; interview of Ruth Mayo Ditto and Grace Mayo Norman, September 12, 1993; interview of Willie Mae Keeling Beaver, October 24, 1986.

40. *Fairfield Recorder,* December 15, 1922; *Teague Chronicle,* December 15, 1922.

41. *Teague Chronicle,* December 15, 1922.

42. Ibid.; *New York News,* December 16, 1922; interview of Harry Hughes and Foreman Carter, April 9, 1995.

43. The lynching of Gay was described in the December 15, 1922 issues of the *Fairfield Recorder* and the *Teague Chronicle.* Additional details were provided by Foreman Carter, Harry Hughes, Uel L. Davis, Jr., and the daughters of Horace Mayo.

44. *New York News,* December 16, 1922.

45. *Fairfield Recorder,* August 17, 1923.

46. *Fairfield Recorder,* September 7, 1923.

Chapter Thirteen: A Place in Blackest History

1. A summary of the beginning of lynching is described by Walter White in *Rope and Faggot: A Biography of Judge Lynch* (Alfred A. Knopf: New York, 1929). Born in 1736, Charles Lynch was a Quaker, a prominent citizen, and a member of the Virginia House of Burgesses. The portion of southwestern Virginia in which he lived was at the edge of the American frontier, and the nearest trial court was two hundred miles away. In order to inject judicial regulation into the community, and to take care of irksome Tories, Lynch and his friends established their own court.

Lynch was chief magistrate, and two neighbors were associate justices. An accused wrongdoer was given the opportunity to testify, summon witnesses, and put on a defense. If acquitted, he was not only freed, he was often given an apology and sometimes reparations. If convicted, the most common punishment was thirty-nine lashes on the bare back. Tories were forced to shout "Liberty Forever" or be strung up by their thumbs. On rare occasions a perpetrator was sentenced to death.

2. Between 1830 and 1840, there were at least three burnings of blacks. Two occurred in Mobile, Alabama, after the victims were sentenced in court for the

murder of two children. The third was a free black in St. Louis who, while helping a slave to escape from bondage, shot two white officers, killing one.

At least twenty-six slaves were lynched for killing their masters during the
1850s; nine of them, one a woman, were burned at the stake. Another twelve
blacks were lynched for rape, four being burned alive. In 1856, however, Lloyd
Garrison reported that the number of whites lynched during the previous twenty
years was over three hundred.

Thousands of lynchings of blacks and whites occurred during Reconstruction.
In Alabama, 107 occurred in two years, and over 2,000 people were murdered by
mobs in Louisiana in 1868. That year, following a "nigger hunt," the bodies of
120 blacks were found in Bossier Parish. Mississippi had at least 124 lynchings
between April 1869 and April 1871. North and South Carolina had 197 in an
eighteen-month period beginning in January 1866. Tennessee mobs hosted 168
lynchings between July 1, 1867 and July 1, 1868, and in Texas, always topping the
list, 1,035 lynchings occurred from the end of the Civil War to 1868 (see White,
Rope and Faggot, pp. 83, 90, and 91–92).

3. The statistics for 1920, for example, were reported in the *St. Louis Argus*
on January 7, 1921, as follows:

There were 56 instances in which officers of the law prevented lynchings. Of
those, 10 were in the northern states and 46 were in the southern states. In 42
of the cases the prisoners were removed or the guards augmented or other pre-
cautions taken. In 14 instances, armed force was used to repel the would-be
lynchers. In 4 of the instances the mob was fired upon and as a result, 7 of the
attackers were killed and several wounded.

There were 61 persons lynched in 1920. Of these, 52 were in the South and
9 in the North and West. This is 22 less than the number, 83, for the year 1919.
Of those lynched, 53 were Negroes and 8 were white. One of those put to death
was a Negro woman. 18, or less than one-third of those put to death, were
charged with rape or attempted rape. Three of the victims were burned to
death. The charges against those burned to death were rape and murder: 1;
killing landlord in dispute: 2.

The offenses charged the Whites were murder: 5; insulting women: 1; no
charge except being a foreigner: 1; killing an officer of the law: 1. The offenses
charged against Negroes were: murder 5; attempted murder 4; killing officer
of the law 5; killing landlord in dispute 6; rape 15; attempted rape 3; assisting
fugitive in escape 3; wounding another 2; insulting women 2; knocking down
guard, escaping from chain gang and then returning and surrendering 2; jump-
ing labor contract 1; threatening to kill a man 1; cutting a man in a fight 1; for
receiving a stay of death sentence because another confessed crime 1; peeping
thru window at women 1; insisting on voting 1.

The states in which lynching occurred and the number in each state are as
follows: Arkansas 1; Alabama 7; California 3; Florida 7; Georgia 9; Illinois 1;

Kansas 1; Kentucky 1; Minnesota 3; Mississippi 7; Missouri 1; North Carolina 3; Ohio 1; Oklahoma 3; South Carolina 1; Texas 10; Virginia 1; West Virginia 1.

4. The following are examples of particularly gruesome stories about early-twentieth-century lynchings:

On February 8, 1904, the *Vicksburg Evening Post* reported the burning of Luther Holbert and his wife:

> When the two Negroes were captured, they were tied to trees and while the funeral pyres were being prepared, they were forced to hold out their hands while one finger at a time was chopped off. The fingers were distributed as souvenirs. The ears of the murderers were cut off. Holbert was beaten severely, his skull was fractured and one of his eyes, knocked out with a stick, hung by a shred from the socket.
>
> Some of the mob used a large corkscrew to bore into the flesh of the man and woman. It was applied to their arms, legs and body, then pulled out, the spirals tearing out big pieces of raw, quivering flesh every time it was withdrawn.

On December 15, 1915, the *Chicago Defender* reported the rape and lynching of Mrs. Cordella Stevenson, near Columbus, Mississippi. The woman's son was suspected of burning a barn, but could not be found, so a mob visited his parents' house at night, dragged Mrs. Stevenson to a tree near the railroad tracks, sexually assaulted her repeatedly, and hanged her.

On January 27, 1921, the *Memphis Press* reported the slow cremation of Henry Lowry:

> With the Negro chained to a log, members of the mob placed a small pile of leaves around his feet. Gasoline was then poured on the leaves, and the carrying out of the death sentence was under way.
>
> Inch by inch the Negro was fairly cooked to death. Every few minutes fresh leaves were tossed on the funeral pyre until the blaze had passed the Negro's waist. . . . Even after the flesh had dropped away from his legs and the flames were leaping toward his face, Lowry retained consciousness. Not once did he whimper or beg for mercy. Once or twice he attempted to pick up the hot ashes in his hands and thrust them in his mouth in order to hasten death. Each time the ashes were kicked out of his reach by a member of the mob.
>
> As the flames were eating away his abdomen, a member of the mob stepped forward and saturated the body with gasoline. It was then only a few minutes until the Negro had been reduced to ashes.

Another paper, the *Nation*, reported on March 23 that Lowry never said a word, until the mob brought his wife and little daughter to see him burning.

5. White, *Rope and Faggot*, vii–viii. A great deal has been written about the practice of lynching during the late nineteenth and early twentieth centuries;

among such books on the subject are: *A Festival of Violence: An Analysis of Southern Lynchings, 1882–1930*, by Stewart E. Talnay and E. M. Beck (Urbana and Chicago: University of Illinois Press, 1995); *The Tragedy of Lynching*, by Arthur F. Raper (New York: Arno Press, 1969, reprint of 1933 edition); and *The Anti-Lynching Movement, 1883–1932*, by Donald L. Grant (San Francisco: Fort Valley State College 1975). The works of Walter White, published in the twenties, are considered to be outdated by some scholars today, but they are relevant to this work because they reveal the mindset of those who were studying the phenomenon of lynching at the time of the Kirven lynchings. In *Rope and Faggot*, White offered ten explanations for how Americans, particularly Southerners, incorporated lynching into the framework of the national folkways, devoting one or more chapters to each explanation. These explanations may be summarized as follows:

First and foremost, lynching was an economic tool, a method of keeping a necessary labor force under complete domination. Coupled with this was the fear of economic success by blacks. A poor white who saw a supposed inferior succeed, by either obtaining a good job, buying a farm, or getting an education, was unable to understand. It did not fit all he'd been taught, and was the source of jealousy, hatred, and violence.

Second, lynching was promoted by the religious beliefs of the day, Biblical verses were seized upon to justify slavery and punishment. Evangelical, primitive religion, led by men described as emotional, hysterical, "bible-beating, acrobatic, fanatical preachers of hell-fire" stirred up "orgies of emotion . . . dangerous passions" that "contribute to emotional instability and play a part in lynching."

Third, vexing sensitivity about sex, and paranoia about racial intermixing, created a complex, defensive mix of attitudes. The dullness of life and lack of diversion in rural areas led to sexual experimentation, but the primitive religious attitudes and bogy of sex crimes turned the much-feared black rapist into a Frankenstein monster who could be controlled only by lynch mobs. A double standard about racial interbreeding existed, with white men mixing freely with black women, black women having little to say about it, and black men being accused of rape at the drop of a glance.

Fourth, the lynching states were populated by officials who would not prosecute. Lynchers had no fear of prosecution, or even of the inconvenience of an investigation.

Fifth, human love of excitement, especially in dull, rural areas lacking modern sources of entertainment, coupled with the general acceptance of mob violence as a type of sport, made lynching a perverse form of community recreation.

Sixth, rural Southerners were unwilling to change their attitudes toward blacks, who were expected to fit into one of three stereotypes: happy but lazy and shiftless; a habitual criminal of unrestrained appetites, kept within the bounds of the law only by extreme brutality; or humble, "befo' de wah" types who knew how to stay in their place. Negroes who did not fit, as well as candidates from the first two types of stereotype, were certain to generate resentment and violence.

Seventh, general attitudes of truculence and belligerency in the South made Southerners more violent, more determined to defend their indefensible position.

Eighth, the loss of the Civil War and emancipation, coupled with the romance and sentimentality of "the lost cause," increased Southern defensiveness of their way of life and attitudes, as well as resentment of Northern attacks and criticism.

Ninth, though totally unsupported in the statistics, belief that blacks were constantly skulking around, planning to rape white women, elevated the act of lynching to one of nobility and gallantry.

Tenth, fear and distrust of outsiders led Southerners to glorify the Klan and the "principles" for which it stood.

6. William Katz, *Eyewitness: The Negro in American History* (Belmont, Calif.: Fearon Education, 1974), 395-396, 410.

7. Ibid.

8. Interview of Lutisia Gibson Foreman and Foster Foreman, January 7, 1995. Mr. and Mrs. Foreman were certain of Floyd Gibson's service during World War I, but did not know his unit. His records, as well as those of thousands more American veterans, were lost, or destroyed by a fire at the military records center in St. Louis during the Vietnam War.

9. Katz, *Eyewitness*, 395-396, 410.

10. *Chicago Defender*, April 5, 1919.

11. John Milton Cooper, Jr., *Pivotal Decades: 1900-1920* (New York: W. W. Norton, 1990), 187; White, *Rope and Faggot*, 112.

12. Grant, *Anti-Lynching Movement*, 150.

13. Ibid.

14. White, *Rope and Faggot*, 152.

15. Eugene P. Trani, *The Presidency of Warren G. Harding*, (Lawrence: Regents Free Press of Kansas, 1977), 59.

16. Grant, *Anti-Lynching Movement*, 158.

17. In July 1921, the Church of Christ launched a campaign to enlist the aid of all churches to put an end to mob violence in the United States. Black women organized a religiously based movement against mob violence, and printed "To Your Knees and Don't Stop Praying" on its letterhead.

18. *St. Louis Argus*, December 9, 1921.

19. *St. Louis Argus*, January 13, 1922.

20. *St. Louis Argus*, January 27, 1922.

21. 32 Congressional Record 6627 (1922).

22. *St. Louis Argus*, May 19, 1922.

23. Ginzburg, *100 Years of Lynching*, 160-162; *Dallas Times Herald*, May 21, 1922, May 23, 1922, and May 27, 1922; *Fairfield Recorder*, May 26, 1922 and June 2, 1922.

24. *St. Louis Argus*, June 16, 1922.

25. Ibid.

26. *St. Louis Argus*, July 21, 1922.

27. Andrew Sinclair, *The Available Man: Warren Gamaliel Harding* (New York: Macmillan, 1965), 256, 258

28. *Fairfield Recorder*, January 5, 1923. The complete editorial read as follows:

> The evidence adduced at the trial of the men charged with murder of thirty or more non-union miners at Herin [*sic*], Ill. makes one's blood run cold. It is hard to believe the sworn testimony. We think of the people of America as a people in whom the milk of human kindness runs and who are sympathetic toward the helpless and the suffering, and we shudder as we read of men being shot down while begging for their lives, and being cursed and stomped when in the agonies of death beg and plead for a drink of water. Yet many men have sworn that this was done. The Herin massacre must remain a black spot on the escutcheon of the United States, a free country whose constitution guarantees the highest and lowest life, liberty and the pursuit of happiness. Surely we have cut loose from the old moorings.

29. Probably Senator Byron P. Harrison. The leading speaker was identified in the *St. Louis Argus* as Senator Harris of Mississippi, but Mississippi's senators in 1922 did not include a Harris, only a Harrison. *Biographical Directory of the American Congress, 1774-1971*, (Government Printing Office, Washington, D.C., 1971).

30. *St. Louis Argus*, December 8, 1922.

31. Lynching totals for the period 1882 through 1927 follow (from White, *Rope and Faggot*, pp. 230ff.):

Year	Total	Whites	Blacks
1882	114		
1883	134		
1884	211		
1885	184		
1886	138		
1887	122		
1888	142		
1889	176		
1890	128		
1891	195		
1892	235		
1893	200		
1894	197		
1895	180		
1896	131		
1897	165		
1898	127		
1899	107		

Year	Total	Whites	Blacks
1900	115		
1901	135		
1902	97		
1903	104		
Totals for 1882–1903:	3,337	1,277	2,060
1904	86	7	79
1905	65	5	60
1906	68	4	64
1907	62	3	59
1908	100	8	92
1909	89	14	75
1910	90	10	80
1911	80	8	72
1912	89	3	86
1913	86	1	85
1914	74	5	69
1915	145	46	99
1916	72	7	65
1917	54	2	52
1918	67	4	63
1919	83	4	79
1920	65	8	57
1921	64	6	58
1922	61	7	54
1923	28	2	26
1924	16	0	16
1925	18	0	18
1926	34	5	29
1927	18	2	16
Totals for 1882–1927:	4,951	1,438	3,513

32. *Time Magazine, The Twentieth Century,* "Lynching." 1994: Compact disc.

Chapter Fourteen: Burning Questions

1. Examples of "shifting perspective" works, which present a story from the viewpoints of multiple witnesses and do not attempt to present a single, over-arching narrative of historical "fact," are *Killing Mister Watson,* by Peter Mat-thiessen (New York: Vintage Books, 1991) and *Stories of Scottsboro,* by James E. Goodman (New York: Pantheon Books, 1994).

2. Page Smith, *Redeeming the Time: A People's History of the 1920s and the New Deal* (New York: McGraw-Hill, 1987), 5.

Chapter Fifteen: Epilogue: A Notoriety Deeply to be Regretted

1. Interview conducted November 19, 1995.

2. Telephone interview conducted June 1, 1996.

3. Interviews of Harry Hughes, January 8 and April 10, 1995; interview of Lura Bess Mayo Sprague, December 3, 1994; interview of Grace Mayo Norman, September 12, 1993; interview of Ruth Mayo Ditto, September 11, 1993; interview conducted October 28, 1986.

Richard Hogan left the county and did not return. Perhaps he was affected by the loss of his friend, or perhaps the story about the missing money was true and he decided to lie low. By some accounts, Hogan died in an accident while a construction worker on Boulder Dam.

4. Sessions was also remembered for being kind to black people, at least by the standards of the day. In an interview on April 9, 1995, B. J. Ausley recalled that one day, as a boy, he was riding horses with Sessions on his ranch when J. R. told him, "Stay right here. I have to take care of something."

B. J. stayed on his horse and watched as Sheriff Sessions rode to the edge of a cotton field. A mule hitched to a plow was standing idle in the furrows, and Sessions called a name. A partially dressed black man rose up from weeds near-by. Sessions called another name and a partially clad black woman stood up beside him.

"I'm not paying you for loving," Sessions called. "I'm paying you to work." He told the woman to go back home and for the man to go back to plowing.

"He didn't do anything else to them," Ausley stated. "He was good to his Negroes."

5. The Texas House of Representatives resolution honoring Sessions, passed in 1949, said, in part:

> He came into . . . office at a time when the county was harassed by illegal liquor traffic and he immediately set up a concerted drive, which, according to a prominent article in a national magazine at that time "succeeded in eliminating at least seventy-five percent of the lawlessness which was making Freestone County notorious over the State." Alert, fearless, calm, and with a poise and dignity that commanded respect, he continued his record of maintaining law and order until the end. Friend and enemy, free man and prisoner, accuser and accused, all who came in contact with this officer of the law knew that in him they would find fairness, justice, fearlessness, honesty and truth. (*History of Freestone County*, vol. 1, 696.)

Jim Sessions' son, J.R., Jr., or "Sonny," was elected sheriff of Freestone County in 1964, and is still in office in 1998. All of the statements describing the fearlessness, calm, poise, and dignity of Jim, Sr. in the foregoing resolution could just as accurately be said about Sonny.

6. Interview conducted October 28, 1986. Alva may have left before the

troubles. As J. C. Whatley told it, "when it [the burnings and lynchings] happened, he was gone up yonder, see, and what caused him to go was that his wife was a one of those 'postolics, roley-holeys, and he didn't believe it and they separated and he just went off, and he didn't come back for all those years."

7. Interview of Lutisia Gibson Foreman, January 7, 1995. J. C. Whatley, always at the center of things, may have claimed in his interview on May 5, 1987 that his father helped Floyd escape. According to him:

My daddy had been in the gin business or connected with the gin business all his life, see, and he had an' ole nigger named Gibson that run the, fired the boilers for him, see, to run the engine, the steam engine, and he was gettin' too old to do the work. This was a lot of work, and he brought one of his boys up to do that work. He asked my daddy to take that boy and make him the same engineer and everything out of him, and he did, and he taught him so much. And he died. The old man died, see? Well, we had that nigger here, and we kept him. We didn't let him out of here, see, or nothin'. We had him around here, and it got so hot, they went off down here and killed one of his brothers, see. The King brothers an' all were just goin' down, and if they saw a damned nigger, well they just shut him down. All the way from Streetman back down into this country, here.

Well, my daddy said they better not do it, so he carried that nigger to Mexia, to Munger's oil mill. Munger had one in Teague and one in Mexia, and Daddy told 'em the story, and a course they knew all about it, about his daddy an' ever'thing else. So they took him in at Mexia, at the oil mill, and they kept him over there where nobody bothered him. They did send him to Teague, but then they moved them oil mills to west Texas, see, and this nigger went with them, see, and the last I heard he was still out there with Munger. I haven't seen him in fifty or sixty years. After he went to Mexia, I didn't see him.

If Whatley was not referring to Floyd Gibson, then perhaps the story, though garbled, is true, and another brother of Leroy or Allie Gibson was assisted by Mr. Whatley.

8. Interview of Lura Bess Mayo Sprague, December 3, 1994.

9. J. C. Whatley was the only genuine member of the lynch mob who was still living and could be located to be interviewed, but he went out of his way to deny hands-on involvement during my interview with him on May 5, 1987. Still, he liked being at the center of events, and may have been more of a participant than he admitted. I was told by a member of the county historical commission that he "knows where a lot of skeletons are buried." It was also whispered that he was a member of "the Dixie Mafia" in Dallas.

Whatever he was or was not, he was colorful, and had a saying about life that he repeated twice during the interview: "This is a great life, if you don't weaken." Once or twice during the interview he slipped into harsh invective against blacks, and another time he said something curious, or very suggestive regarding his involvement during the reign of terror following the lynchings, the exact meaning of which was known only to him.

We were discussing the search for Eula's body, and right after saying there were others searching, but not in the right place, he trailed off, saying thoughtfully, "You just don't have no idea how many gun barrels you'd look down, see, and I have looked down . . . uh, just like I said . . . [long pause]. I wasn't a segregate [segregationist], and that's the cause of it right there. I never harmed a nigger that I know about. I have made them do . . . I have looked down their gun barrels and they told me not to do it and I done it anyway, in my life."

10. Interview of B. J. Ausley, April 9, 1995.

11. Harry Hughes remembered the tree and described it, but neither he nor I could locate any trace of it.

12. *History of Freestone County*, vol. 1, 134.

Epilogue to the New Edition

1. Doris Nealy, Lovie White, Ruth Sloan, Mary Sample, and Wanda Lynah.

2. Letter to the editor from Quentin D. Morrow, *Fairfield Recorder*, March 4, 1999.

3. Letter to the editor from Betty M. Morrow, *Mexia Daily News*, May 11, 1999.

4. Quentin D. Morrow letter, supra. The "truth of the matter" was a copy of a 1922 newspaper account about Eula's murder and the subsequent lynchings.

5. See note 137.

6. I am indebted to all the readers and others who made the effort to provide me with additional information, and want to particularly single out Gode Davis and Betty Cochran. The former has doggedly and expertly pursued filming and writing about lynching in America for nearly two decades and has generously shared information and guidance involving the Kirven incidents. Ms. Cochran is related to Johnny Cornish and has carefully researched and shared her information regarding the remarkable Cornish family and the multiple tragedies its members experienced.

7. Otis King's descendants were not the only family members who heard that Snap Curry was a well-known troublemaker. A grandson of Drew King, who said he always wondered if the Prowells were involved in the murder instead of Cornish and Jones, asserted nevertheless that Curry was a menace and that he was "a bad actor." He had also never heard any suggestion that his grandfather or great uncles ever mistreated their hired hands. Telephone interview of Dr. Terry King, July 7, 2008.

8. E-mail from Betty Cochran to Monte Akers, July 16, 2008, quoting the recollections of Mary Helen Malone.

9. E-mail from Clara King to Monte Akers, July 24, 2008.

10. Interview of Roland King, March 6, 1999; this incident was confirmed by Clara King in the e-mail of July 24, 2008.

11. Letter from Steve McConnico to Monte Akers dated April 20, 1999.

12. Letter from Clara King to Monte Akers postmarked March 25, 1999.

13. Ibid.

14. Letter from Steve McConnico to Monte Akers, April 20, 1999.

15. This information was attributed to the *Corsicana Daily Sun,* May 6, 1922, p. 1, by V. Wayne Oakes, *Mob Hysteria—Kirvin, Texas, 1922* (term paper for History 5390, Professor William C. Pool, Southwest Texas State College, March 21, 1967), 10. It was questioned by the King family, however, who knew Agnes and had never heard that she was jailed. E-mail from Clara King to Monte Akers, July 24, 2008.

The Oakes term paper was provided by a gentleman named Greg Olds, who also reported that its author, who was from near Mexia, died in 1992. Letter from Greg Olds to Monte Akers, July 2, 2001. The Kirven story was the subject of at least two other college papers written prior to this book's publication. One was written in the 1970s by Greg Cooke for a history course at Baylor University in Waco. Cooke, who was the Region 6 Administrator of the Environmental Protection Agency when the book was published in 1999, called to tell me this surprising news the day after I gave him a copy of the book, unaware of his connection to the story. The other paper was by Jacqueline Jones, who was a great-great niece of Johnny Cornish, for a course on African American history taught in 1990 or 1991 by Dr. Norbert Brockman at St. Mary's University in San Antonio. E-mail from Jacqueline Jones to Monte Akers, April 30, 1999.

16. This claim was questioned by members of the Cornish family, who believed that Mose Jones was a closer friend. E-mail from Betty Cochran to Monte Akers, July 16, 2008, quoting the recollections of Mary Helen Malone, who was closely acquainted with Johnny's mother, Nettie Cornish, and his sister, Lovie Cornish Proctor.

17. E-mail from Gode Davis to Monte Akers, June 1, 2008. Davis and David McCartney interviewed Hobart Carter in 2002, prior to his moving to the retirement home in Worthham.

18. The relatives of Johnny Cornish also dismissed Hobart's claim of his being with Johnny when Eula was murdered, saying that he was actually with Dr. Billy Sneed, as claimed by Dr. Sneed. E-mail from Betty Cochran to Monte Akers, July 16, 2008.

19. Interview of Hobart Carter, July 18, 2002.

20. Telephone interview of Dr. Terry King, July 7, 2008.

21. Ibid.

22. Oakes, *Mob Hysteria*, 2.

23. Photograph of Eula Ausley and Layton Smith furnished by Clara King.

24. Tom Chatham, Jr., a native of Mexia who was a director of numerous plays on Broadway for many years, retired to Corsicana, Texas, in the 1990s and

e-mailed me on April 19, 1999, to discuss the book and to mention that "[m]y two dear old/talkative neighbors suddenly not available. The one from/reared at Dew, Texas (near Fairfield/Teague), had a brother who 'called on'/'dated' Eula Ausely. His name was Walter Yerby . . . died years and years ago." I notified Clara King of this information by e-mail dated April 20, 1999, but she had not heard of the connection. If nothing else, the information indicates that Yerby was not one of the two men killed by Floyd Gibson at Simsboro on June 2, 1922.

25. E-mail from Clara King to Monte Akers, July 24, 2008.

26. Ibid.

27. Ibid.

28. Oakes, *Mob Hysteria*, 3.

29. E-mail from Clara King to Monte Akers, July 24, 2008. An example of how details of the crime were enhanced and exaggerated was supplied by Grady Cotton, who was an eight-year-old boy in 1922. Cotton heard at the time and recalled eighty years later that it was Otis King who found his niece and that when he did he screamed and ripped his shirt from his body. Interview of Grady Wayne Cotton in Pasadena, Texas, July 18, 2002.

30. Oakes, *Mob Hysteria*, citing the *Waco Times-Herald*, May 5, 1922, p. 1.

31. Ibid., 4, citing *Corsicana Daily Sun*, May 6, 1922, p. 1.

32. Telephone interview of Dr. Terry King, July 7, 2008.

33. Roland King, March 6, 1999.

34. E-mail from Clara King to Monte Akers, June 9, 2000. Drew and Otis King married sisters, Rena and Corrie Roland, creating the double-cousin relationship and providing a first name for Otis's son. E-mail from Clara King to Monte Akers, July 24, 2008.

35. Oakes, *Mob Hysteria*, 5–6, citing the *Fort Worth Star-Telegram*, May 7, 1922; and page 7, quoting G. D. Davis, staff correspondent to the *Dallas Morning News*.

36. Ibid., 12.

37. Ibid., 12–13, citing the *Corsicana Daily Sun*, May 6, 1922, p. 1; and the *Fort Worth Star-Telegram*, May 7, 1922, p. 4.

38. Ibid., 13, citing the *Fort Worth Star-Telegram*, May 7, 1922, p. 4.

39. Ibid., 14, citing the *Waco Times-Herald*, May 5, 1922, p. 1.

40. Ibid., 15, citing the *Dallas Morning News,* May 7, 1922, p. 2.

41. Ibid.

42. Ibid.

43. Ibid., 16.

44. Ibid., 18, citing the *Fort Worth Star-Telegram*, May 6, 1922, p. 1.

45. *Flames*, 61.

46. E-mail from Gode Davis to Monte Akers, June 1, 2008. Mr. Davis spoke to Mack in September 2002, but did not record the telephone conversations or take notes. The graphic nature of the information caused much of it to become imprinted on Gode's mind, but some details were lost, or nearly lost. With regard

to Smith, Gode's first recollection was that his name was Louis Smith, but when asked if it might not have been Layton, a natural candidate to have urged on the mob, he responded, "Yes, that rings a bell. I think he did say Layton; all I was sure of was Smith, so that seems likely."

47. E-mail from Gode Davis to Monte Akers, June 1, 2008. This startling detail, if correct, raises a rash of new questions. As with Layton Smith's name, there is some room for doubt, because Gode thought at the time that Mack called him "Powell" rather than "Prowell." However, he consistently referred to him as being the older of two brothers, the other of whom was inexplicably absent. If accurate, Prowell's presence suggests either that he and his brother were not guilty of Eula's murder or that he realized that by being active in the burning of the three men he could further misdirect attention from his and his brother's guilt.

48. His real name is not included for two reasons: first, he still has family living in and around Freestone County who have long felt shame and discomfort for what Mack did on May 6, 1922. Second, and more important, another man who lives in the area and is only a few years younger has the same first and last names. The second man visited the site of the lynching after it was over, but he was only nine years old. However, to state Mack's real name gives rise to legal risk of defamation of the second man's character.

49. Ibid.

50. Ibid.

51. Oakes, *Mob Hysteria,* 19, citing the *Fort Worth Star-Telegram,* May 6, 1922, p. 2.

52. Ibid., 19, citing the *Corsicana Daily Sun,* May 6, 1922, p. 1.

53. Grady, the youngest, was actually just a few days shy of his ninth birthday. Interview of Grady Wayne Cotton in Pasadena, Texas, July 18, 2002.

54. Ibid.

55. Ibid.

56. E-mail from Gode Davis to Monte Akers, May 27, 2008.

57. Interview of Grady Cotton by Monte Akers and Gode Davis, July 18, 2002.

58. E-mail from Gode Davis to Monte Akers, May 27, 2008.

59. E-mail from Clara King to Monte Akers, July 24, 2008.

60. Ibid.

61. E-mail from Gode Davis to Monte Akers, June 1, 2008.

62. It is also possible that Tom Prowell was present. If the two Prowell brothers really did return to the Kirven area shortly before Eula was killed, if they murdered her, and particularly if Claude Prowell was a leader of the lynching team, there seems to be no reason for the father to be absent. If there really was a deathbed confession that was subsequently told to Jenkins Carter (pp. 119–121), the elder Prowell was the most likely confessor. Furthermore, Gode Davis recalled that Mack said the members of the core group of the mob were contemptuous of the younger Prowell brother, Audey, for not participating, that they called

him a coward, and, Gode wrote, "Now that you've jogged my memory, it is possible that the elder Prowell (Andrew Thomas) might also have been involved in the lynching as I believe he was mentioned—making the absence of the younger Prowell more significant." It is entirely possible, of course, that Audey was in jail in Fairfield during the burnings because he was arrested earlier in the day, as Sheriff Mayo was quoted as saying in the story published in the *Brooklyn Citizen*, May 6, 1922, pp. 114–115.

63. E-mail from Gode Davis to Monte Akers, June 1, 2008.

64. Ibid.

65. Ibid.

66. Mack stated that Osterhous died during the Second World War, and any confirmation that he did so would have added credibility to the rest of his report. However, an Internet search for that confirmation was fruitless, largely because the correct spelling of the man's name is not known and available research sites ask for more information, such as the county and state from which he enlisted.

67. Ibid.

68. Ibid.

69. Ibid.

70. Interview of Grady Cotton, July 18, 2002.

71. Ibid.

72. Oakes, *Mob Hysteria*, 20, citing the *Dallas Morning News*, May 7, 1922, p. 1.

73. Interview of Clara King, March 6, 1999.

74. Cotton interview, supra.

75. Oakes, *Mob Hysteria*, 21, citing the *Fort Worth Star-Telegram*, May 6, 1922, p. 1.

76. Grady Cotton, then aged eighty-eight, was interviewed on film on July 18, 2002, at the home of his daughter in Pasadena, Texas, before which he was asked to summarize his recollections off-camera. He made the "like a woman's hair" comparison before filming began, but did not repeat it on the tape. Although not reported by any newspapers or other sources, this incident was corroborated by Mack in his testimony to Gode Davis.

77. Jones was identified as the second victim on page 65 in this volume. Both the *Fort Worth Star-Telegram* and Mack said the second victim was Cornish.

78. E-mail from Gode Davis to Monte Akers, June 1, 2008.

79. *Flames*, 67.

80. E-mail from Gode Davis to Monte Akers, June 1, 2008.

81. Wayne Oakes wrote that "[i]n fact, editor Paul Moore of the *Corsicana Daily Sun*, who lived in Waco at the time, stated that scores of men were leaving Waco to join in the hunt" earlier in the day. Oakes interviewed Moore in November 1966, but it is not clear whether Moore was one of those men, whether he wrote anything for the *Sun* about the incident, or exactly when Moore was editor of that paper. Oakes, *Mob Hysteria*, 11.

82. Oakes, *Mob Hysteria*, 21, citing the *Fort Worth Star-Telegram*, May 6, 1922, p. 1.

83. Ibid., 22, citing the *Corsicana Daily Sun*, May 6, 1922, p. 1.

84. E-mail from Gode Davis to Monte Akers, June 1, 2008.

85. Oakes, *Mob Hysteria*, 21, citing the *Corsicana Daily Sun*, May 6, 1922, p. 1.

86. Ibid, citing the *Fort Worth Star-Telegram*, May 6, 1922, p. 1.

87. Ibid., 22–23, citing the *Corsicana Daily Sun*, May 6, 1922, p. 1.

88. E-mail from Gode Davis to Monte Akers, June 1, 2008.

89. Oakes, *Mob Hysteria*, 2, citing the *Corsicana Daily Sun*, May 6, 1922, p. 1.

90. Copies of two of the postcard photos, one being essentially the same as that sold on eBay but taken from the opposite side of the pyre, and the other being the photo of Otis King and Sergeant Simmons, were provided to the author by a reader named Charlotte Roppolo, who obtained them from an aunt living in Boston, Massachusetts.

91. E-mail from Linda Kuczwanski to Monte Akers, April 1, 1999. She identified the man who burned the camera as her grandfather.

92. This odd incident, described by Mr. Cotton on July 18, 2002, was mentioned by one other person interviewed for the book who was not an eyewitness and was dismissed at that time as apocryphal.

93. Mack identified Tom Cornish as Johnny's brother, but a member of the family who researched its genealogy confirmed that he was an uncle. Phone interview of Betty Cochran, June 6, 2008; U.S. Census of 1920. However, considering that Tom Cornish was reported to be alive and well by local newspapers in the autumn of 1922 (see p. 143), it follows that he was not lynched as reported by Mack; or there was more than one Tom Cornish; or the man whom Mack identified as Tom Cornish was actually Tom Barry, who was identified as a lynching victim by Dan Kelly (p. 108).

94. Oakes, *Mob Hysteria*, 24, citing the *Fort Worth Star-Telegram*, May 6, 1922, p. 2.

95. Ibid., citing the NAACP *Annual Report* for 1922. Mr. Oakes concluded that Tom Cornish was killed instead of Shadrick Green. Considering the testimony of Bertha Williams, who knew both men, it seems more likely that each met the same fate.

96. E-mail from Gode Davis, May 27, 2008, supra.

97. Interview of Roy L. Green by Betty Cochran in Forney, Texas, October 2006, described to Monte Akers by Ms. Cochran in a telephone interview on June 6, 2008. Mr. Green died a few weeks after talking to Ms. Cochran.

98. Ibid.

99. Oakes, *Mob Hysteria*, 26, citing interview with Walter Hayes by Oakes on November 25, 1966.

100. Ibid., 27, citing interview with Anna Chambers by Oakes on November 19, 1966.

101. Letter from Steve McConnico, grandson of David Nettle, to Monte Akers, April 20, 1999.

102. See *Flames*, pp. 84–85.

103. E-mail from Clara King to Monte Akers, April 1999.

104. Both portraits ended up in the possession of Eula's nephew, B. J. "Bill" Ausley, and somewhere along the line, the portrait of Eunice was labeled "Eula Ausley" on its verso in pencil. This latter fact came to my attention after the book had gone to print, and I was temporarily convinced that the portrait of Eula that appears on page 88 was actually an image of her mother. When I met Roland King on March 6, 1999, I mentioned that Eula was considered to be an attractive girl, and Roland retorted "Oh no, she was a homely woman," thus sealing the error in my mind. All was made well by Clara King, however, when she subsequently furnished copies of the photos of Eula and Layton Smith, as well as the scrap of photo that served for Eunice's portrait, and the chain of events regarding the portraits' reproduction was unraveled. The woman depicted on page 88 is, in fact, Eula Ausley.

105. See *Flames*, p. 211, note 7.

106. E-mail from Clara King to Monte Akers, June 9, 2000.

107. Phone conversations with Dr. Terry D. King, Monroe, Louisiana, on unrecorded date in 2002 and on July 7, 2008.

108. *Flames*, 171.

109. Interview of Roland and Clara King, March 6, 1999.

110. Phone interview of Steve McConnico, April 1999.

111. Letter from Don Marberry to Monte Akers, postmarked April 1, 2002.

112. Telephone interview of Betty Cochran, June 6, 2008. Uncle Charlie later became an outcast from the Cornish family after he shot and killed his nephew, Ben Huckaby, supposedly by accident but probably because Charlie suspected Ben of romancing his girlfriend.

Ms. Cochran provided extensive genealogical information about the Cornish family. Nettie, Johnny's mother, was born in May 1885 and was the eighth of ten children of Jubilee Cornish and Susan Compton Cornish. Jubilee was probably born in May 1860 in Arkansas and Susan was probably born in March 1865 in Texas. Nettie's siblings, in birth order, were Donie Cornish Huckaby, Janie Cornish, Bennie Cornish, Phyliss Cornish Stevenson, Charlie Cornish, Sam Cornish, Tom Cornish, Walter Cornish, and Arvinie Cornish. Nettie gave birth to seven children: Johnny Cornish, born about 1904; Lovie Cornish Proctor, born on January 25, 1907; Heddly Thompson, born in 1909; Eddie Thompson, born in 1912; Robert F. Thomas (or Thompson), born on February 28, 1915; Eloise Thompson, born March 16, 1916; and Frank Cornish, born about 1919.

Johnny and Tom's fates were not the only tragedies visited on the Cornish family. The youngest brother, Frank, committed suicide, as did a great-great nephew. Furthermore, Shadrick Green was part of the Cornish family, having married Lela Stevenson, the daughter of Phyllis Cornish Stevenson, Nettie's sister, making him Nettie's nephew, and Johnny's cousin, by marriage. Nettie Cornish endured great trials and troubles, first living in the Keechi Creek bottoms on property owned by her white lover, Bud Thompson, then moving to Fairfield during the troubles, and later taking up with J. R. Sessions. Her daughter, Lovie, opened what may have been the first store in Fairfield owned by a black person. E-mail from Jacqueline E. Jones to Monte Akers, April 30, 1999; e-mails from Betty Cochran to Monte Akers, June 27 and 28 and July 18, 2008.

113. Robert Martin, *Howard Kester and the Struggle for Social Justice in the South, 1904–1977* (Charlottesville: University of Virginia Press, 1991), 5, 19.

114. E-mail from William Coleman to Monte Akers, March 7, 1999.

115. Jerry Turner, "Flames After Midnight: A Study in Horror," *Mexia Daily News*, April 2, 1999.

116. E-mail from Gode Davis to Monte Akers, May 27, 2008.

117. Book review, *Southern Art & Soul* (May/June 1999), 11.

118. Letter from Monte Akers to Fred W. Marks, May 20, 1999.

119. Significant reviews include the following: *Austin Chronicle*, March 12, 1999; *Fairfield Recorder*, February 25, 1999; *Grand Prairie News*, March 28, 1999; *USA Today*, April 1, 1999; *Mexia Daily News*, April 2, 1999; *Amarillo News Globe*, April 18, 1999; *Southern Art & Soul*, May/June, 1999; *Houston Chronicle*, August 30, 1999; *Texas Observer*, August 25, 2000.

120. Erin Capps, *Kirven and Streetman: A New History of the Northwest Section of Freestone County, 1900 to 1950* (master's thesis, Baylor University, 2006), 42–43.

121. Melissa Hall, "When the World Stopped Turning in Kirven, Texas" (Texas History 4035, University of Houston at Clear Lake, 2007).

122. See www.americanlynching.com.

123. Capps, *Kirven and Streetman*, supra.

124. Mack rather enigmatically described Sonny's father, J. R. Sessions, as "a busybody." E-mail from Gode Davis to Monte Akers, May 27, 2008.

125. Ibid.

126. Ibid. The "irrelevant story" apparently being the account of J. R. Sessions being tried and acquitted for the murder of the Miller brothers two and a half months before the lynchings in Kirven (pp. 24–26).

127. Nevertheless, J. C. Whatley's sister, Ruby Kate Richardson, reported that Sheriff Sessions came by to tell her to keep her door closed when Mr. Akers came around to interview her. Mrs. Richardson shared Sheriff Sessions' disdain for the witnesses interviewed for the book, but expressed it as "He interviewed every Nigger in Streetman." She also admitted that her brother "colored things considerably when he told a tale." E-mail from Michael Ditto to Monte Akers, March 16, 1999.

128. Capps, *Kirven and Streetman*, 44. Another possible reason for Sheriff Sessions' animosity toward revelation of the story was provided by members of the Cornish family who researched their family tree. According to their account,

Johnny's mother, Nettie, gave birth to four children by Bud Thompson, who died before Johnny was killed, after which Nettie took up with and had children by J. R. Sessions. According to the recollections of Cornish family members, Mr. Sessions made a point of being seen in Nettie's company openly in Fairfield, as if to challenge anyone who would criticize him. He was said to have had a son and a daughter by her, both of whom were older than Sonny. Telephone interview of Betty Cochran, June 6, 2008; telephone interview of Cornish family member who requested anonymity, August 3, 2008.

129. Letter from Sherry Byrd to Monte Akers, April 5, 1999.

130. Capps, *Kirvin and Streetman*, 45.

131. E-mail from Clara King to Monte Akers, June 9, 2000.

132. Ibid. Mrs. King added, "God, I wish that you had gotten both sides of the story before you wrote your book. But it didn't happen so. . . ."

133. Brian Anderson, "Author Proposes Taking Down Segregation Fence in Central Texas," *Waco Tribune-Herald*, May 6, 1999.

134. Ibid.

135. David McCartney of Tehuacana led the charge on the issue, but reported in a letter on May 19, 1999, that those associated with the African American portion of the old burial ground were not truly interested in doing anything but "clean up of their cemetery, straighten up stones, cut the fence row, haul in dirt for sunken graves, etc." He quoted one of the daughters of Lutisia Gibson Foreman as saying, "I don't blame the whites for not wanting the fence down when they take beautiful care of theirs and we don't ours." Similarly, in an e-mail dated April 22, 1999, Clara King reported that "I have not talked to anyone that is in favor of taking the fence down between the two cemeteries. . . ." She also mentioned that she recently talked about the fence with a lady who "had been coming to the cemetery for several years" who "did not know there was another cemetery over there." By the time she was interviewed about the fence in May by a reporter for the *Waco Tribune-Herald,* she referred to her original suggestion to tear it down by saying, "I shouldn't have opened my mouth."

The possibility that the Cotton Gin fence might be removed was part of what prompted Mrs. Morrow to send her "stinky can of worms" letter to the editor of the *Mexia Daily News* in May 1999, declaring that "an individual living and operating his personal business in other than Freestone Co. should not publicize erroneous information stating it as true facts." The other contents of Mrs. Morrow's long letter demonstrate that she was a devoted researcher and expert on Freestone County cemeteries and the County's genealogy.

In 2010, Betty Cochran and Mary Helen Malone were responsible for erecting a headstone—and holding a ceremony—for Johnny Cornish in the Fairfield Cemetery. That same year the Texas Historical Commission selected the story of the Kirven incident for a state historical marker, although as of early 2011 it has not been erected.

136. Equally barren were a few flirtatious inquiries from Hollywood. A film and TV agent represented the book for several months, but the lack of success of

the 1997 movie *Rosewood*, starring Jon Voight, which explored a similar, or more horrific, outrage that occurred in Florida in 1922, helped ensure lack of serious interest. Another agent called in early June 1999 to explore the book's potential but lamented that what the story needed for box office success that was totally lacking was a happy ending. E-mail to Kathleen Niendorff from Monte Akers, June 4, 1999.

137. In reality, I thought long and hard about what I should do, if anything, about this man. Should he, like Byron De La Beckwith, who was convicted thirty-one years after shooting Medgar Evers in 1963, or Bobby Frank Cherry and Thomas Blanton, who were convicted thirty-seven years after helping bomb a Birmingham church in 1963, be brought to trial eighty-plus years after participating in the Kirven burnings? If not, why not? When I analyzed the matter like a lawyer, my initial questions were: With what crime might he be charged? Has the statute of limitations run out so that prosecution is barred? If not, is there evidence to support a conviction? If so, would a local prosecutor accept the case and seek an indictment from a Freestone County grand jury?

The man's crime was not murder. The horrible act for which he took credit was, at least under current law, aggravated assault, for which the statute of limitations is only three years. There is no statute of limitations for murder or sexual assault, but it is unlikely that his acts conformed with the elements of either of those offenses. His actions might be consistent with the elements of either "conspiracy to murder" or manslaughter, neither of which have a statute of limitations, but the law of 1922 was different than it is today with regard to conspiracy, leaving only manslaughter as a possible charge. Accordingly, while it is not possible to say with final certainty that passage of time barred prosecution for all crimes for which he might have been prosecuted, it is probable that it had.

As for evidence, there was nothing physical after so many years, but there were his statements to Gode. The statements were hearsay, but it meets one of the exceptions to the hearsay rule, whereby a statement that another person heard may be admitted into evidence for a jury to consider as an "admission against interest." Hearsay would not be admissible, for example, if a witness tried to testify that he or she heard someone say that this person castrated two of the lynching victims. But if Gode testified that he had heard it directly from "Mack," who gave statements contrary to his own legal interest, then a judge would probably allow the testimony to be admitted.

However, it is unlikely that a local prosecutor, who is an elected official dependent for his future on the support of local voters, would view any applicable criminal charge as a career-boosting opportunity; and whereas a federal prosecutor might be willing to try the man for a civil rights violation, that particular federal offense did not exist in 1922.

Finally, by the time I learned of the extent of the man's involvement and that he had actually admitted to a crime that might still subject him to prosecution, he had been dead for two years. Nevertheless, I could have learned the extent of his involvement and taken action while he was still alive had I elected to do so.

The ironic truth is that I was no better than the hundreds of Freestone County citizens in 1922 who knew what was happening at Kirven, who attended the burnings or heard of them, and who learned about the killings that continued for nearly another month thereafter. Many locals knew the identities of core lynch mob members and other killers, but they did nothing, looked another direction, and rationalized and justified their own behavior.

138. E-mail from Gode Davis to Monte Akers, May 27, 2008.

139. Ibid.

140. Identity withheld by request, interviewed March 6, 1999.

141. E-mail from Betty Cochran to Monte Akers, June 28, 2008.

142. Oakes, *Mob Hysteria*, 28.

Index

Index to the Epilogue,
Revised Edition